AF761068

OECD Economic Surveys: Indonesia 2015

BETTER POLICIES FOR BETTER LIVES

Please cite this publication as:
OECD (2015), *OECD Economic Surveys: Indonesia 2015*, OECD Publishing, Paris.
http://dx.doi.org/10.1787/eco_surveys-idn-2015-en

ISBN 978-92-64-22968-6 (print)
ISBN 978-92-64-22969-3 (PDF)

Series: OECD Economic Surveys
ISSN 0376-6438 (print)
ISSN 1609-7513 (online)

OECD Economic Surveys: Indonesia
ISSN 2072-5116 (print)
ISSN 2072-5108 (online)

Photo credits: Cover © Teguh Hardi Sujono/Dreamstime.com.

Corrigenda to OECD publications may be found on line at: *www.oecd.org/about/publishing/corrigenda.htm*.

Table of contents

Thematic chapters

Boxes

Tables

Figures

This Survey was prepared in the Economics Department by Petar Vujanovic and Richard Dutu under the supervision of Peter Jarrett.

Research and editorial assistance was provided by Anne Legendre and secretarial assistance by Mee-Lan Frank.

The Survey was discussed at a meeting of the Economic and Development Review Committee on 23 February 2015.

The Survey is published on the responsibility of the Secretary-General of the OECD.

BASIC STATISTICS OF INDONESIA, 2013

(Numbers in parentheses refer to the OECD average)[a]

LAND, PEOPLE AND ELECTORAL CYCLE					
Population (millions)	249.9		Population density per km²	129.6	(34.8)
Under 15 (%)	28.9	(18.3)	Life expectancy (years, 2012)	70.7	(80.2)
Over 65 (%)	5.2	(15.7)	Men	68.6	(77.5)
			Women	72.7	(82.3)
Latest 5-year average growth (%)	1.3	(0.6)	Latest general election	October 2014	
ECONOMY					
Gross domestic product (GDP)			Value added shares (%)		
In current prices (billion USD)	916.8		Primary	25.7	(2.5)
In current prices (billion IDR)	9 524.7		Industry including construction	34.5	(26.8)
Latest 5-year average real growth (%)	5.8	(0.8)	Services	39.9	(70.2)
Per capita (current prices, 000 USD PPP)	9.9	(38.2)			
GENERAL GOVERNMENT Per cent of GDP					
Expenditures[b, c]	17.3	(42.5)	Gross financial debt[b]	24.9	(110.4)
Revenue[b, c]	15.1	(36.8)			
EXTERNAL ACCOUNTS					
Exchange rate (IDR per USD)	10 390		Main exports (% of total merchandise exports)		
PPP exchange rate (USA = 1)	3 687		Mineral fuels, lubricants and related materials	31.4	
In per cent of GDP			Machinery and transport material	12.1	
Exports of goods and services	23.7	(53.4)	Manufactured goods classified chiefly by material	12.1	
Imports of goods and services	25.7	(49.4)	Main imports (% of total merchandise imports)		
Current account balance	-3.3	(-0.1)	Machinery and transport equipment	30.3	
Net international investment position	-42.5		Mineral fuels, lubricants and related materials	24.4	
			Manufactured goods classified chiefly by material	15.3	
LABOUR MARKET, SKILLS AND INNOVATION					
Employment rate for 15-64 year-olds (%)	62.7	(65.0)	Unemployment rate, Labour Force Survey (age 15 and over) (%)	6.2	(7.9)
			Youth (age 15-24, %)	21.6	(16.2)
Participation rate for 15-64 year-olds (%)	66.8	(71.1)	Tertiary educational attainment 25-64 year-olds (%, 2012)	7.9	(31.5)
ENVIRONMENT					
Total primary energy supply per capita (toe, 2012)	0.9	(4.2)	CO_2 emissions from fuel combustion per capita (tonnes, 2012)	1.8	(9.7)
Renewables (%, 2012)	33.4	(8.6)			
Fine particulate matter concentration (urban, PM_{10}, µg/m³, 2011)	48.0	(28.0)			
SOCIETY					
Income equality (Gini coefficient)	0.41	(0.31)	Education outcomes (PISA score, 2012)		
Relative poverty ratio at USD 2 a day (PPP) (%, of population, 2011)	43.3	(1.0)	Reading	396	(497)
			Mathematics	375	(494)
Public and private spending (% of GDP)			Science	382	(501)
Health care (2012)	3.0	(9.0)	Share of women in parliament (%,September 2014)	16.8	(28.7)
Education (public, 2012)	3.6	(5.3)			

Better life index: *www.oecdbetterlifeindex.org*

a) Where the OECD aggregate is not provided in the source database, a simple OECD average of latest available data is calculated where data exist for at least 29 member countries.

b) 2012 for the OECD average.

c) Central government for Indonesia.

Source: Calculations based on data extracted from the databases of the following organisations: OECD, International Energy Agency, World Bank, International Monetary Fund and Inter-Parliamentary Union.

Executive summary

- *Main findings*
- *Key recommendations*

Main findings

Macroeconomic policy challenges. Indonesia's economy performed exceptionally well over the decade following the Asian Crisis on the back of the prudent macroeconomic framework and solid policy reforms of the time, and from which dividends continue to flow. However, growth has moderated in recent years, reflecting weaker international demand and slow investment growth due to lower commodity prices but also heightened regulatory uncertainty and infrastructure bottlenecks. Indonesia is still in the catch-up phase of growth, but the pace of reform has slowed in recent years, and some protectionist measures have been adopted. Both internal and external factors will continue to challenge the implementation of monetary policy. Ensuring continued increases in living standards for all Indonesians will require maintaining macroeconomic stability, adopting a broad range of structural reforms, and creating fiscal space to expand government expenditures in priority areas such as education, health, poverty alleviation and infrastructure. The recent removal of most fuel subsidies was a laudable step in this direction. However, low commodity export prices and slower growth mean that further space will need to come from carefully designed increases in tax revenues from current low levels. There is also room to improve the efficiency and targeting of public spending at both central and sub-national levels.

Implementing policies for inclusive and sustainable growth. Indonesia has made impressive inroads into poverty, aided by strong per capita income growth and increasingly efficient and well-targeted poverty-reduction programmes. However, income inequality is high and even rose in the past decade. The current mix of social programmes, including cash transfers conditioned on school attendance and a subsidised rice programme, are not well targeted, although encouraging headway is being made in developing a single registry of vulnerable households. Transport congestion and logistics bottlenecks are preventing better integration with global value chains and inhibiting growth more generally. Investment in power generation and water treatment is also lagging. While PISA outcomes are in line with Indonesia's current stage of development, the education system still suffers from serious quality and access problems.

Improving the regulatory framework and dealing with corruption. Some institutional arrangements hinder economic and social development, inhibiting the formation of new firms and the investment plans of existing businesses. The lack of harmonisation and conformity between national and sub-national laws and regulations continues to be an issue. The authorities have been stepping up the fight against corruption, notably with the establishment and expansion of the Corruption Eradication Commission. The capacity of the civil service is inconsistent in some areas, impeding business and discouraging both domestic and foreign investment. Budget execution at all levels of government also remains a problem; measures have recently been taken to address this issue.

Managing natural resources and combating environmental degradation. Indonesia has an abundance of natural resources, but its geography and underdeveloped transport infrastructure prevent it from taking full advantage of them for the benefit of all Indonesians. Under-exploitation and mismanagement are responsible for the decline in the energy sector. The efficiency of coal-fired power plants is low. The 2014 enforcement of the 2009 export ban on mineral ore (in order to foster onshore processing) has increased uncertainty. The agricultural sector suffers from lagging productivity, misplaced support for staple food crops (e.g. rice, maize and soybeans) and lack of diversification. Environmental outcomes, including greenhouse gas emissions and deforestation, are aggravated by the central role played by fossil fuels and uneven enforcement of existing laws and regulations.

Key recommendations

Confronting macroeconomic policy challenges

- Bank Indonesia should remain cautious with regards to monetary and macro-prudential policies, taking into account both external and internal factors.
- Raise government tax revenues in order to fund a needed longer-term increase in government spending. Revenue could be raised by bringing more self-employed into the tax net and by improving the effectiveness of tax collection.

Implementing policies for inclusive and sustainable growth

- Raise public spending on infrastructure. Focus on transportation and logistics to support industry, as well as natural disaster prevention and water treatment.
- Avoid protectionist measures that inhibit openness to trade and foreign investment with uncertain development payoff.
- Increase, and further improve targeting of, spending on poverty alleviation and health measures.
- Direct more public resources to improving education access and outcomes. Continue regular teacher assessments and professional development, and link teacher salaries more closely to qualifications and performance.
- Increase financial inclusiveness by further developing branchless banking, drawing lessons from such countries as India, Mexico, the Philippines and Kenya.
- Tackle labour market informality by reducing rigidities in the formal sector, and by enhancing the effectiveness of the tax-transfer system for poverty alleviation and channelling other social benefits.

Dealing with corruption and improving the regulatory framework

- Improve mechanisms to prevent corruption, while further increasing efforts to combat all forms of corruption.
- Expand support to sub-national governments for capacity building, including the provision of technical and administrative assistance by the central government.

Managing natural resources and combating environmental degradation

- Refocus the mineral ore export ban based on an evaluation of the costs and benefits of onshore processing for each mineral. Provide infrastructure and electricity to the new smelters.
- Increase agricultural productivity by providing technical assistance and training, including through agreements between smallholders and large estates. Increase farmers' access to credit by accelerating land titling. Lower food prices by decreasing trade restrictions.
- Devote more resources to enforcing laws against illegal forest clearing, logging and mining.
- Reduce greenhouse gas emissions by further developing clean power, especially geothermal.

Assessment and recommendations

Indonesia has enjoyed strong and stable growth in the decade and a half since the Asian Crisis (Table 1). This performance was in no small measure due to policy reforms put in place over this period, notably a robust macroeconomic framework. Much of the growth was domestically driven, with household consumption in particular providing a steady and solid base. Labour market conditions improved, and this, in combination with increasingly effective poverty-alleviation programmes, helped to bolster household incomes and confidence. The external sector also played an important role, especially through global demand for commodity exports. The pace of reform has eased, and this may in part account for the recent slowing in output growth.

Strong per capita gains and increasingly efficient and well-targeted government measures have been instrumental in reducing poverty. However, income inequality as measured by the Gini coefficient has risen over the past decade. Annual per capita income is around USD 9 300 in purchasing power parity terms, and a significant share of the workforce is still engaged in low-productivity agriculture. Indonesia is thus still well within the catch-up phase of economic development. Ensuring continued strong and inclusive growth will require sustained increases in spending on education, health, poverty alleviation and infrastructure. This, in turn, will require revenue increases, as well as reprioritising spending. The recent decision to cut fuel subsidies was a laudable step in this direction. Indonesia's abundant natural resources also need to be harnessed to support development, by raising investment and improving the regulatory environment. Environmental outcomes remain poor due to the central role in played by fossil fuels, as well as weak enforcement of existing laws and regulations, especially in forestry.

The key messages of this *Economic Survey* are:

- Growth has been strong in the decade and a half since the Asian Crisis but has slowed in recent years, reflecting weaker international demand, the fall in commodity prices and low investment growth, due in large part to heightened regulatory uncertainty and infrastructure bottlenecks.
- The pace of reform needs to accelerate as the backlog of necessary structural reforms and public investments has accumulated. But some of the directions policymakers have headed are worrisome, with protectionist tendencies sometimes coming to the fore.
- Healthy per capita growth and expanding social security programmes have helped to reduce poverty significantly. However, income inequality has risen, and the social safety net needs to be further developed.
- Indonesia's abundant natural resources can be better harnessed by raising productivity in agriculture, increasing efficiency in coal-fired power plants, and progressively shifting to renewable energy, especially geothermal.

Recent macroeconomic developments and short-term prospects

Since 2012, the Indonesian economy has encountered a good deal of turbulence. In 2013, GDP growth fell below 6% for the first time since the financial crisis, and growth

Table 1. **Selected indicators for Indonesia**

	1995	2000	2005	2011	2012	2013	2014[1]
Population							
Total, million	205.9	208.9	224.5	243.8	246.9	249.9	252.8
Age distribution							
0-14	33.6	30.7	30.0	29.6	29.3	28.9	28.5
15-65	62.2	64.7	65.1	65.3	65.6	65.9	66.2
65+	4.2	4.7	4.9	5.1	5.1	5.2	5.3
Absolute poverty rate (per cent)[2]		19.1	16.0	12.4	11.7	11.5	11.0
Gini coefficient		0.30	0.36	0.41	0.41	0.41	
Net enrolment ratio (secondary education, per cent)				67.5	70.7		
Employment and inflation							
Employment (million)	80.1	89.8	95.4	107.4	112.5	112.8	114.6
Informal employment, per cent of employment			70.5	63.9	61.4	60.1	59.6
Unemployment rate (per cent)	7.2	6.1	10.5	7.5	6.1	6.2	5.9
Inflation (CPI, end of year, per cent)	9.0	9.3	17.1	3.8	4.3	7.7	8.4
Supply and demand							
GDP (in current trillion rupiah)	546.4	1 520.7	3 035.6	7 831.7	8 615.7	9 524.7	10 542.7
GDP (in current USD billion)	243.6	182.4	313.2	894.3	921.4	916.8	888.8
GDP growth rate (real, in per cent)	8.2	4.9	5.7	6.2	6.0	5.6	5.0
GDP growth rate (real, in per capita terms, per cent)	6.1	5.1	4.2	4.8	4.7	4.3	3.8
Demand (growth in per cent)							
Private consumption	12.6	1.6	4.0	5.1	5.5	5.4	5.3
Public consumption	1.3	6.5	6.6	5.5	4.5	6.9	2.0
Gross fixed investment	10.3	10.8	9.5	7.9	12.2	3.9	6.3
Exports	14.0	16.7	10.9	8.9	9.1	5.3	4.1
Imports	7.7	26.5	16.6	14.8	1.6	4.2	1.0
Supply (in per cent of nominal GDP)							
Agriculture		14.3	13.1	14.7	14.5	14.4	14.3
Mining		11.0	11.1	11.8	11.8	11.3	10.5
Manufacturing		25.4	27.4	24.3	24.0	23.7	23.7
Services[3]		49.4	48.3	49.1	49.7	50.6	51.5
Public finances (central government, in per cent of GDP)							
Revenue	13.1	13.5	16.3	15.5	15.5	15.1	15.5
Expenditure	12.0	14.6	16.8	16.5	17.3	17.3	17.8
Nominal balance (central government)	1.1	-1.1	-0.5	-1.1	-1.8	-2.2	-2.3
Gross debt (general government)		81.1	43.3	23.1	23.0	24.9	24.4
Balance of payments (in per cent of GDP)							
Trade balance (goods)	2.7	13.7	5.6	3.8	0.9	0.6	0.8
Current account balance	-2.6	4.9	0.1	0.2	-2.8	-3.2	-3.0
In USD billion	-6.4	8.0	0.3	1.7	-24.4	-29.1	-26.2
International reserves (gross, USD billion)			34.7	110.1	112.8	99.4	111.9
Outstanding external debt		77.7	41.7	25.2	27.4	29.0	32.9

1. Estimates.
2. Per cent of people below the national poverty line, where the latter is the value of per capita expenditure per month needed for a person to enjoy decent living conditions.
3. Includes electricity, gas, water and construction.

Source: Statistics Indonesia, Government financial statement (audited), World Bank, and OECD calculations.

continued to soften through 2014. Despite the slowdown, Indonesia's economic growth has outperformed its ASEAN peers (Figure 1). This performance can be attributed to both a robust consumer base and to sound macroeconomic policies, such as inflation targeting and fiscal prudence. Until mid-2014, consumption had been supported by firming

Figure 1. **Level of real GDP in selected ASEAN countries**

2008 Q1 = 100

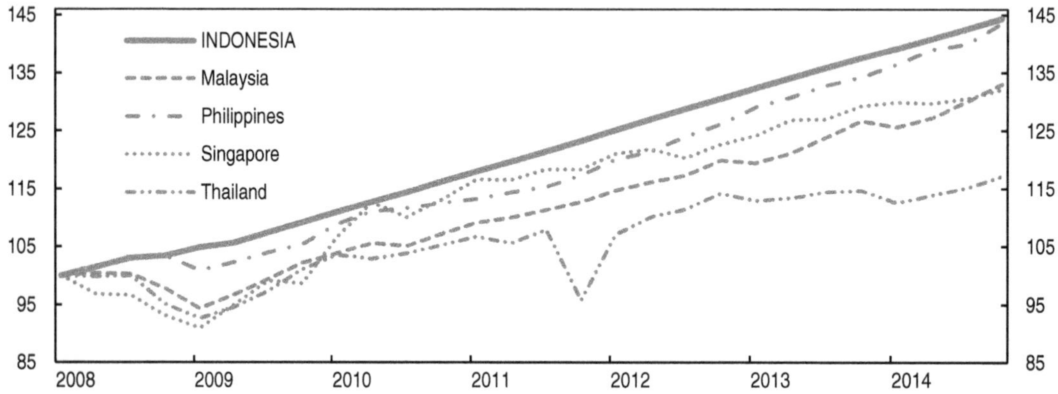

Source: National statistics offices.

StatLink http://dx.doi.org/10.1787/888933199951

confidence, cash transfers to poor families, strong wage gains and improving labour market outcomes. Despite a surge in exports in late 2013, as exports of mineral ores were bought forward before the enforcement of the export ban, the contribution of external demand to growth has been disappointing, exacerbating current account worries starting in mid-2011 and again in the mid-2014. Investment also weakened in 2013-14, led by slowing investment in machinery and transportation equipment (Figure 2). This deceleration in investment should be a concern, not only because of its effect on productivity but also its growing share in GDP: one quarter in 2013, up from one fifth in 2000.

Figure 2. **Indonesian real GDP, consumption and investment growth**

Year-on-year percentage changes

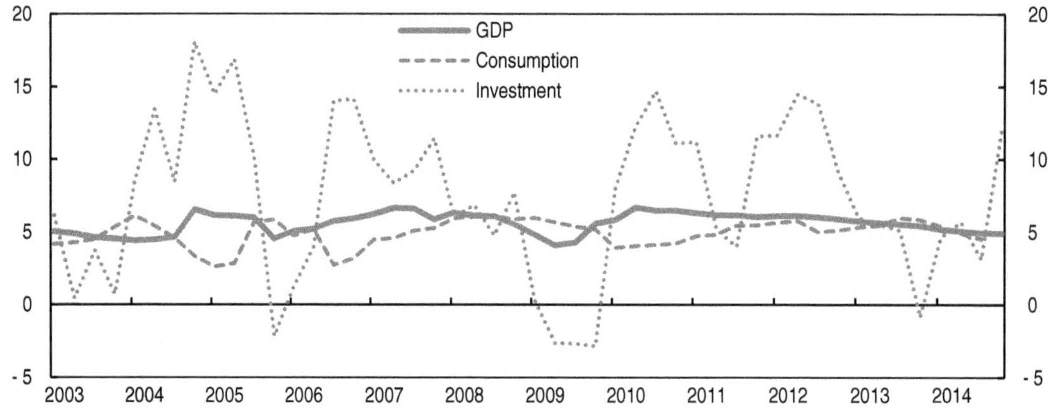

Source: OECD *Quarterly National Accounts Database.*

StatLink http://dx.doi.org/10.1787/888933199961

The economy grew at 5% in 2014 and is projected to accelerate somewhat in 2015 and 2016, as exports accelerate, thanks to the lower exchange rate, and a pickup in government investment (Table 2). A rapidly expanding middle class, combined with improving confidence, will help to sustain consumption and lift private investment. While the depreciated currency will help to curb imports, robust domestic demand will offset this to

Table 2. **OECD economic projections for Indonesia**

	2012	2013	2014	2015	2016
Real GDP growth	6.0	5.6	5.0	5.3	5.9
Inflation rate (CPI)	4.3	6.4	6.4	4.8	4.0
Short-term interest rate	5.9	6.3	8.8	7.0	6.6
Fiscal balance (% of GDP)	-1.9	-2.2	-2.4	-2.0	-1.8
Current account balance (% of GDP)	-2.8	-3.2	-3.0	-2.8	-2.5

Note: Real GDP growth and inflation are defined as percentage changes from the previous period.
Source: OECD staff estimates.

some extent, with the current account deficit persistently high. Even if core inflation remains low and the current account is stabilising, Bank Indonesia (BI) needs to remain cautious about official interest rates, especially in light of the continuing reliance on external sources of funding in the context of global financial uncertainty. The 2014 budget deficit remained elevated, in part due to lower revenues from the extraction sector, as commodity prices declined. The fiscal balance is expected to remain in moderate deficit, as is appropriate.

Risks to the outlook are tilted to the downside and mainly external. Trading partner demand, especially from China, may not recover as quickly as assumed, and commodity prices could weaken further. While financial markets have partly factored in imminent monetary policy normalisation in the United States, Indonesia is still vulnerable to an increase in international interest rates, as external funding requirements remain significant. Natural disasters are also an omnipresent risk to the resilience of growth. Indonesia is particularly prone to catastrophic natural disasters, such as earthquakes, tsunamis and volcanic eruptions. Between 2000 and 2014, close to 200 000 people died from natural disasters in Indonesia. This is a per capita death rate four times higher than both the Asian and world averages (CRED, 2015). Finally, the 2014 elections resulted in an unclear balance of political power, leaving the new President with the challenge of getting his ambitious reform agenda through a parliament in which his allies do not hold a majority. Related to this, the temptation remains strong to resort to misguided but politically popular protectionist actions whose long-run consequences are inimical to inclusive and sustainable development.

Monetary and financial policies

Monetary policy: Balancing internal and external constraints

The authorities' approach to managing external imbalances changed over the past three years. As the current account worsened starting in mid-2011 (Figure 3, Panel A), Bank Indonesia (BI) used its foreign currency reserves to intervene heavily in the foreign exchange market in order to cushion the fall in the rupiah (Panel B). In the second half of 2013, Indonesian shares, bonds and the domestic currency came under strong pressure after the Fed signalled that it would begin scaling back its bond-buying programme. This led to a change in policy as interest rates were raised, and BI started rebuilding its reserves. The current account deficit widened again in the second quarter of 2014 to 4.0% of GDP, and the rupiah has been adjusting downwards in an orderly manner, consistent with the IMF (2013) view that it was overvalued. This was assisted by strong portfolio capital inflows through 2014. The current deficit improved to below 3% of GDP at the end of 2014.

Current policy rates are appropriate, given residual tensions on financial markets, including the need to attract capital to fund the current account deficit, and moderating

Figure 3. **Current account and exchange rate developments**

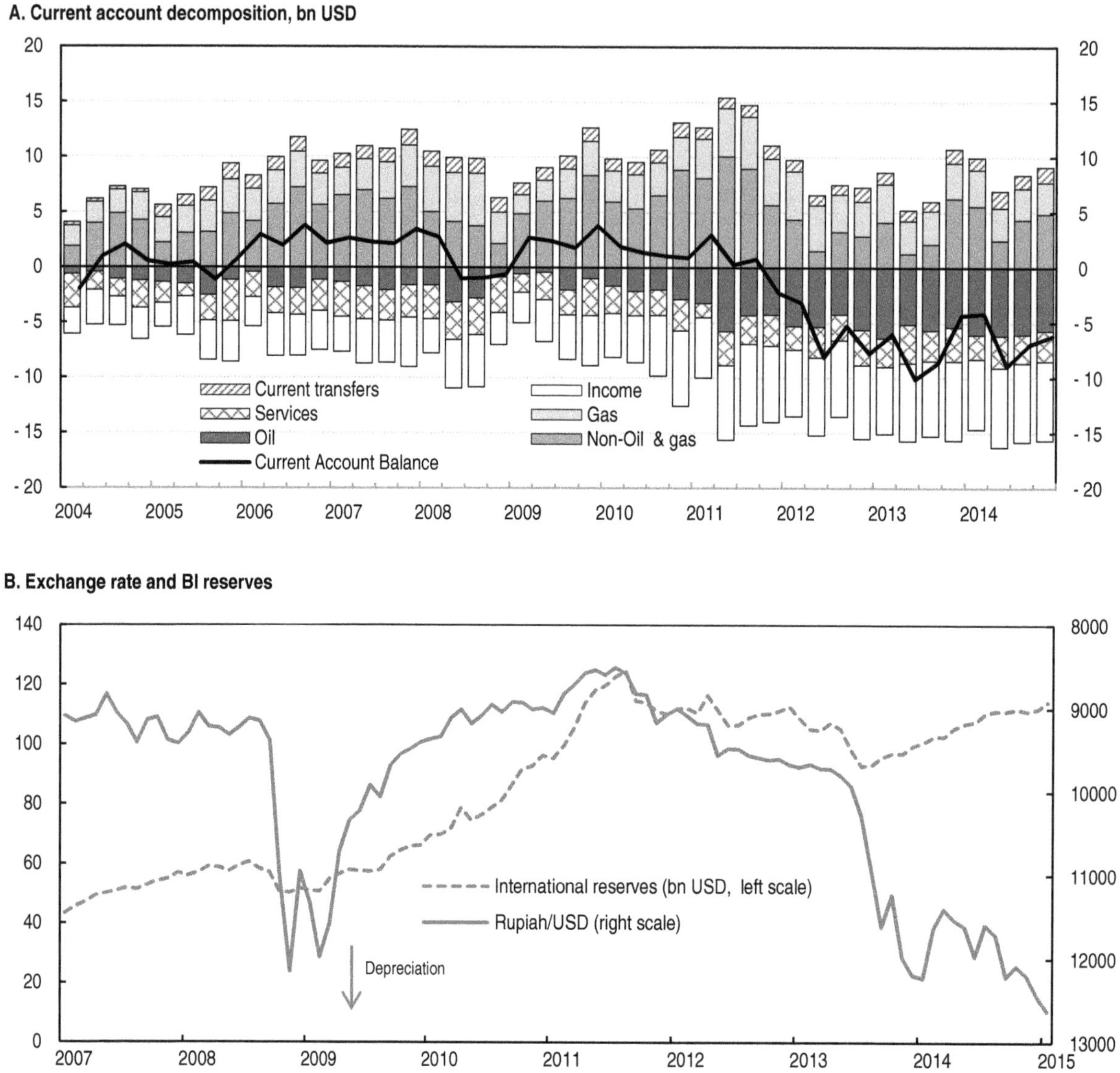

Source: Bloomberg and CEIC.

StatLink http://dx.doi.org/10.1787/888933199976

underlying inflation (Figure 4, Panels A and B). The small quarter-point point increase in November 2014, which followed a cut in fuel subsidies, was consistent with the inflation-targeting framework and signalled the Bank's determination to anchor inflation expectations. And the quarter-point point decrease in February 2015 was in response to inflation declining more rapidly than expected, mainly because of falling global oil prices. Going forward, BI should remain cautious in changing its policy settings, taking into account both external and internal factors, especially in light of signs that any reacceleration in domestic growth will be more tepid than previously projected.

Broadening and deepening the financial system

The financial system is dominated by banks, which held 79% of financial-sector assets in 2013 (compared to 50% in Malaysia, for example), leaving little room for other financial

Figure 4. **CPI inflation, decomposition and target**

A. CPI decomposition[1], year-on-year growth

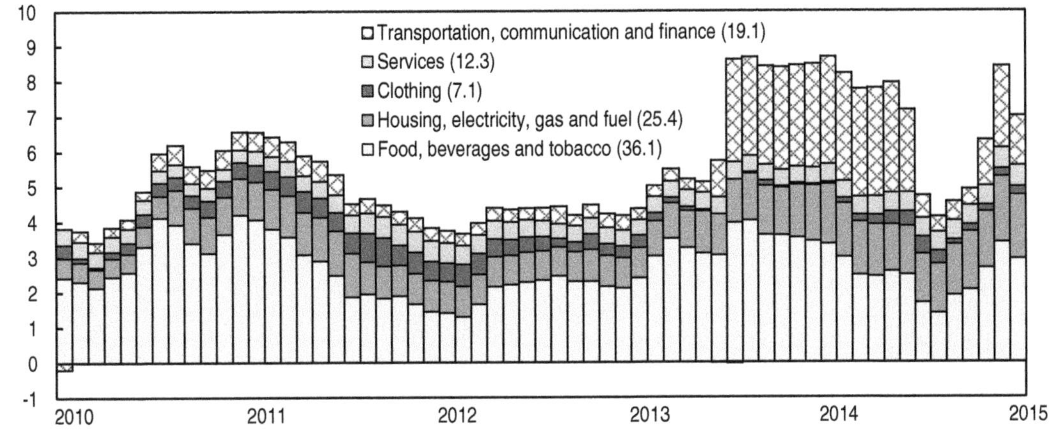

B. CPI inflation, target, year-on-year growth

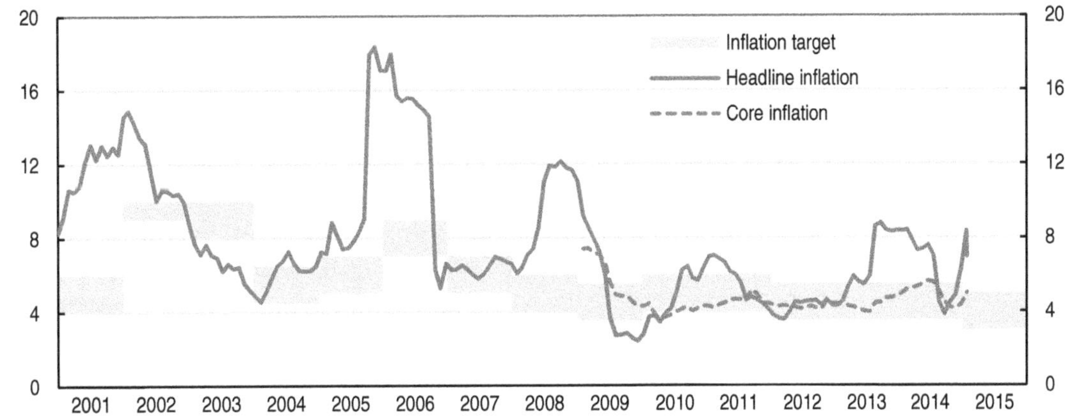

1. CPI component weights in brackets.

Source: CEIC and Bank Indonesia.

StatLink http://dx.doi.org/10.1787/888933199986

institutions. Insurance companies on the other hand hold about 10% of financial-sector assets, and less than 3% are held by pension funds (IMF, 2013). Indonesia needs to accelerate the deepening and broadening of its financial system by encouraging formal domestic savings (which requires a low-inflation environment) and facilitating the mobilisation of funds from non-bank institutions to finance investment, especially in infrastructure. This would enhance financial stability and increase liquidity. Volatility in capital inflows has contributed to the periodic sharp swings in the rupiah, bond and stock prices. Despite being the largest economy in the Southeast-Asian region, Indonesia's forex transactions are less than 5% of neighboring Singapore. Authorities thus need to continue efforts to develop the foreign exchange market and decrease the risk premium on rupiah-denominated assets underlying the transactions, generalising hedging and options to reduce the dominance of spot transactions and progressively eliminating remaining restrictions on foreign-currency-denominated bank deposits.

Indonesian banks have higher margins between borrowing and lending interest rates than those from other ASEAN countries (Figure 5). This reflects their need to cover higher operating costs (between 2.5% and 4% of their assets, as against 2% in Malaysia and 1% in

Figure 5. **Banks' interest rate margins on lending to private customers**
Percentage points, 2012

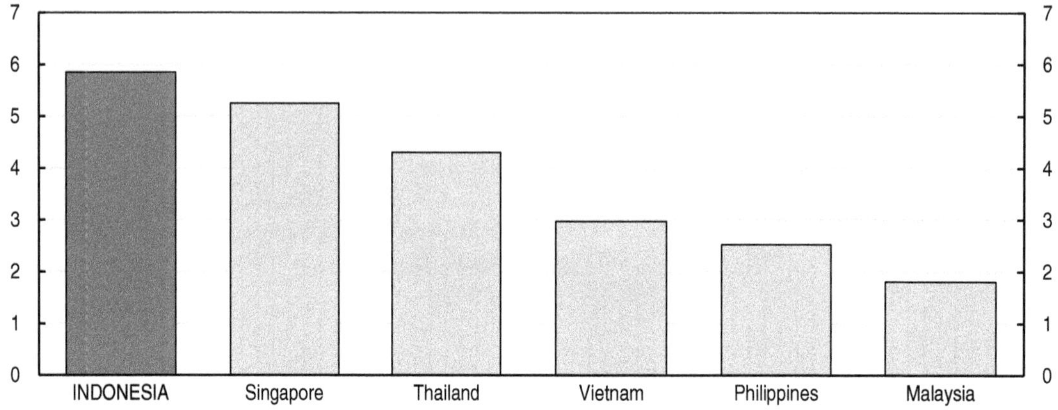

Source: World Bank, *World Development Indicators.*

StatLink http://dx.doi.org/10.1787/888933199997

Singapore), due to Indonesia's unique geography and inefficiencies: they have some of the highest ratios of operating expenses to total assets among banks in the G20 (Bloomberg, 2013). However, Indonesian banks are also the most profitable among the G20 economies, with an average return on equity at 23%, ahead of China at 21% and more than double the United States at 9% (Bloomberg, 2013). The high returns in Indonesia are driven by net interest margins, which at an average of 7 percentage points, are the highest in the G20 (the average interest rate on loans is 12%, while the average rate paid to depositors is 5%). Recent steps taken by authorities towards encouraging more competition and transparency in order to bring down spreads were appropriate, but measures to cap foreign ownership in banking should be reconsidered.

Domestic credit as a percentage of GDP is significantly below that of neighbouring ASEAN peers, suggesting that there is much room for financial deepening (Figure 6). The financial system shrank in the aftermath of the 1997-98 crisis. Between 1997 and 2012, domestic credit to the private sector fell from 61% to 35% of GDP and the number of commercial banks from 239 to 122. But rapid economic growth since then, combined with a clearer and stronger supervisory regime, makes it appropriate to expand the banking sector once again and to further encourage a greater role by non-depository institutions in providing credit. Indonesian households are also lagging on a range of financial and credit-access indicators (Figure 7). Overall, 20% of adults have an account at a formal financial institution, compared to 35% in India, 56% in Brazil and 64% in China (Demirguc-Kunt and Klapper, 2013). Moreover, only 8% of the bottom two quintiles of Indonesian households hold an account at a formal financial institution. Governments in other emerging-market economies are moving forward with plans to improve this situation. For example, in August 2014, the Indian government introduced the Jan Dhan Yojana scheme, which aims at opening 75 million bank accounts by end-January 2015. Opening an account through the scheme will entitle a holder to an accidental insurance cover and, after six months of operations, to an overdraft facility. In Indonesia, a large proportion of poor households, micro-businesses and SMEs are excluded from formal banking and lending services, or use shadow banks, which charge much higher rates. The outstanding value of SME loans was worth just 0.7% of GDP in 2010, compared with 30.7% in Thailand and 17.4% in Malaysia. Finally, the high margins enjoyed by Indonesian banks may also be a sign that credit

Figure 6. **Credit and stocks traded for selected ASEAN countries**

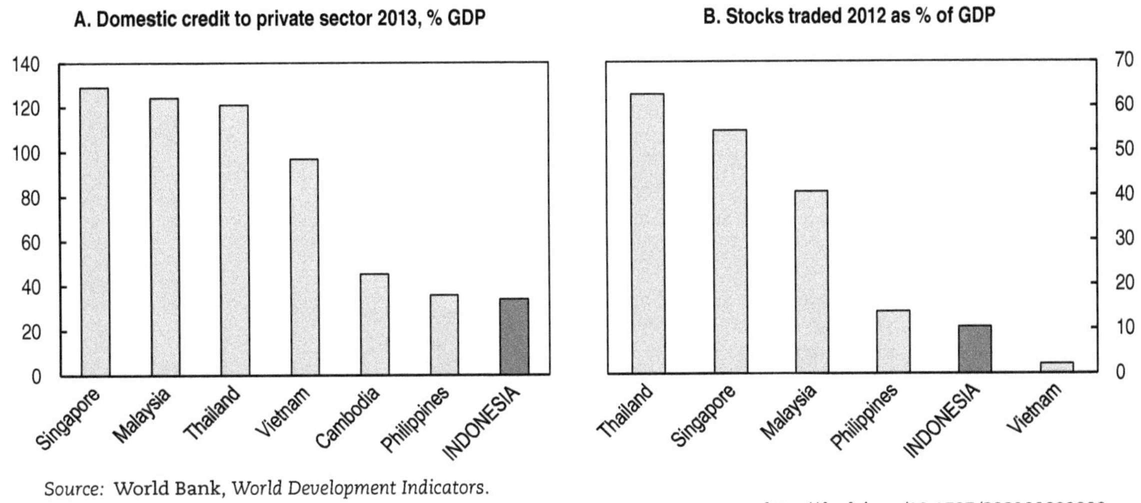

Source: World Bank, *World Development Indicators*.

StatLink http://dx.doi.org/10.1787/888933200000

growth is being constrained by the lack of deposits (Bloomberg, 2013). Improving financial inclusiveness may assist in this regard.

By eliminating the need for costly branch infrastructure, branchless banking could foster financial inclusion by making serving poor and isolated, unbanked households and businesses profitable (World Bank, 2014c). To enhance financial inclusion, more attention could be given to less costly methods of service provision such as mobile phone banking. This has been a success in countries like Kenya and the Philippines (World Bank, 2012b; and BBVA, 2015). Financial services could also be offered through local gas stations or shops, as in Mexico or Brazil. In Mexico, new regulations enabling the use of nonbank correspondents (also known as banking agents) make it possible for financial institutions to increase their reach at lower costs both for banks and potential customers. BI recently conducted a pilot in some provinces (Stapleton, 2013), and if it is judged successful, branchless banking should extended. Branchless banking can also be used by the government for tax collection for unbanked segments of the population. Government ministries' early adoption of branchless banking would also accelerate social security payments in areas where the unbanked are concentrated.

Banking oversight was strengthened with the implementation of all three pillars of Basel II, and Basel III is to be implemented before 2018. In 2014, banking supervision was transferred from BI to the newly established Financial Services Authority (Otoritas Jasa Keuangan, OJK), which oversees capital market regulation, banks and non-bank financial institutions. The financial system has come a long way in improving its health and coherence, as evidenced by its ability to withstand the global financial crisis, in sharp contrast with the turmoil seen in 1997-98. However, non-bank corporations have again started to accumulate foreign currency denominated debt. To confront these risks, in October 2014 BI introduced rules for such borrowing that require a minimum hedging ratio in order to mitigate currency risk, a minimum foreign exchange liquidity ratio to allay liquidity risk and a minimum credit rating to lessen overleverage risk.

At 2% of GDP in 2014, the local currency bond market is very small, in contrast with Thailand at 19% and Malaysia at 42% (ADB, 2015). Indonesia's corporate bond landscape remains shallow, dominated by mining firms and state-owned utilities, which issued more

Figure 7. **Financial development indicators for selected ASEAN countries, 2011**

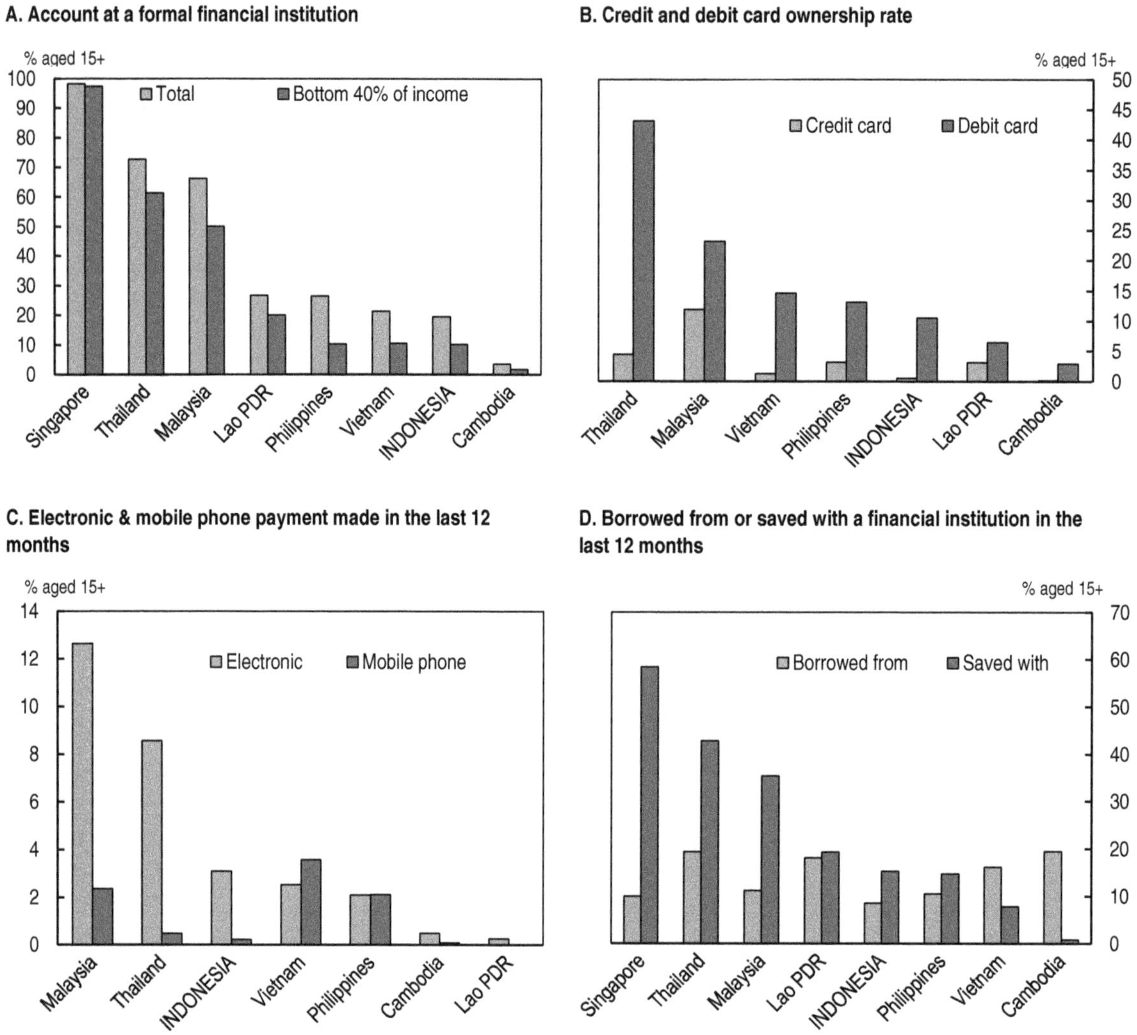

Source: World Bank, *Global Findex (Global Financial Inclusion Database).*

StatLink http://dx.doi.org/10.1787/888933200019

than half of all such bonds in 2009-13, and the 20 largest issuers were responsible for around 90% of total bond issuance in 2013. Only 30% of corporate bonds issued in Indonesia in 2012-13 were denominated in local currency (RBA, 2012). Efforts to develop a local corporate bond market should therefore be stepped up.

The fiscal position is strong, but the government budget is small

Thanks to strong growth prospects and well-entrenched fiscal prudence, exemplified by a fiscal rule limiting the budget deficit to no more than 3% of GDP, the fiscal outlook is solid, with government debt stabilising at an enviable 26% of GDP. But revenue is low, and spending needs are increasing; the deficit has been rising for the past four years (Figure 8). Under current circumstances, this stimulus is broadly appropriate, but only to the extent it does not signal a significant structural deterioration in the budget.

Until end 2014, over 20% of spending had been on fuel and electricity subsidies, to keep energy affordable for the poor and to raise household purchasing power. But the

Figure 8. **Central government revenue, expenditure and balance**

Per cent of GDP

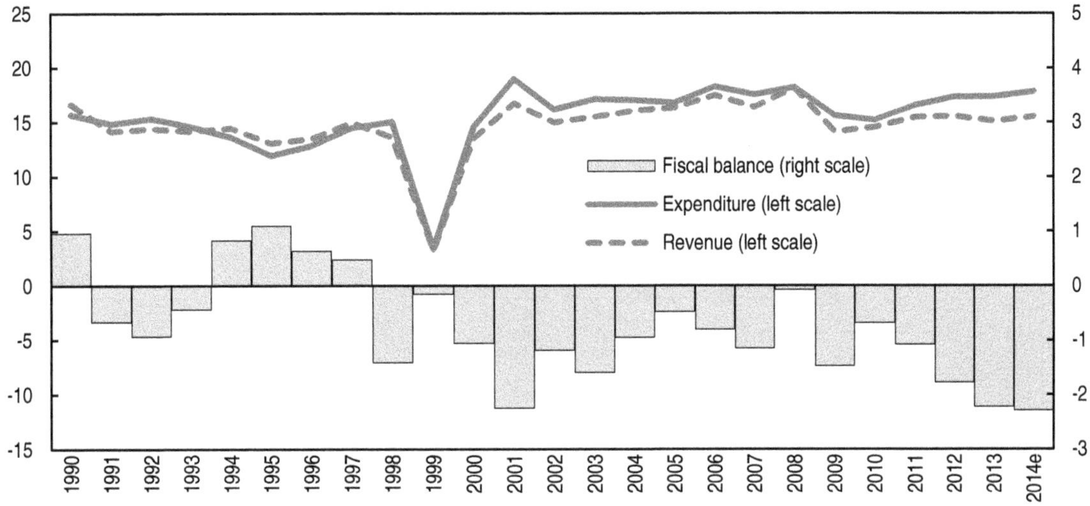

Source: CEIC data; Bank Indonesia; DPJU; and *OECD Economic Outlook 96.*

StatLink http://dx.doi.org/10.1787/888933200021

subsidies did not work as intended, as 40% of subsidy benefits went to the top income decile and less than 1% to the poorest (World Bank, 2014a). Subsidies also had unintended consequences in the form of increased demand, traffic congestion and environmental damage, whose deadweight loss had been estimated at USD 4-8 billion annually (Davis, 2014). Declining production from maturing oil fields (requiring more imports) added to the problem. Fuel subsidies were reduced in June 2013 and again in November 2014, bringing subsidised fuel prices closer to market prices. Then, at the beginning of 2015, the government dexterously grasped the opportunity offered by falling world oil prices and scrapped its existing petrol and diesel price-setting regime. Both domestic petrol and diesel prices are now linked directly to world prices, with only diesel getting a fixed subsidy of IDR 1 000 (USD 0.08) a litre. The small subsidy on diesel has been retained because of its use in public and freight transport. A programme is in place to phase out diesel use in favour of liquefied natural gas (LNG).

The 2015 budget originally contained fuel subsidies worth more than 13% of total government expenditure, but this has now been whittled down to only 1%. The government has allocated the savings from the fuel subsidy cut largely to infrastructure and the remainder to social spending, local-level projects and deficit reduction. Electricity subsidies remain an issue, and because most generation capacity takes the form of coal- and oil-fired power plants, this is indirectly a fossil fuel subsidy. Electricity subsidies amount to around 8% of total government expenditure. The ongoing reforms in this area should continue, including gradual price reforms until electricity pricing fully recovers the ongoing costs of maintaining and improving Indonesia's electricity system.

Raising government revenues

The government budget is small, even by the standards of peer countries. Central tax revenue (excluding non-tax resource revenue) is around 12% of GDP where it has remained for the past decade, despite increasing efforts to combat tax fraud (see below). The vast majority of revenue is raised at the central government level, rather than by provincial or municipal governments. Its tax effort (the ratio of actual tax revenues to their potential), estimated at around 50%, is among the lowest for peer countries (Figure 9; Fenochietto and Pessino, 2013). Indonesia, as a resource rich country, relies heavily on corporate taxes on the large and profitable extraction sector. Correspondingly, personal taxes comprise a low share of total revenues; this may reflect the very large informal sector.

Figure 9. **Tax effort versus GDP per capita, 2011**

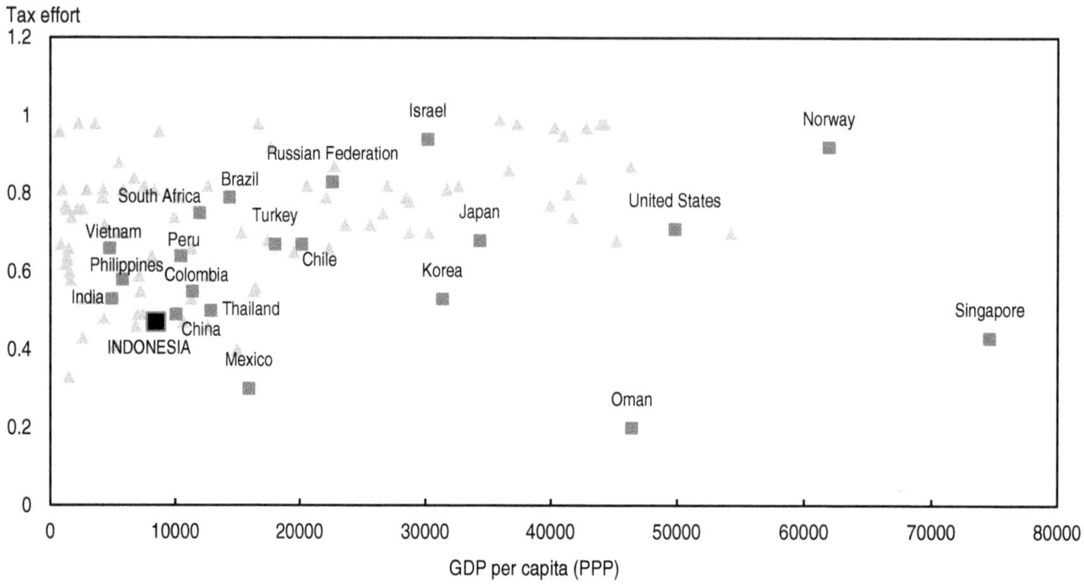

Note: Tax effort is the ratio of actual tax revenues to estimated potential tax revenues.
Source: Fenochietto, R. and C. Pessino (2013), "Understanding Countries' Tax Effort", *IMF Working Paper*, WP/13/244; World Bank, *World Development Indicators*.

StatLink http://dx.doi.org/10.1787/888933200030

Realising the new government's economic agenda, which includes expanding social services, improving education and lifting infrastructure spending, requires more revenues. To that end, the President has pledged to lift the tax-to-GDP ratio to 16% by 2019 (BAPPENAS, 2015). The 2012 *Economic Survey* (OECD, 2012) included a chapter on the tax system. It recommended increasing tax compliance by bringing more self-employed into the tax net and by both boosting the efficiency of and increasing resources for tax collection. The performance of the tax office could be further improved by greater empowerment of tax officials (including through heightened legal protection), more frequent and targeted auditing, better access to third-party sources of information, and enhanced co-operation with local authorities. Indonesia should continue to be actively engaged in the OECD's Base Erosion and Profit Shifting (BEPS) Project.

Recommendations for fiscal, monetary and financial policy

Key recommendations

- Bank Indonesia should remain cautious with regards to monetary and macro-prudential policies, taking into account both external and internal factors.
- Raise government tax revenues in order to fund a needed longer-term increase in government spending. Revenue could be raised by bringing more self-employed into the tax net and by improving the effectiveness of tax collection.

Other recommendations:

- Deepen and broaden financial markets by making more room for non-banks and the stock market in financing the economy. Further develop the foreign exchange market by reducing the role of BI, generalising hedging and options, and enlarging the class of assets underlying the transactions.

Improving living standards by sustaining long-term inclusive growth

Indonesia's level of real per capita GDP (adjusted for purchasing power) has doubled from around 5% of US levels in 1960 to 10% in 2012, rising from 130th of 143 countries in 1960 to 90th (Penn World Tables, 2013). However, with per capita income of around USD 9 300, it is still in the catch-up phase. The growth dividend for multi-factor productivity (MFP) accruing from earlier policy reforms in sustaining convergence continues to be high but is slowly decreasing (Box 1). Moreover, sustained and robust growth is a vital ingredient in eliminating poverty, which is still widespread, even when compared to other countries at similar levels of per capita income.

Indonesia's per capita GDP gap with high-income OECD countries reflects lower hourly labour productivity. The new government has set itself the target of raising labour productivity by 40% by 2019. Per capita hours worked are already close to high-income countries (Figure 11). As in Japan, Korea and Chinese Taipei in the past, the process of convergence in Indonesia will involve the continued transfer of labour resources from low-productivity sectors, like agriculture, to manufacturing and services. However, convergence is conditional on the right economic fundamentals, put in place by an appropriate mix of policies. Indonesia is benefiting from an ongoing demographic "bonus" (Figure 12), with the labour force participation rate expected to peak only around 2030. Youth unemployment is high at over 20%. Sufficient high-quality formal-sector jobs will need to be created in order to absorb the continuing large inflow of young people into the labour force. Chapter 1 of this *Survey* explores the types of policies Indonesia needs to promote sustainable and inclusive growth.

The large productivity gap is, at least in part, due to large segments of the labour force still engaged in agriculture. Indeed, Indonesia's comparative advantage has been in primary products, as is indicated by their rising share of exports. In that regard, the recent fall in the mining and energy share is for the most part due to the sharp decline in coal prices, Indonesia's top export (Figure 13). Indonesia also has the lowest export share of manufactures among ASEAN countries. Part of the MFP catch up will involve fostering robust manufacturing and services sectors. And manufacturing FDI has risen substantially since 2009 and accounted for nearly half of all FDI in 2012.

Box 1. **A new decomposition of growth**

Using a dynamic stochastic general equilibrium (DSGE) model of Indonesia, growth can be decomposed into four main components: changes in supply factors (capital, labour and multi-factor productivity), changes in external conditions (such as the risk premium on domestic bonds and world growth), changes in monetary conditions (in particular interest rates) and changes in consumption decisions by households (Figure 10). As expected, most of Indonesia's growth over the last decade has been driven by supply factors, especially rising multi-factor productivity (MFP) as Indonesia reaped the benefits of post-Asian-crisis structural reforms. The pace of multi-factor productivity growth has slowed since 2010, however, a decelerating trend reinforced by slower world growth and less dynamic domestic consumption. A series of interest rate cuts has successfully managed to offset those headwinds. Absent further structural reforms to revive productivity growth, the current supportive monetary environment will not be sufficient to sustain long-term growth and poses inflation risks.

Figure 10. **Sources of growth**

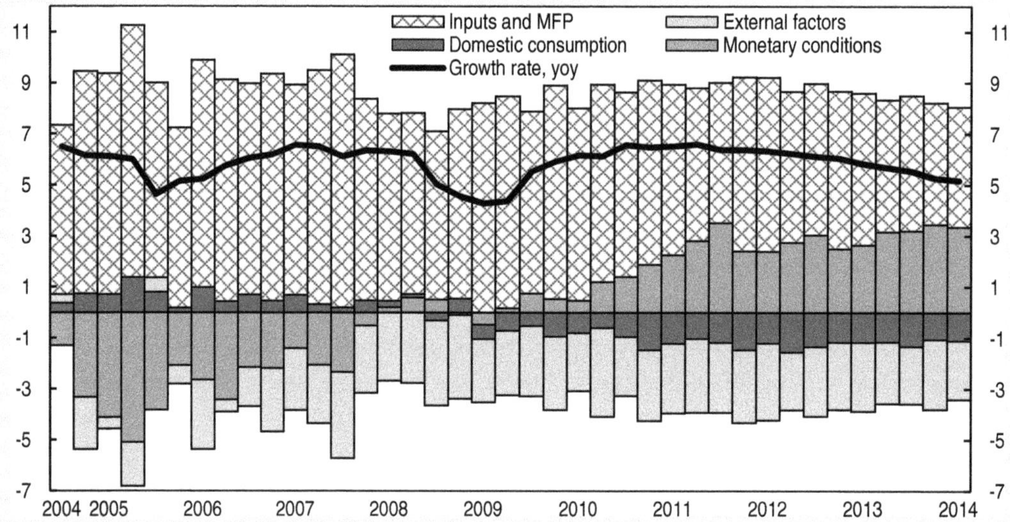

Source: Dutu, R. (2015), "Decomposing Shocks to the Indonesian Business Cycle Using an Estimated DSGE Model", *Technical Background Paper* (2015).

StatLink http://dx.doi.org/10.1787/888933200049

Protectionist sentiment has long been evident in policy making in Indonesia. This sentiment comes from the arguments that recent policy measures introduced by the government are aimed at increasing value-added to some of its strategic commodities, reaching self-sufficiency, and climbing up its value chain to diversify economic activity and create jobs as mandated by its Constitution. Having said this, Indonesia has taken concrete steps to liberalise trade, both unilaterally and through regional free trade agreements (ASEAN, and ASEAN + Japan, China, Australia and New Zealand). These trade agreements account for a large proportion of Indonesia's traded goods and to some extent render unilateral protectionist policies ineffective. Moreover, self-sufficiency does not necessarily mean protectionism. In some contexts, self-sufficiency can be directed towards enhancing production efficiently, sustainably, and environmentally friendliness.

Figure 11. **Differences in income per capita for selected emerging economies, 2013**

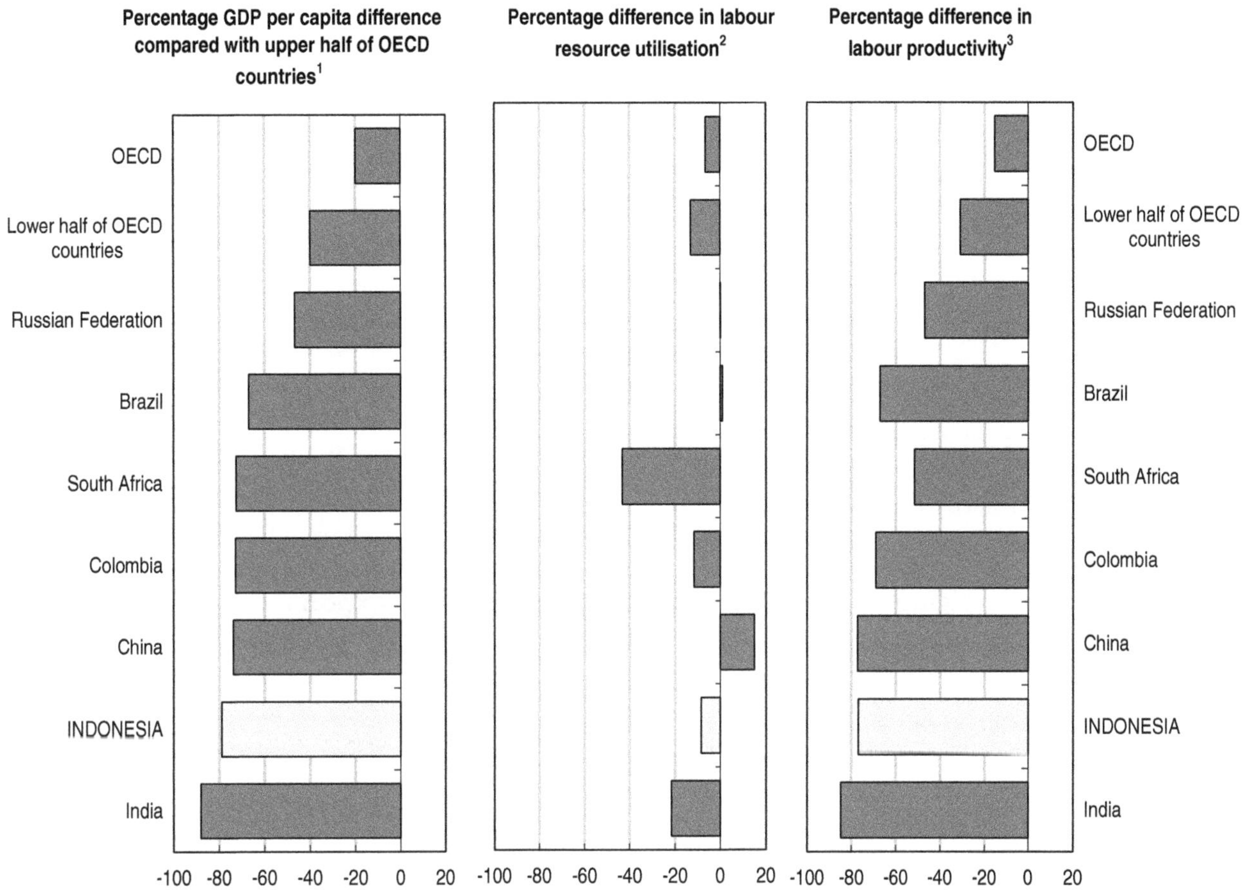

1. Compared to the simple average of the 17 OECD countries with highest GDP per capita in 2012, based on 2012 purchasing power parities (PPPs). The sum of the percentage difference in labour resource utilisation and labour productivity do not add up exactly to the GDP per capita difference since the decomposition is multiplicative.
2. Labour resource utilisation is measured as employment as a share of population.
3. Labour productivity is measured as GDP per employee.

Source: OECD National Accounts, OECD Economic Outlook and OECD Employment Outlook Databases.

StatLink http://dx.doi.org/10.1787/888933200051

However, the 2014 Trade Law establishes a new legal basis for the government to manage exports and imports of tradable goods by authorising the restriction of imports to protect and promote local industries; to impose tariffs where necessary; to limit or halt exports of strategic commodities to ensure adequate local supplies; to act in the general interest of the country's trade balance. Agriculture has long been the sector in which self-sufficiency and protectionist measures have been most evident. These policies often conflate and confuse different objectives, including protecting farmers' incomes, managing food price volatility and achieving national food self-sufficiency by minimising reliance on foreign imports. The New Food Law No. 18/2012 articulated the general principle of food security (*kemandirian pangan* or self-reliance) and established domestic production of staples as the priority. Production targets were set for 39 products, and for five (rice, corn, soybean, sugar and beef) the targeted levels aim to achieve self-sufficiency. The law imposed restrictions on the import of fruits and vegetables resulting in high domestic prices. Rice is a case in point, with estimates that in mid-2014, the domestic price of rice was 60% higher than world prices

Figure 12. **Demographic projections for Indonesia**

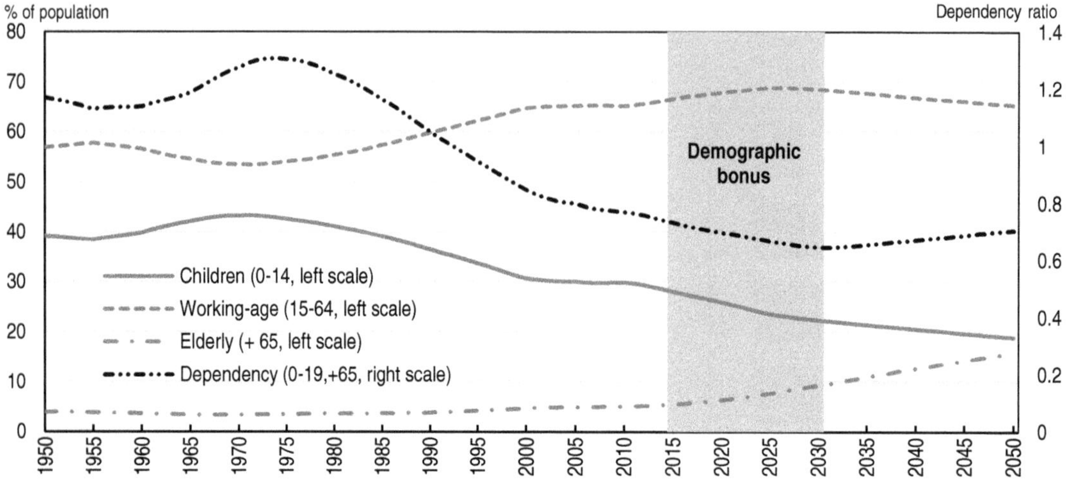

Source: United Nations, *World Population Prospects: The 2012 Revision*.

StatLink http://dx.doi.org/10.1787/888933200064

Figure 13. **Composition of Indonesian goods exports**[1]

Per cent of goods exports

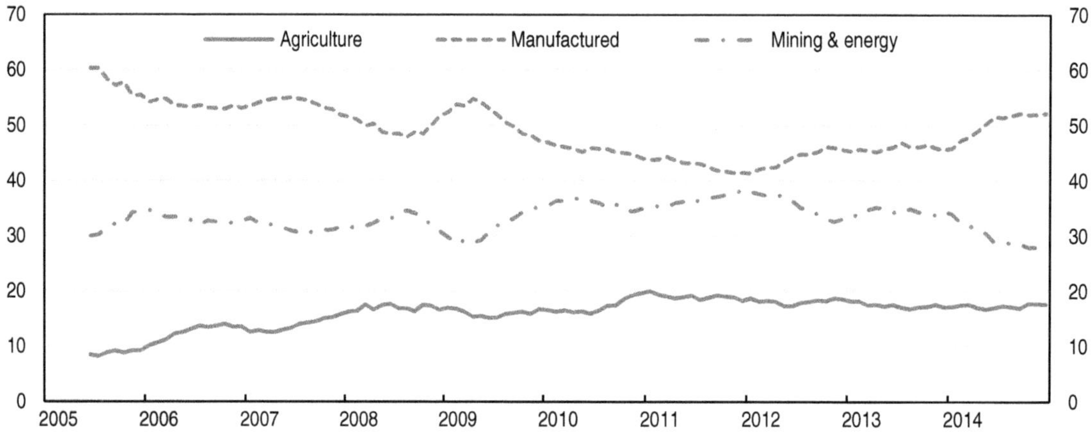

1. Palm oil and processed rubber are included in Agriculture, and oil products are in Mining & Energy.

Source: Bank Indonesia.

StatLink http://dx.doi.org/10.1787/888933200074

(Timmer, 2014). This imposes a significant burden on poor households, for whom expenditure on rice comprises a large proportion of their budget.

Many other sectors of the economy are also protected from foreign competition. For example, limits on the foreign ownership of mines have hampered investment in the sector (see Chapter 2). The inauguration of the ASEAN Economic Community (AEC) free trade area in 2015 has prompted some changes, including a revision of the Negative Investment List (NIL), which sets out sectors of the economy that are either wholly closed to foreign direct investment or in which foreign direct investment is limited to a certain share. In May 2014, changes to the NIL reflected both national development priorities and AEC obligations. Restrictions on foreign investment in some infrastructure sectors such as ports, electricity generation and waste treatment were relaxed, and special provisions were made for ASEAN investors. However, the May 2014 revision of the NIL also included tightening of restrictions in other sectors, including in the oil industry and in logistics.

In 2013, Indonesia had the fourth most restrictive FDI regime among 58 countries, according to the OECD FDI regulatory restrictiveness index. As noted above, the December 2013 revision to the list of sectors requiring official approval for FDI (the Negative Investment List) is more restrictive than its predecessor in several key sectors, such as oil and gas. Nevertheless, FDI inflows have remained high, as strong growth prospects and favourable funding conditions triggered an FDI boom beginning in 2010 (Figure 14). Growth in FDI in the manufacturing sector has been particularly strong since 2010.

Figure 14. **Foreign direct investment**

USD billions and per cent of GDP

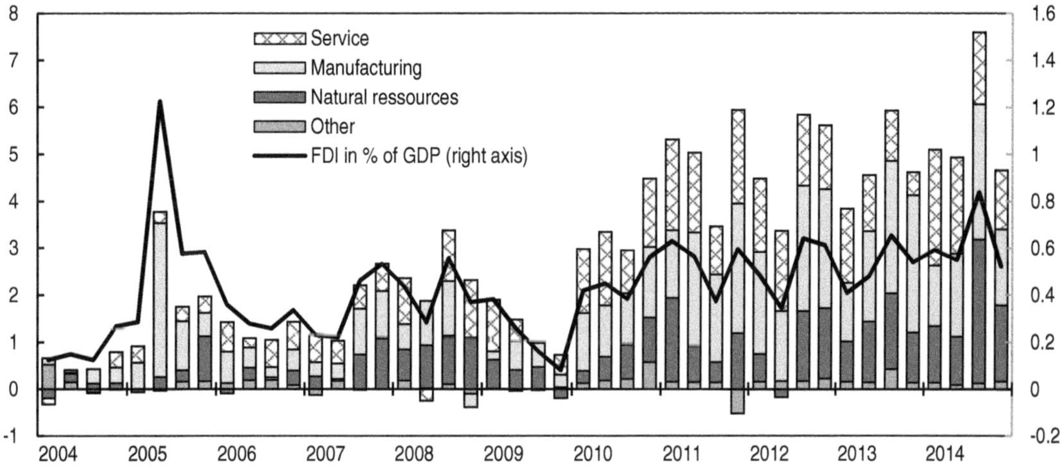

Source: Bank Indonesia.

StatLink http://dx.doi.org/10.1787/888933200088

Boosting education outcomes and participation

The accumulation of human capital provides labour with the skills to move into more capital-intensive industry and services. Countries like Japan, Korea, Singapore and Chinese Taipei all put enormous resources (both public and private) into raising educational outcomes. In 2002, Indonesia put in place a spending floor on education of 20% of all public expenditure, but this has been only rarely met. In 2011, this share was around 15%, which compares with around 21% for both Malaysia and Vietnam, 24% for Thailand, but only 10% in India. In terms of GDP, Indonesia's education spending is particularly low compared to other countries – in 2011, it was 2.8% compared to 6.3% in Vietnam, 5.9% in Malaysia, 5.8% in Thailand and 3.2% in India (Figure 15, Panel A).

Indonesia has made many education reforms in the past two decades, with significant innovations in both organisational policy and practice, and pedagogic practices (OECD, 2014b), and these reforms have had positive returns. While its educational outcomes tend to lag those of other countries in the region and beyond, adjusting for its level of per capita GDP, Indonesia performs fairly well. For instance, while it ranks second-lowest among those countries that participated in PISA 2012, relative to its per capita income level, its performance is quite good: its PISA outcomes are on par with those of Peru and Brazil, both of which have higher per capita income (Figure 15, Panel B). Likewise, tertiary educational

Figure 15. **Education outcomes and enrolment versus GDP per capita, 2012**

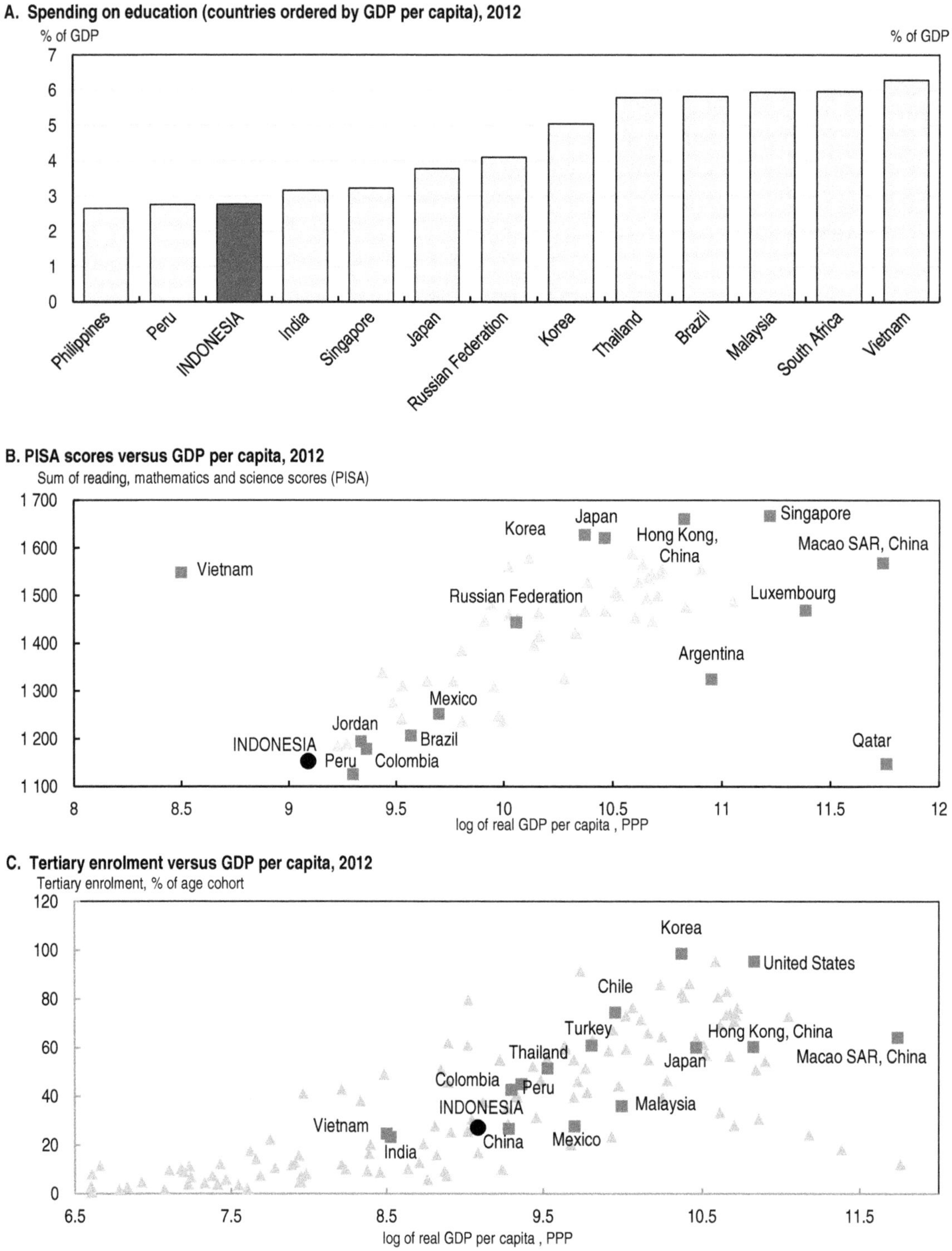

Source: *PISA Database 2012*; World Bank, *World Development Indicators.*

StatLink http://dx.doi.org/10.1787/888933200091

enrolment and attainment are quite low, but not relative to per capita income (Panel C). Moreover, most educational performance indicators have been improving steadily over the past few decades: tertiary enrolment was 3% in 1970, 9% in 1990 and 27% in 2011. Gender outcomes have also been relatively equal. However, policymakers cannot be complacent. Indonesia's educational performance started from a low base, and the easiest gains, such as achieving universal primary school enrolment, have now been made. Serious policy challenges lie ahead, and if these are not tackled, the progress seen to date will stall, and improvements in economic outcomes, including inclusive growth, will slow. The OECD *Education Policy Review of Indonesia* (OECD, 2015) goes into these issues in more detail, including expanding vocational schemes aimed at promoting youth employment.

While participation at all levels of education has risen in recent decades and is consistent with Indonesia's level of economic development, there is significant variation in enrolment and outcomes across the country. Social programmes are currently in place to assist students from poor families and isolated communities in attending educational institutions. The BSM (*Beasiswa untuk Siswa Miskin*) programme is a mix of several independent initiatives designed to help children to stay in school. It includes bursaries and scholarships, providing transfers directly to students or the schools that they attend, contingent on enrolment, attendance and other criteria. Currently around 4.6 million students are covered. However, the individual initiatives within the BSM are independently administered and budgeted and poorly co-ordinated, even when run by the same institution (see Chapter 1).

The quality of educational resources, including school infrastructure and teaching, is also an issue. The efficiency of public spending on education needs to be re-examined, as it has increased substantially in the past decade but outcomes have remained largely static. Around one in ten children repeat their first year of primary school and 6% their second year (UNICEF, 2012). Class sizes tend to be large relative to OECD countries (OECD, 2012a). Around one-third of all elementary school teachers have not undertaken any professional teacher training beyond a high school diploma, and three-quarters lack an undergraduate degree (Baedhowi, 2009). Improving teaching quality will require regular teacher assessments. Limited teacher retraining and certification programmes are in place, but coverage should be expanded to all 2.8 million teachers, although this may be unachievable by the 2015 target mandated in the 2005 national teacher law (World Bank, 2013b). Continuous professional development programmes should become the norm, linked to salary increments and promotion opportunities. Local authorities should also be helped to develop the capacity to better monitor the quality of instruction.

Raising infrastructure investment

As discussed in detail in the 2010 *Survey* (OECD, 2010), a second priority is the provision of high-quality infrastructure through greater investment, and better maintenance – especially in light of Indonesia's difficult geography and slowing infrastructure spending since the Asian Crisis. Infrastructure increases productivity and attracts business activity by lowering transport and production costs and facilitating market access. It not only facilitates greater engagement in global value chains (GVCs), but also promotes personal mobility across the archipelago and hence makes growth more inclusive. In the three years immediately prior to the Asian Crisis infrastructure spending averaged around 9% of GDP, but since 1999 it has averaged only around 4% (World Bank, 2012a). Road and rail transport are underdeveloped and overburdened, both between and within cities. Given Indonesia's maritime character, with some 17 500 islands, 6 000 of them inhabited, the new administration's focus on sea-based infrastructure is welcome. A lack of electricity generating capacity is also inhibiting capital investment, and delays at the country's outdated airports and ports are increasing the cost of international trade and hindering the formation of national value chains.

Given the opportunities offered by integration into GVCs, both in terms of generating well-paid jobs and boosting high value added exports, efficient communication and logistics are extremely important. Although progress has been made, including the introduction of a single window for port clearances, the World Bank's Logistics Performance Index (LPI) recently ranked Indonesia 53rd out of 160 countries in logistics, well behind other middle-income countries in the region in all aspects considered. Indeed, Indonesia ranks lowest in all sub-components of the LPI among such countries. Moreover, it scores poorly in openness to trade in the types of services that promote integration into GVCs. According to the OECD Services Trade Restrictiveness Index (STRI), Indonesia scores below the average of peer countries (Brazil, Chile, China, India, Mexico, Russian Federation, South Africa, Turkey) in 16 of the 18 service sectors included in the STRI. Indeed, it is in the logistics sectors like road freight transport and distribution services that Indonesia performs comparatively the worst.

In 2011, the government launched the Master Plan for Acceleration and Expansion of Indonesia Economic Development 2011-25 (MP3EI), which listed infrastructure as a national priority. The plan detailed the government's intention to build economic corridors, each supported by industry clusters, thereby optimising agglomeration advantages and strengthening national and international connectivity across those corridors. Its costs were estimated at USD 450 billion over 15 years; the government would directly finance 30%, and the private sector the rest. The government's aim should be to increase public spending on infrastructure to the levels that prevailed prior to the Asian Crisis, with a focus on transportation and logistics, and on poverty-alleviating infrastructure, such as natural disaster abatement, water treatment and sanitation.

The growing realisation that the government alone does not have the resources to meet all of the country's infrastructure needs means that the private sector is expected to play an important role. This is especially true given the 3% of GDP cap on government deficits. However, there remain major impediments to expanding the role of the private sector, both domestic and foreign. Greater efforts will need to be made to better channel available funds from public, private and Official Development Assistance (ODA) sources towards more productive infrastructure investments. Creating more transparent regulatory frameworks, improving accessibility to capital through more supportive financial markets and increasing the capacity to absorb capital inflows are all issues that need to be addressed. Allowing state-owned enterprises to borrow directly from ODA donors, under the supervision of Ministry of Finance, is a step in the right direction.

The government is strongly promoting the use of public-private partnerships (PPPs) to deliver infrastructure investment. A range of state-owned entities have been created to assist with PPP financing, including PT Penjamin Infrastruktur Indonesia (PT PII), which can provide project guarantees to improve the creditworthiness of the public-sector participants, thereby increasing private-sector participation and ring-fencing the government's contingent liability. Indonesia's sovereign wealth fund, *Pusat Investasi Pemerintah* (PIP), is capable of financing land acquisition for PPPs, and a Viability Gap Fund has also been established to provide additional capital to ensure projects' financial viability. Despite these initiatives, as of October 2013, of the 21 PPPs that have been tendered since 2009, only seven had reached the final stage of negotiations (BAPPENAS, 2013).

Moreover, although the central government's capacity to deliver PPPs has been strengthened, more needs to be done to boost the resources and capacities of sub-central governments, which are often the contracting authorities in PPP agreements. The recently established PPP centre within the Ministry of Finance is a timely step. This will focus on developing a pipeline of bankable government-supported infrastructure projects. Likewise, the recently instituted Infrastructure Prioritising Body (KP2IP) is welcome. It will assess and prioritise project proposals, and allocate them for implementation to line agencies, state-owned enterprises or the PPP centre in the Ministry of Finance. It will also provide guidance on how each project can be appropriately financed. Key challenges to improve the business environment and encourage good decision-making are to ensure that its deliberations and decisions are transparent and that it succeeds in enhancing co-ordination among infrastructure-related government bodies.

Given the complexities, including dealing with regional governments, a central co-ordinating entity is needed to help champion and shepherd PPP projects, including offering direct assistance to private firms tendering for them, but it remains unclear if the new PPP Centre or KP2IP will play this role. In any case the government's contingent liabilities need to be made public to avoid the temptation to hide them away from public scrutiny.

A major impediment to infrastructure investment and other fixed investment in Indonesia has been the long and arduous process of land acquisition. The 2011 Land Acquisition Act seeks to address this. It allows the government to acquire private land for public works projects and establishes a fair and transparent framework for compensating landowners, including spelling out a simplified and accelerated appeals procedure using prescribed time frames for each stage of the process. The Widodo government has announced plans for a land bank which would facilitate government purchases of land required for infrastructure development.

Improving inter-governmental co-ordination and regulations to promote infrastructure investment

Decentralisation, which started in 2001, devolved numerous expenditures, such as local roads and water treatment, to sub-national governments. Central government's share in infrastructure investment fell from around 80% to about 35% (World Bank, 2013a). While local governments are in a better position to assess regional infrastructure needs, this poses the challenge of effective integration of sub-national measures and regulations with national plans, such as MP3EI. Regulatory bottlenecks have been identified in at least nine national laws, six national government regulations, five presidential regulations, decrees and instructions, nine ministerial regulations and a number of sub-national regulations and permits (OECD, 2012b). The 2015-19 National Medium Term Development Plan (RPJMN 2015-19) (BAPPENAS, 2015) makes explicit the government's commitments for regulatory "debottlenecking" in order to overcome barriers that inhibit investment and business development in each sector and region. The government should not only accelerate the process of regulatory streamlining but make explicit efforts to ensure regulatory reforms are coherent across levels of government.

Recommendations for promoting inclusive and sustainable economic growth

Key recommendations

- Direct more public resources to improving education access and outcomes. Continue regular teacher assessments and professional development, and link teacher salaries more closely to qualifications and performance.
- Raise public spending on infrastructure. Focus on transportation and logistics to support industry, as well as natural disaster prevention and water treatment.
- Avoid protectionist measures that inhibit openness to trade and foreign investment with uncertain development payoff.

Reducing poverty and inequality

Indonesia has performed admirably in reducing absolute poverty. Over the past three decades per capita GDP growth has averaged around 3.5% annually, and this, in combination with government poverty-reduction programmes, has reduced the USD 2 per day poverty headcount from around 85% of the population to 43% since 1980 (Figure 16, Panel A). For

Figure 16. **Poverty and inequality**

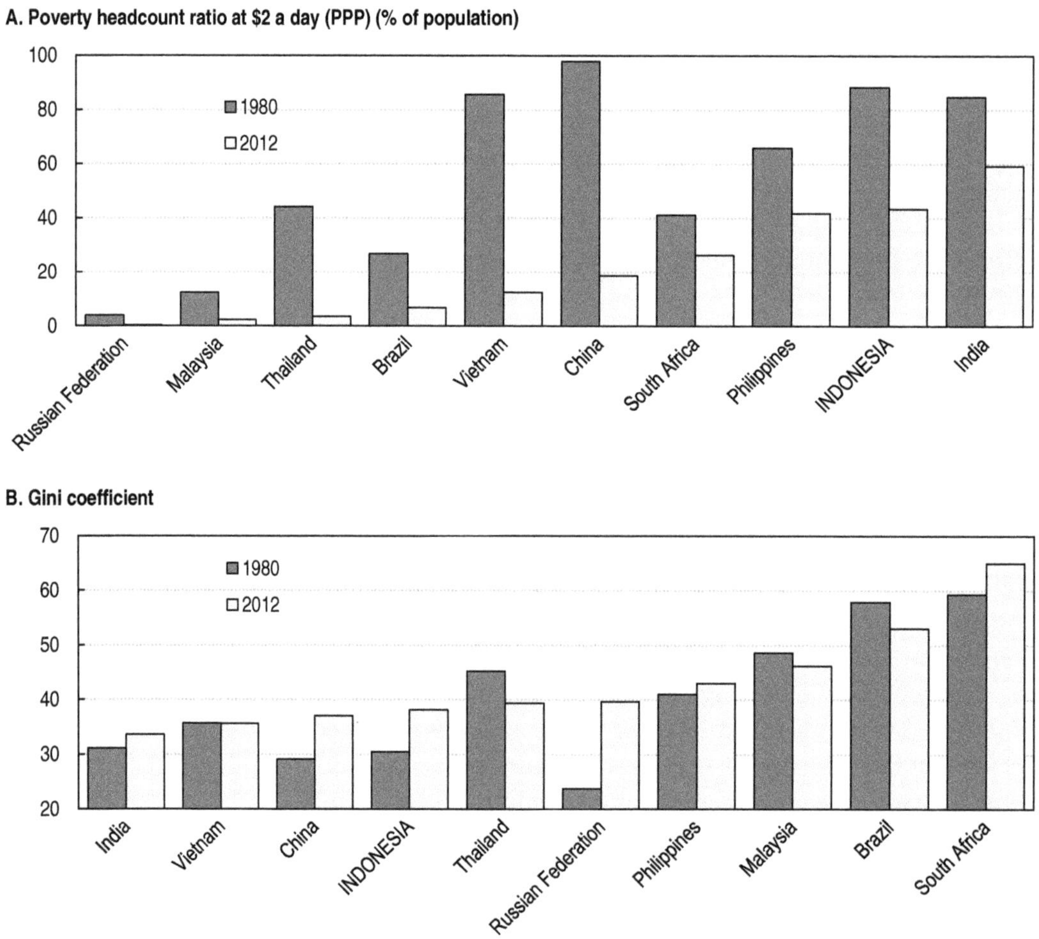

Source: World Bank, *World Development Indicators.*

StatLink http://dx.doi.org/10.1787/888933200106

Indonesia, poverty is mostly, but not exclusively, found in the rural and agricultural areas where about half the population lives. In 2012, 14.3% of the rural population were below the rural poverty line, compared to only 8.4% of the urban population.

However, income alone is not the sole measure of the well-being of the poor. For example, less than half of the rural poor have access to clean water, only three-quarters of all Indonesians have access to electricity, and only 55% of poor children complete junior high school. Moreover, the falling absolute poverty rate masks a high degree of vulnerability: much of the population is clustered just above the official poverty line, consuming approximately IDR 248 000 per month in March 2013 (about USD 22). Around 22% of Indonesians live below or within 20% of it, while 34% of the population lives below 1.5 times the poverty line and is almost equally vulnerable. The World Bank (2012) estimated that 40% of Indonesians are highly vulnerable to poverty.

Indonesia's record in reducing income disparity has been less impressive, particularly over the past decade when the Gini coefficient rose significantly (Figure 16, Panel B). However, in comparison with many other developing countries, income inequality remains low. Nevertheless, top income shares rose sharply in the late 1990s, coinciding with the economic crisis and remain generally higher than in other countries (Leigh and van der Eng, 2009).

Indonesia currently operates two large conditional cash transfer (CCT) schemes: BSM, focusing on education, and PKH (*Program Keluarga Harapan*), for health and education. These schemes are being facilitated by the recent rollout of smart cards and have a number of advantages. First, they typically focus on investment in the education, nutrition and health of children from households in extreme poverty. They therefore help reduce intergenerational poverty transmission and improve efficiency and productivity on a much broader scale. Second, they are typically well targeted, as they are by definition designed to provide resources to those most in need. Verification of need can therefore often be built into the scheme. However, the government should take measures to improve targeting of social assistance programmes, including CCT schemes, by continuing efforts to develop a single registry of vulnerable households (PPLS11), which will result in better cost-effectiveness.

Indonesia has made steady and significant progress on several key population health measures over the past few decades. However, poor nutrition and stunting remain serious issues among the poor, and universal access to good-quality health care across the entire archipelago is still inadequate. Total spending on health care as a share of GDP is low, as is the number of physicians per thousand inhabitants. While the new health insurance scheme and the rollout of *Healthy Indonesia* cards are welcome, these programmes need to be monitored closely to ensure that they properly protect households (including those that have children, elderly, non-salaried and informal workers) from catastrophic medical costs and ensure satisfactory accessibility to affordable health-care services.

There are several other priority areas where Indonesia could focus efforts to further tackle poverty and inequality. These include improving access to schooling, continuing to formalise land tenure and titles, improving infrastructure particularly in rural areas, and better using the tax and transfer system to improve assistance to the poor. Chapter 1 examines these policy options in depth.

Labour informality exacerbates poverty and inequality

The International Labour Organisation (ILO) estimates that 60% of all non-agricultural jobs in Indonesia are informal. While this is less than in India (68%) and the Philippines (73%), it is much higher than in China (33%) and Vietnam (44%) (Figure 17, Panel A). Informality in Indonesia arises from several factors. The minimum wage, which according to ILO data was 63% of the average wage in 2010, is very high by international standards (Panel B). The high minimum-wage cascades through the economy, as it is used as a reference in broader wage negotiations; recent large increases have thereby propagated across the wage structure. In addition to hurting competitiveness more generally, this is likely to have retarded job creation in the formal sector and encouraged informal employment. Rigid labour- and product-market regulations, including stringent hiring and firing rules, also exacerbate labour-market informality and encourage unregistered micro-enterprises by raising the cost of taking on formal workers. At the same time, policies aimed at formalisation, such as stricter enforcement of laws and regulations, may actually

Figure 17. **Labour market informality and minimum wages in selected EMEs**

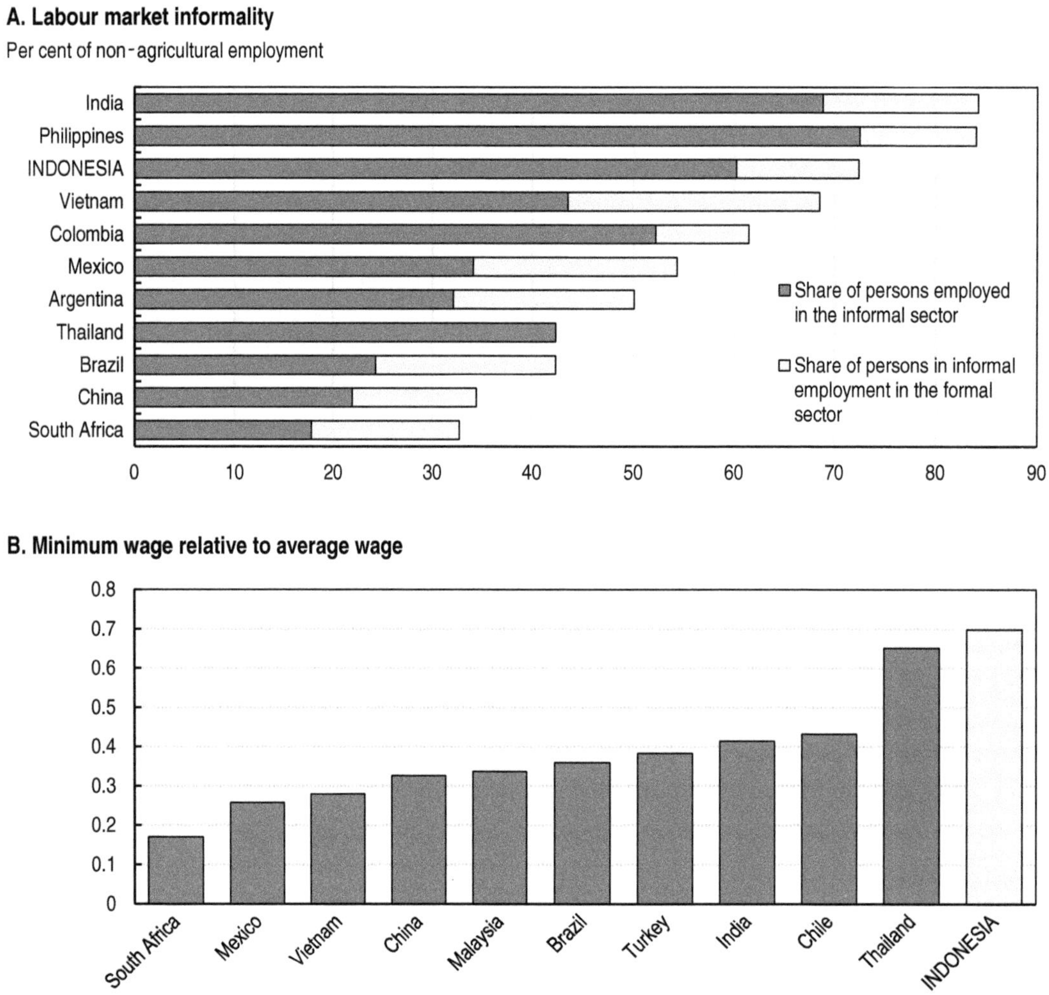

Source: ILO (2012), *Statistical Update on Employment in the Informal Economy*, June; and ILO, *Wages Database*.

StatLink http://dx.doi.org/10.1787/888933200117

increase poverty and vulnerability by pushing already vulnerable people into even more difficult situations.

The tax and transfer system can affect the livelihood of the poor beyond the public provision of goods and services that both directly and indirectly target poverty. To the extent that workers are in the formal sector and therefore within the tax net, the progressivity of personal income tax and the social transfers can have a direct and immediate impact. However, with over 60% of the total labour force outside the formal sector, and a much greater percentage of poor workers, the reach of the tax and transfer system is likely to be limited. So a first step in boosting its effectiveness as a tool for poverty alleviation is to take measures to promote workforce formalisation.

Recommendations for reducing poverty and inequality

Key recommendations

- Increase, and further improve targeting of, spending on poverty alleviation and health measures. Direct more public resources to improving education access and outcomes.
- Increase financial inclusiveness by further developing branchless banking, drawing lessons from such countries as India, Mexico, the Philippines and Kenya.
- Tackle labour market informality by reducing rigidities in the formal sector, and by enhancing the effectiveness of the tax-transfer system for poverty alleviation and channelling other social benefits.

Other recommendations

- Continue building a single registry of vulnerable households to better target assistance.

Ensuring the regulatory framework and civil service perform better

Weaknesses in the legislative, legal and bureaucratic processes remain impediments to inclusive and sustainable growth and development. On several other measures of good governance, Indonesia lags many of its neighbours as well as other emerging economies (Table 3). The Rule of Law Index Report 2014 released by the World Justice Project indicates that corruption is still widespread in the judiciary and law enforcement (WJP, 2014). Moreover, while decentralisation of government to the regions in 1999 has been a political success, it has also exacerbated the problems of bureaucratic capacities and inefficiency and led to an increase in local-level corruption (Martini, 2012; Rinaldi et al., 2007; Rock, 2007). Indonesia Corruption Watch estimates that around one-third of the country's education budget is misappropriated, largely through the improper procurement of goods and services. The consultancy firm A.T. Kearney estimates that Indonesia loses USD 4 billion every year (0.5% of GDP) due to poor public procurement practices. Around 30% of the cases handled by the Corruption Eradication Commission (KPK) over the past decade were related to poor procurement practices (A.T. Kearny, 2010).

Administrative and governance reform had top priority in the 2010-14 National Medium Term Development Plan (RPJMN 2010-14) and continues to do so in RPJMN 2015-19. The RPJMN 2010-14 aimed to achieve this by ensuring the adequate capacity of government personnel. The Government Public Procurement Agency (LKPP) was established in 2010 to

Table 3. **Governance and corruption indicators, selected regional and emerging economies**

Ease of doing business rank[1]		Corruption perception index[2]		Control of corruption index[3]		Government effectiveness index[4]		Global competitiveness report rank[5]	
Malaysia	18	Malaysia	52	Brunei	0.6	Malaysia	1.0	Malaysia	20
Thailand	26	Brazil	43	Malaysia	0.3	Brunei	0.8	China	28
S. Africa	43	S. Africa	42	Brazil	-0.1	S. Africa	0.3	Thailand	31
Russia	62	India	38	S. Africa	-0.2	Thailand	0.2	**Indonesia**	**34**
Vietnam	78	Philippines	38	Thailand	-0.3	Philippines	0.1	Philippines	52
China	90	Thailand	38	China	-0.5	China	0.0	Russia	53
Philippines	95	China	36	Vietnam	-0.6	Brazil	-0.1	S. Africa	56
Brunei	101	**Indonesia**	**34**	India	-0.6	India	-0.2	Brazil	57
Indonesia	**114**	Vietnam	31	Philippines	-0.6	Vietnam	-0.3	Vietnam	68
Brazil	120	Russia	27	**Indonesia**	**-0.7**	**Indonesia**	**-0.3**	India	71
Cambodia	135	Laos	25	Russia	-1.0	Russia	-0.4	Laos	93
India	142	Cambodia	21	Laos	-1.0	Cambodia	-0.8	Cambodia	95
Laos	148	Myanmar	21	Cambodia	-1.0	Laos	-0.9	Myanmar	134

Sources: 1. World Bank "Ease of Doing Business" 2015. 2. Transparency International 2014. 3. World Bank *Worldwide Governance Indicators* 2012. 4. World Bank *Worldwide Governance Indicators* 2012. 5. World Economic Forum 2014-15.

monitor and evaluate procurement practices within the public sector. The new government has also articulated a particularly strong focus on these issues. Its goal is to ensure a professional and adaptive government bureaucracy that is neutral, clean and corruption-free. The RPJMN 2015-19 not only addresses financing issues but also necessary regulatory and institutional reforms to support the government's cross-cutting, sectoral and regional priorities.

There has been progress in improving the performance of the civil service (World Bank, 2012a). However, overstaffing, nepotism and difficulties laying off staff mean that progress in adjusting ministerial and agency staffing has been slow. Early retirement, offering severance packages to surplus staff, giving lower-level managers more responsibility for recruiting and terminating employees, and decentralising personnel budgets to individual ministries could provide the flexibility needed to enhance performance. The government has committed to review the functions and structures of all central government ministries and agencies by 2019. Central government, perhaps the Ministry of Administrative Reform and Bureaucratic Reform (PAN Kemeneg), should be tasked with providing guidance on severance procedures, as individual ministry-level programmes may face conflicts of interest.

A pilot bureaucracy reform programme was started in 2004 in the Ministry of Finance, and in 2008 the programme was rolled out to many other ministries and agencies before extension to the regional level in 2013. Its principle objectives are to: i) tackle corruption, collusion and nepotism; ii) improve service delivery; iii) improve civil servants' capacity and accountability; iv) upgrade human resource management policies and practices; and v) address overlapping, inconsistent and vague laws and regulations. The reform programme has been a success, and rolling it out to the regions should continue. The government has committed to publish a "Grand Design and Roadmap for Bureaucratic Reform" by 2019.

Box 2. **Corruption Eradication Commission (KPK)**

The KPK was established in 2002 as an ad hoc corruption fighting agency, independent from the executive, legislature and judiciary. It works alongside incumbent agencies such as the Attorney General's Office and national police and is authorised to conduct pre-investigation, investigations and prosecutions against corruption cases that: i) involve law enforcers, state officials and other individuals; ii) have generated significant public concern; and/or iii) have lost the state at least IDR 1 billion (USD 70 000). Moreover, based on Article 6 Law No. 30/2002, KPK has mandates to conduct investigation and prosecution of corruption cases, to prevent corrupt practices, to co-ordinate with government agencies, supervise corruption case handled by other law enforcement authorities (the national police force and Attorney General's Office) and also to monitor the implementation of good governance throughout the country.

The KPK is led by five commissioners and has a staff of around 1 200, including some 250 investigators and prosecutors. The commissioners operate as a panel and all investigations need to be vetted by it. The investigators and prosecutors of the KPK are typically experienced agents recruited mainly from the Indonesian National Police and the Attorney General's Office. Experts from other government agencies are also taken on, particularly financial experts. While not ideal from the point of view of independence and avoiding possible contagion of corruption from one agency to the next, thorough testing and vetting has been largely successful in avoiding this problem. Following their selection, investigators and prosecutors are engaged on fixed-term contracts and after three to five years they are expected to return to their home agencies. KPK funding has more than doubled since 2008. Its budget in 2014 was IDR 559 billion (USD 43 million).

The KPK's focus has been on high profile cases, and the public perception of its effectiveness is high. Since its inception in 2002, the KPK has prosecuted only around 320 cases but has achieved a conviction rate of 100%. The convictions it has obtained include government ministers, top management and officials from private companies, provincial governors, police, judges and prosecutors. As stipulated in the 1999 Governance Law, all state officials are obliged to submit a wealth report to the Commission within two months of starting or finishing their tenures. This includes the President and government ministers. President Joko Widodo was the first president to require all ministerial candidates to be vetted by the KPK, as well as by the Financial Transaction Reports and Analysis Centre (PPATK) which tracks international money transfers with a view to uncovering corruption, fraud and tax avoidance.

The authorities have made great strides in battling corruption (through both enforcement and preventative measures), which has long been an impediment to growth. Indonesia improved on the Corruption Perception Index from 1.9 in 2001 to 3.0 in 2011 (USCS, 2012). The KPK was established in 2002 as part of broader anti-corruption legislation and has had significant success in raising public awareness by pursuing high-profile cases (Box 2). Decisive action has been taken to stamp out corruption in customs and tax administration, including by the dismissal of senior public officials and a significant increase in compensation for civil servants working there. Nevertheless, perceptions of corruption remain, especially regarding the lower rungs of the civil service and in the regions.

Devolving some political and revenue-raising powers to the regions increased the potential for inconsistent and incompatible regulations across levels of government. The 2004 law on the Establishment of Laws and Regulation sought to address this issue, and further measures have been taken since, including setting up mandatory *ex ante* central government reviews of sub-national regulations that impose new taxes and charges (OECD, 2012b). However, there is no national institution that has formal responsibility for co-ordinating and providing oversight of these reviews and for providing best-practice guidelines. Indeed, a major issue remains sub-central governments' lack of capacity (as can be seen in administering PPPs). This is another area in which the central government could provide direction and assistance to its sub-national counterparts.

The new President has identified improving the business climate as a major priority. Indonesia lies in the bottom half of the World Bank's "Ease of Doing Business" rankings (Table 3) although its position has improved. Indonesia performs poorly in the subcategories of "Starting a business", "Paying taxes" and "Enforcing contracts". The government plans to expand the number of one-stop shops for business to streamline the permit and licensing process by combining these functions into a single office. The government should consider adopting a "silence is consent" policy whereby a license is deemed to be granted if a response is not received from the agency after a certain pre-defined number of days.

Recommendations for better regulation and reducing corruption

Key recommendations

- Improve mechanisms to prevent corruption, while further increasing efforts to combat all forms of corruption.
- Expand support to sub-national governments for capacity building, including the provision of technical and administrative assistance by the central government.

Making the most of natural resources while preserving the environment

Indonesia abounds with natural resources, but they are spread over a vast country composed of thousands of islands. The unique nature of its geography coupled with the lack of transport infrastructure makes exploitation of natural resources challenging. The agricultural sector, despite progress, suffers from lagging productivity and misplaced support for staple crops. Unwieldy regulations make the exploitation of mineral deposits difficult. In the last Fraser Institute's (2013) survey, mining companies ranked Indonesia last out of 96 jurisdictions when evaluating the attractiveness of its mining policies.

Increasing productivity and encouraging diversification in agriculture

Indonesia has become a global player in many key farm and food markets (e.g. palm oil, rubber, fishery products). Improvement in agricultural yields has varied widely across crops, however. Rice yields have surpassed Malaysian levels but remain below Vietnamese and Chinese counterparts (OECD, 2012c). On the other hand, crude palm oil yields have declined (Figure 18). Boosting productivity growth will be crucial, as it will be increasingly difficult to expand agricultural land, given environmental concerns. Indonesia should encourage more partnership arrangements between large estates and smallholders under the so-called "nucleus plasma" scheme [smallholders occupy 87% of cultivated land and produce 90% of total rice and maize output (Jeon, 2013)]. This 30-year old programme has successfully provided large companies (nucleus), both private (such as Unilever) and state-owned, with subsidised capital and long-term leases for public lands for estate crop

Figure 18. **Selected crop output per hectare**

Index, 2000 = 1

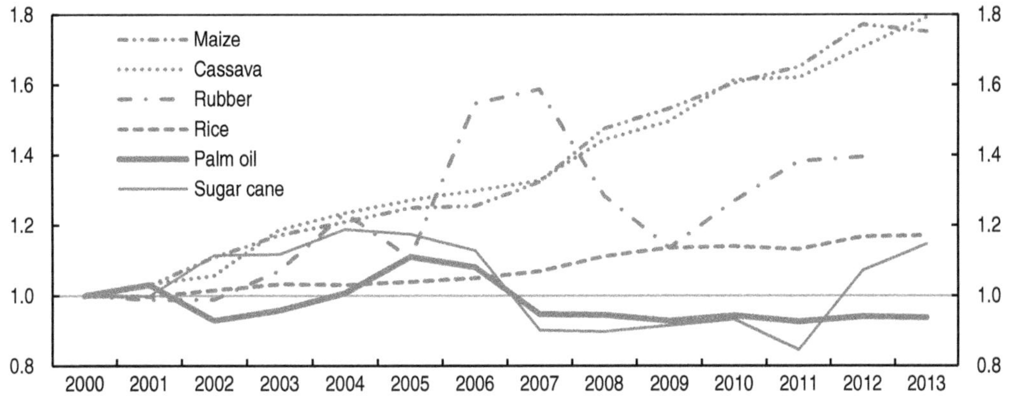

Source: FAOSTAT.

StatLink http://dx.doi.org/10.1787/888933200126

production, on condition that these companies provide technical and marketing services to neighbouring smallholders (plasma).

Productivity growth is also hampered by lack of scale economies due to the large number of small parcels (arable land per farmer is at 1 000 square meters, half the world average). While small farms provide a living to tens of millions of households, smallholders have only limited financial capacity to expand and upgrade production methods. Increasing farm size will require reform of the complex land-tenure system. Most rural households have unregistered land rights usually acquired through inheritance. The situation hinders consolidation of property and accessing credit, and hence fixed capital formation, as farmers must provide collateral to meet bank lending requirements. Creating an agency dedicated to accelerating land rights registration should be a priority.

Diversification away from traditional crops is another avenue for upgrading the agricultural sector. While government support is focused on staple crops (OECD, 2012c), Indonesia should allow farmers to diversify by providing them with better information on high-return specialised crops and corresponding market prices. Diversification would enhance their involvement in international farm trade, and would encourage risk taking and innovation. It could be encouraged by establishing an insurance scheme against adverse climatic or price developments. In addition, fertiliser subsidies (1.3% of total government expenditure on average over the last three years), which are applied disproportionally to staple food crops (rice, maize, soybeans), should be phased out and the savings used to finance a voucher system leaving farmers free to decide how to use those funds. Besides, state-owned fertiliser companies operate at high costs, use obsolete technologies and are often slow in their deliveries. Privatisation of the five fertiliser companies could raise efficiency and help fund the voucher reform as well.

Indonesia has made major improvements in achieving food self-sufficiency. Crop yields have risen, including in staples, and the prevalence of undernourishment is currently estimated at 9% of the population, half of what it was only a decade ago. Food security remains high on the policy agenda. This takes various forms such as rice reserves, priority to domestic production, price support, delivery of rice at subsidised prices to poor households (RASKIN), and foreign trade restrictions and licenses. These policies, however, tend to worsen the situation: the domestic rice price was 60% higher than the reference international price in 2010-12, compared to 8% in 2000-02, and simulations show that such policies would increase the rate of undernourishment under various risk scenarios (OECD, 2014c). In addition, Indonesia imports only 13.1% the cereals it consumes. This percentage has not moved much since 1998, and is on par with Thailand (12%) and Vietnam (13.4%). It is, however, much lower than wealthier countries such as Malaysia and Japan, both at 80.7% (2011 data, three-year average) (FAOSTAT, 2015). By removing trade restrictions and phasing out price support, Indonesia could lower prices for both domestic and imported food, making costly self-sufficiency policies less necessary. Indeed, challenging logistics (e.g. low capacity for refrigerated shipping) play an important role in undermining food security.

As an alternative to RASKIN, which does not always reach its target population and bears high administrative costs, food vouchers or cash transfers would improve diversity and be more cost effective (Hidrobo et al., 2014). They would also further encourage crop diversification. In order to reduce food poverty through trade, trade restrictions should be eliminated over time, in co-ordination with other ASEAN members. Import restrictions, especially in areas where Indonesia has no comparative advantage, are especially burdensome.

Policy should better acknowledge differences in refining profitability among minerals

In January 2014, the government began enforcing the ban on the export of unprocessed mineral resources, first legislated in 2009. While mineral ore exports such as nickel and bauxite are now banned, exports of so-called mineral concentrates (copper, iron, manganese, lead and zinc) will be permitted for the next three years under a new regulation taxing semi-processed mineral exports at 20-25% of sales revenues, rising to 60% by 2016 unless firms guarantee they will build a smelter. To show their commitment Newmont has paid a bond of USD 25 million and Freeport USD 115 million, and both are currently discussing possible locations for the smelters. These measures aim to foster processing in Indonesia, rather than overseas.

Such import-substitution strategies have been used elsewhere, although with mixed effects. If successful, they can raise long-term growth by launching new growth engines. Examples of successful policies protecting infant industries can be found, although mainly in developed countries. Airbus successfully entered the world aircraft market thanks to strong support from European governments. In Indonesia the tax on crude palm oil (CPO) exports succeeded in keeping it as an affordable input into many domestic industries rather than being exported at high prices. In all instances the global context needs to be taken into account. In Airbus' case, it penetrated an uncompetitive market characterised by high monopoly rents, making the rationale for government support stronger. However, in the case of the Indonesia ore export ban, the benefits may depend on the details of the extraction and refining processes. For example, nickel and bauxite refining generates more value than that of copper for which most market value comes from concentration, which is already conducted in Indonesia (USAID, 2013). The industry also suffers from mismanagement and corruption. A KPK audit of Indonesia's mining industry earlier in 2014 uncovered more than USD 2.3 billion in tax fraud, leading to the revocation of more than 4 000 mining permits. The new government has asked the KPK to undertake a comprehensive study of the management of the entire oil and gas sector, including the state-owned energy company (Pertamina).

The ore export ban has direct costs. The mineral extraction sector, and the tax revenues it provides, are being hurt because of falling exports. Successful import substitution will require large investments in refining capacity and supporting infrastructure. The announcement appears to have caused a sharp drop in business expectations (Figure 19), and such policies risk damaging Indonesia's international reputation as a good place to invest and do business. Mineral exploration investment is already quite low by comparison: it was only USD 80 million in 2011 (Energy and Mining Journal, 2012), in contrast with USD 2.9 billion in Australia (Australian Bureau of Statistics, 2014). To maximise the benefits and contain the risks, the government should reconsider its strategy based on the expected profitability of onshore processing for each metal.

Figure 19. **Business expectations**

Above 100 corresponds to improving business conditions

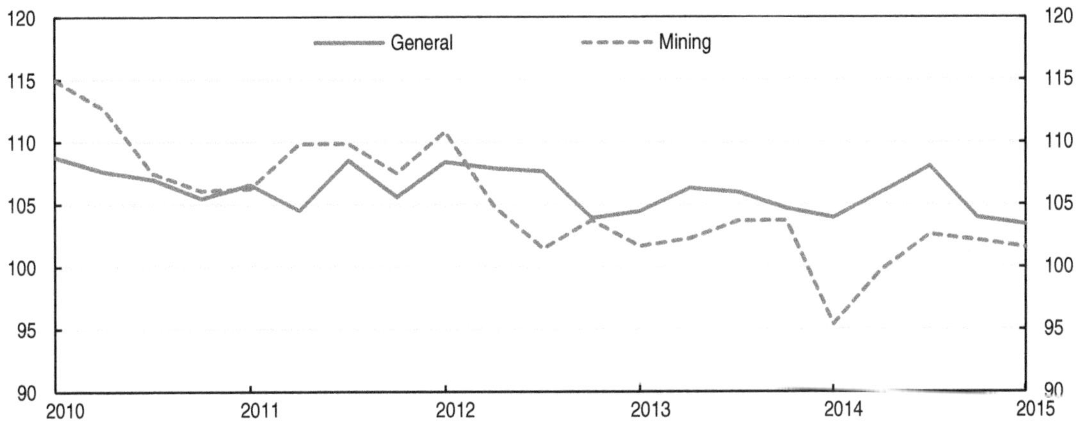

Source: CEIC.

StatLink http://dx.doi.org/10.1787/888933200137

Protecting the environment and tapping the potential for renewables

Rapid economic and population growth and rising urbanisation are putting pressure on the environment. The 2010 ADB-ILO-IDB Environmental Performance Index positioned Indonesia 134th of 163 countries (OECD, 2012c). One major issue is the growing role of fossil fuels in Indonesia's energy mix, challenging its 2009 G20 commitment to reduce greenhouse gas (GHG) emissions by 26% by 2020 against a business-as-usual trajectory. Indeed, CO_2 emissions from fossil fuel combustion were already 12.3% greater in 2011 than in 2009 (IEA, 2013). Indonesia is the world's fifth largest fossil-fuel-based electricity producer, ahead of the United States. The trend is reinforced by an implicit negative carbon price for coal due to Indonesia's electricity subsidy system (OECD, 2014a). Phasing out all subsidies would raise the implicit price and reduce consumption. Coal-fired electricity generation efficiency, which lags both by world and Asian standards, is also a concern and could be improved by transitioning to cleaner and more efficient plants.

Deforestation is a major contributor to Indonesia's poor emissions record. Its forest cover as a share of land area shrank by more than 10 percentage points from 1990 to 2011. The government should increase the resources devoted to reforestation and combatting illegal logging, and punish illegal deliberate forest fires more severely. New agricultural activities should be authorised only on scrub land and abandoned agricultural land. The KPK recently announced that 89% of the nation's 128 million hectares of forest were under no regulation or permit, making them difficult to protect (Jakarta Post, 2013). The government should ensure that all privately and publicly owned land has well defined property rights and is under clear regulation.

Mining is also contributing to environmental degradation, mostly through water pollution and damage to the ecosystem. Most coal mining operations are open-cast and carried out in remote, pristine areas, increasing the risk of environment damage. However, some major mining companies who belong to the Indonesian Coal Mining Association are pursuing ambitious rehabilitation programmes. Nevertheless, smaller, often illegal mines lack the incentives and the means to repair the damage done by their activities. More resources should be devoted to combating illegal mining.

Indonesia's geothermal energy reserves, which are estimated at 40% of the world total (IEA, 2008), should be developed more aggressively. Although expensive to develop, geothermal energy is clean and abundant. In August 2014, the House of Representatives approved a revised geothermal law allowing for the exploitation of geothermal sources in the country's conservation forests. It also returned the power to issue permits or conduct tenders related to geothermal energy exploitation to the central government. As the new regulatory environment becomes operational, the government should accelerate the exploration and tendering of new geothermal projects. In order to attract investors the ceiling price for electricity generated from geothermal power plants should be raised. Other underutilised renewable energies include hydropower and solar. Given agriculture's important role, the potential for biomass is also vast, as any unused agricultural by-product is potentially biomass. Several initiatives have already begun, such as the recent signing of an agreement between state-owned energy companies and General Electric for the development and deployment of biomass gasification systems.

Recommendations for making the most of natural resources while preserving the environment

Key recommendations

- Refocus the mineral ore export ban based on an evaluation of the costs and benefits of onshore processing for each mineral. Provide infrastructure and electricity to the new smelters.
- Increase agricultural productivity by providing technical assistance and training, including through agreements between smallholders and large estates. Increase farmers' access to credit by accelerating land titling. Lower food prices by decreasing trade restrictions.
- Devote more resources to enforcing laws against illegal forest clearing, logging and mining.
- Reduce greenhouse gas emissions by further developing clean power, especially geothermal.

Bibliography

Australian Bureau of Statistics (2015), *ABS Database*, available at *www.abs.gov.au/*.

ADB (2015), Asian Development Bank: Asia Bonds Online, *http://asianbondsonline.adb.org*, accessed 25 February.

BAPPENAS (2013), *Public–Private Partnerships: Infrastructure Projects Plan in Indonesia 2013*, Badan Perencanaan Pembangunan Nasional (Bappenas), *http://pkps.bappenas.go.id/attachments/article/1154/PPP%20BOOK%202013.pdf*.

BAPPENAS (2015), *Medium Term National Development Plan (RPJMN) 2015-2019.*

BBVA (2015), *Mexico Banking Outlook*, January 2015, *www.bbvaresearch.com/wp-content/uploads/2015/02/1501_MexicoBankingOutlook_Jan15.pdf.*

Bloomberg (2013), "World's Most Profitable Banks in Indonesia Double U.S. Returns", 5 February.

CRED (2015), Centre for Research on the Epidemiology of Disasters EM-DAT: International Disaster Database. *www.emdat.be/database*, accessed 25 February.

Davis, L. (2014), "The Economic Cost of Global Fuel Subsidies", *American Economic Review: Papers & Proceedings*, Vol. 104, Iss. 5, pp. 581-585, May.

Demirguc-Kunt, A. and L. Klapper (2013), "Measuring Financial Inclusion – Explaining Variation Across and Within Countries", *www.brookings.edu/~/media/Projects/BPEA/Spring-2013/2013a_klapper.pdf?la=en.*

Dutu, R. (2015), "Decomposing Shocks to the Indonesian Business Cycle Using an Estimated DSGE Model", *Technical Background Paper* (forthcoming).

Energy and Mining Journal (2012), "Transforming the Nation's Mining Industry. Indonesian Coal Giants Look to Take the Next Step", pp. 52-59.

FAOSTAT (2015), *FAOSTAT Database*, available at *http://faostat3.fao.org/faostat-gateway/go/to/home/E.*

Fenochietto, R. and C. Pessino (2013), "Understanding Countries' Tax Effort", *IMF Working Paper*, WP/13/244.

Fraser Institute (2013), *Survey of Mining Companies 2012/2013*, Vancouver.

Hidrobo, M., J. Hoddinott, A. Peterman, A. Margolies and V. Moreira (2014), "Cash, Food, or Vouchers? Evidence from a Randomized Experiment in Northern Ecuador", *Journal of Development Economics* Vol. 107, pp. 144-156.

IEA (2008), *Energy Policy Review of Indonesia*, OECD/IEA Publishing.

IEA (2013), *CO_2 Emissions From Fuel Combustion Highlights 2013*, OECD/IEA Publishing.

IMF (2013), "Indonesia Staff Report for the 2013 Article IV Consultation", *Country Report*, No. 13/362.

Jakarta Post (2013), "REDD+ Agency to Begin Work Soon", 20 December.

Jeon, S. (2013), "Agricultural Transformation and the Escape from the Middle-Income Country Trap: Challenges Facing Small Farmers in Indonesia in a Time of Green Restructuring", PhD thesis, The Graduate Institute, Geneva.

Johansson, A., Y. Guillemette, F. Murtin, D. Turner, G. Nicoletti, C. de la Maisonneuve, G. Bousquet and F. Spinelli (2013), "Long-Term Growth Scenarios", *OECD Economics Department Working Papers*, No. 1000, OECD Publishing.

Leigh, A. and P. van der Eng (2009), "Inequality in Indonesia: What Can We Learn from Top Incomes?", *Journal of Public Economics*, Iss. 1-2, Vol. 93, pp. 209-12, February.

Martini, M. (2012), "Causes of Corruption in Indonesia", *Transparency International U4 Expert Answer*, 7 August, No. 338, *www.u4.no/publications/causes-of-corruption-in-indonesia/downloadasset/2890.*

OECD (2012a), *Education at a Glance 2012: OECD Indicators*, OECD Publishing.

OECD (2012b), "Indonesia: Government Capacity to Assure High Quality Regulation", *OECD Reviews of Regulatory Reform*, September, OECD Publishing.

OECD (2012c), *OECD Review of Agricultural Policy, Indonesia*, OECD Publishing.

OECD (2012d), *OECD Economic Surveys: Indonesia*, OECD Publishing.

OECD (2014a), *Toward Green Growth in Emerging and Developing Asia*, Chapter 2, OECD Publishing.

OECD (2014b), *Measuring Innovation in Education: A New Perspective*, OECD Publishing.

OECD (2014c), *Transitory Food Insecurity in Indonesia*, OECD Publishing.

OECD (2015), *Education Policy Review of Indonesia 2015*, OECD Publishing.

RBA (2013), "East Asian Corporate Bond Markets", *Reserve Bank of Australia Bulletin* – September Quarter.

Rinaldi, T., M. Purnomo and D. Damayanti (2007), *Fighting Corruption in Decentralised Indonesia*, The World Bank, Jakarta.

Rock, M. (2007), "Corruption and Democracy", *United Nations/Department of Economic and Social Affairs Working Paper*, No. 55, August.

Stapleton, T. (2013), "Unlocking the Transformative Potential of Branchless Banking in Indonesia", *Bulletin of Indonesian Economic Studies*, Vol. 49, No. 3, pp. 55-80.

Timmer, C. (2014), "Rice Price Stabilization in Indonesia: A Century-Long Perspective", presentation to World Bank conference "Food Price Volatility, Food Security and Trade Policy", 18-19 September.

UNICEF (2012), *Indonesia: Annual Report 2012*, New York.

USAID (2013), *Economic Effects of Indonesia's Mineral-Processing Requirements for Exports*, April, Washington, DC.

USCS (2012), "Doing Business in Indonesia: 2012 Country Commercial Guide for U.S. Companies", US Commercial Service and US State Department, Washington, DC.

WJP (2014), "WJP Rule of Law Index 2014", World Justice Project, Washington, DC.

World Bank (2012a), *Indonesian Economic Quarterly*, October, Washington, DC.

World Bank (2012b), *India Economic Update*, September, Washington, DC.

World Bank (2013a), *Indonesia Economic Quarterly FY13*, May, Washington, DC.

World Bank (2013b), *Spending More or Spending Better: Improving Education Financing in Indonesia*, March, Washington, DC.

World Bank (2014a), "Why Is Reducing Energy Subsidies a Prudent, Fair, and Transformative Policy for Indonesia?", *Economic Premise*, No. 136, Washington, DC.

World Bank (2014b), "Investment in Flux", *Indonesian Economic Quarterly*, March, Washington, DC.

World Bank (2014c), "The Opportunities of Digitizing Payments: How Digitization of Payments, Transfers, and Remittances Contributes to the G20 Goals of Broad-Based Economic Growth, Financial Inclusion, and Women's Economic Empowerment", World Bank Development Research Group.

World Bank (2014d), "Delivering Change", *Indonesian Economic Quarterly*, December, Washington, DC.

ANNEX

Progress in main structural reforms

This Annex reviews progress in the area of structural reform based on the policy recommendations made in the 2012 Survey.

Monetary and fiscal policy and financial markets

Survey recommendations	Action taken since last *Survey*
Achieve the inflation target and, as planned, reduce it over time. This would be achieved by relying on interest rate, liquidity management and macro prudential measures.	Bank Indonesia has strengthened monetary, liquidity management and macroprudential policy mix and increased inflation control co-ordination with the central government and regional governments.
Step up efforts to pass a micro finance law, and expand the sectoral coverage of the regulatory framework.	Law No. 1/2013 on Microfinance Institutions has been stipulated and followed by the enactment of relevant implementation regulations.
Significantly diminish fossil fuel and electricity subsidies, and implement enhanced compensatory cash transfer programmes to prevent a rise in poverty. Communicate widely on the efficiency and distributional benefits of reform. As an interim measure, re-establish a rule linking fuel prices to developments in international oil markets, to remain valid until subsidies are markedly reduced.	A fixed subsidy system has replaced the subsidy that fixed the price of fossil fuels. In the transition to the new regime, conditional cash transfers were used to cushion the impact on low income households.

Tax revenues

Survey recommendations	Action taken since last *Survey*
Continue efforts to expand the number of taxpayers, in particular among the self-employed. Adopt a single taxpayer number for individuals, and eliminate the need to apply for one, e.g. by using the national identity card number. Consider removing the need to file a tax return for employees with a single source of income. Temporarily reduce penalties for previous non-compliance for first-time taxpayers only.	National Identification Number and Taxpayer Identification Number synchronisation programme is still in process. Filing a tax return is an obligation for every taxpayer in Indonesia. Exceptions for this obligation are applied only for very limited type of taxpayer, i.e. individual taxpayers who derive income in a tax year that is not exceeded non-taxable income.
Subject employer-provided fringe benefits and allowances to personal income taxation, and move towards equal tax treatment of interest and dividend incomes, for example by considering the withholding tax on dividends as final, as is the case for interest.	Employer-provided fringe benefits and allowances are subject to personal income tax under three conditions. *First,* if the employer is not a taxpayer. *Second,* if the employer only derives income which is imposed with final tax. *Third,* if the employer only derives incomes which is imposed tax by calculating deemed profit of the income. Since revision of the Income Tax Law in 2008, dividend received by individual taxpayer is final tax. Therefore, some of the issues on this recommendation have been implemented.
Reconsider tax incentives and in particular tax holidays for specific sectors or investment projects. If investment incentives are granted, make them broadly available to all companies, and give preference to investment tax credits over tax holidays.	A regulation of the Minister of Finance regarding income tax facilities for investment in certain business segments and certain areas was signed in September 2012 to include 129 business segments, expanded from 38 segments in the previous regulation (PMK 144/2012). Tax holiday facilities have been extended one year until 2015 (PMK 192/2014).
Reduce the compliance burden for small firms by introducing a specific tax system, combining simplified procedures with a low tax rate and decisive action to enforce compliance, as planned by the government.	A government regulation to simplify taxation procedure, promote transparency and compliance for small firms has been enacted with 1% rate of sales turnover (PP 46/2013).
Take exploration and development risks into account by allowing full recovery of the associated costs from production revenues.	Full cost recovery has been allowed if working area of oil and gas have started oil and gas production.
Move away from revenue-based royalties and give greater weight to taxing economic rents, at higher rates than at present.	Royalties for 111 mining companies are in the process of being renegotiated.
Reconsider local processing requirements and local ownership requirements in the mining sector, and focus on raising the government's tax take instead.	No action taken. These requirements are important to create value added for mining commodities.
Review export taxes, considering their implication for the whole economy, including international trade.	Export taxes has been continuously reviewed with the main consideration to fulfil domestic needs, preservation of natural resources, maintaining price stability of certain commodities, and anticipating drastic price fluctuations of certain commodities in international market.
Reduce the number of activities that are exempt from VAT to a minimum.	Activities that are exempt from VAT have been reduced gradually.
Introduce a carbon tax at an initially low rate.	This is under consideration.
Update the property value registry to increase the tax take from recurrent taxes on immovable property. Consider moving towards a simplified area-based assessment of tax liabilities.	The property value registry is updated every three years. Starting at 1 January 2014 property taxation is fully managed by local government.

Survey recommendations	Action taken since last *Survey*
Allocate more tax audits on the basis of risk assessments, and eliminate automatic audit requirements. Increase the number of government auditors.	No notification of action taken.
Make greater use of third-party information and indirect ways of assessing tax liabilities, e.g. by using information on assets or consumption items to trigger tax audits even for those not registered as taxpayers.	No notification of action taken.
Move forward with the planned tax census to expand the tax base beyond current taxpayers, and establish additional tax offices specialised in affluent individuals beyond Jakarta.	A tax census was held in mid-2012. It was undertaken in three priorities areas: business district, high rise building and luxury residential area. Observation from this tax census lead to a number of modifications, Standard Operating Procedure for data utilisation were revised, data cleansing and data matching for taxpayer census data were enhanced, and back office application for census was improved. Starting 2012, back office application was able to classify respondents of census based on respondent's potential, follow up census data and evaluate the follow-up. A tax census was held in end-2013. The priorities were business district, luxury residential area, and other potential area. This Census also aimed to improve the respondent's understanding of the tax system. No census was undertaken in 2014 but the tax office had to follow up census data. Starting from 2014, DGT is expanding coverage by using several third party data such as National Identification Number and luxurious good ownership, as well as withholding tax slip.
Continue efforts to improve the human resource management of the tax authorities by reducing disparities in training across tax offices and officials. Enhance the administration's litigation capacity, and consider the use of external legal services in important appeal cases, while moving forward with plans to establish tax courts outside of Jakarta.	The capacity development programs at DGT are organised in various teaching methods which has passed the series of the improvement, based on annual evaluation. Enhancement and improvement of the capacity development activities that organised by the DGT are explained below: i) The materials of in-class training which organised by Finance Education and Training Agency (FETA) has passed the validation with the Technical Job Competencies Standards. Based on the validation, the teaching materials are expected to comply with Job Competencies Standards; ii) The standardisation of In House Training (IHT) materials organised at internal DGT, has been complied with competencies need in accordance with Technical Job Competencies Standards for 8 job families based on the Decree of DGT ref. KEP-165/PJ/2012; iii) The review and additional of the On The Job Training (OJT) materials is conducted annually to Renew the material of coaching; iv) The review and additional e-learning interactive modules as a learning media, are comply with the needs of the competencies of each position; v) The improvement of Learning Media System (LMS) for the needs of Training Needs Analysis (TNA) and implementation assessment of competencies by assessment Centre. Moreover, DGT has also done several techniques to conduct DGT's employee capacity building such as: i) Using Information Technology (IT) in shifting training participants in order to ascertain that DGT's employees have the same opportunity and meet all necessary requirements to follow training; ii) DGT consistently continue working together with FETA and donor country in enhancing employees training and/or educational capacity; iii) In House Training program which are held in DGT should always be based on Internal Control and Apparatus Transformation. Additionally: i) Training Court Communication Skills for Case officers in Jakarta, Surabaya, Yogya dan Medan; ii) Training in special subject such as Transfer Pricing, etc.; iii) Conducting workshop and Co-ordination Forum for case offers periodically; iv) Inviting legal experts from prominent universities such as University of Indonesia, Gajah Mada University, Diponegoro University and Parahyangan University to support DGT in Tax Court; v) DGT is considering to design Standard Operating Procedure to support tax court administration outside Jakarta.

Survey recommendations	Action taken since last *Survey*
Strengthen internal control systems and disciplinary action within the tax administration. Improve the transparency of administrative decisions by allowing taxpayers access to their tax-related information, publishing all decrees and implementing regulations and using publicly accessible precedent rulings.	This recommendation has been implemented. The Directorate of Internal Compliance and Apparatus Transformation has taken various steps to strengthen the DGT's internal control and disciplinary measures including: Applying the code of conduct, internalising the organisational values, implementing the whistle blowing system, handling complaints both directly and indirectly, performing compliance testing, applying risk management, monitoring the wealth report obligation, applying early detection of possible misconduct/ indisciplinary cases, developing the Internal Compliance Units in DGT's offices, monitoring the obligation to report gifts/gratifications, spreading the "Clean DGT In Our Hands" campaign, investigating misconduct/indisciplinary cases, recommending punishment the related units, developing co-operation with the commission of Corruption Eradication. Additionally, DGT has promulgated Director General Circular Letter Number 8 Year 2013 to ascertain that the employee punishment system follows sound governance principles. Moreover, DGT's span of control will be decrease which is in line with Initiative Number 15 of Structural Reform Program. In tax offices under Large Tax Payer Regional Tax Office, there is a means of DGT's Service Monitoring Progress which allow tax payers access their related information. However, currently it only monitors sort of services which are Certificate of Tax Clearance request, exemption Certificate request for article 22 import, Exemption Certificate request for article 23, and Exemption certificate request for Fixed Deposit Interested, Deposits and Discount Interest of bank Indonesia Certificate. In addition, all decrees and implementing regulations can be accessed through DGT's official website *www.pajak.go.id.*

Education and trade

Survey recommendations	Action taken since last *Survey*
Ease access to education and training for students from disadvantaged backgrounds. Rigorously assess the cost efficiency of all existing programmes aimed at upgrading dropouts' and workers' skills, and phase out those found to be inefficient.	Although social assistance strategic plan targets have not been reached, the participation of the community in organising courses and training have contributed to improving skills of the unemployed to help integration into the labour market, as well as the starting independent businesses. Provide scholarships to the communities for quality improvement programs and institutional organisation of courses and training. Policies to improve skills and competence for workers and unemployed workers are done through training in various vocational training centres. With the competency-based training programme, cost efficiency can be monitored.
Assess the impact of non-tariff barriers on trade and the domestic economy and remove those that are found detrimental to growth. Remove the new regulations that restrict the range of products a general importer can import. Relax remaining barriers to foreign direct investment, unless they address valid public interest concerns.	Indonesia has acceded the International Convention on Simplification and Harmonization of Customs Procedures (Revised Kyoto Convention), the Convention on Temporary Admission (Istanbul Convention), and the ASEAN Agreement on Customs. This means that customs procedures are in line with international standards.

SME development and others

Survey recommendations	Action taken since last *Survey*
Systematically review all significant existing business licensing requirements at the national and local levels, with a view to simplification and ensuring they remain cost effective. Sanction regional governments that fail to make significant progress in simplification and consolidation.	In December 2013, the Minister of Trade has issued a regulation for business licensing simplification. The aim is to reduce the procedure period for processing a license to 3 days. There will be sanctions if local governments, who issue business licenses, fail to meet this target.

Survey recommendations	Action taken since last *Survey*
Public finances permitting, increase public outlays on cost effective infrastructure projects beyond what is already planned.	In the 2015 Revised Budget, the Government strengthened the role of SOEs in infrastructure development in order to accelerate the implementation of the government's priority programs through schemes such as state capital investment schemes, public-private partnerships, and the subsidiary loan agreements. Priorities areas are national infrastructure connectivity, maritime, food sovereignty, and energy.
Lower electricity subsidies and have recourse to cash transfer schemes to compensate poor households for the rise in electricity price.	The government has lowered subsidies for electricity and is moving toward a cost-reflective tariff. In 2013, the MEMR raised tariffs by an average of 5% in quarterly phases, and in 2014, the government announced a further average tariff hike of almost 13% which is to be phased in during the course of the year.
In provinces where minimum wages are high in relation to average wages, resist increases that exceed trend productivity gains. Introduce a sub-minimum wage for youth directly linked to the general minimum wage. Reduce onerous severance payments and ease dismissal procedures in the formal labour market. In return introduce unemployment benefits coupled with individual unemployment savings accounts.	No notification of action taken.
Improve the enforcement of intellectual property rights.	No notification of action taken.
Make the information collected by the credit bureau available to all non-bank financial institutions.	The Indonesia Finance Services Association (APPI) with PT Pemeringkat Efek Indonesia (Pefindo), PT Telkom Sigma, CIC (Credit Information Center) Indonesia, and PT Pegadaian have agreed to set up a credit bureau, to be named PT Pefindo Biro Kredit, which will provide data such as credit scoring report (debtor's information and profile). This information will be able to be accessed by non-bank financial institutions. The principal permit was granted by Otoritas Jasa Keuangan (OJK) on 5 August 2014. PT Pefindo Biro Kredit is targeted to be fully operational in the third quarter of 2015.
Remove the tax exemptions granted to venture-capital companies to support investments in some industries and the existing restriction of 85% on foreign ownership of such companies.	Currently, Indonesia has no tax exemption specifically aimed for venture-capital companies. However, under article 4 paragraph 3 subparagraph Income Tax Law, dividends or distribution of profit received by or accrued by a resident limited corporation, co-operative, state-owned enterprises, or local government-owned enterprises trough ownership in enterprise established and domiciled in Indonesia, provided that: Dividends are paid out from retained earnings; Limited corporations and state-owned enterprises and local-owned enterprises receiving the dividends must own at least 25% of the total paid-in capital.
Extend conditionality in income support programmes to include attendance in secondary education. Increase the per student transfer under the School Operations Fund (BOS) programme for schools located in remote areas and catering for poor students or alternatively increase conditional cash transfers.	BOS allocation has been transferred to secondary schools is based on the number of students in each school. BOS accommodates fee waivers for the poor students. Unit cost of BOS in 2014 was IDR 1 000 000 per student per year and in 2015 it has been increased to IDR 1 200 000; a 20% increase from the previous year. The Financial Aid for Poor Students Programme (BSM) covers personal expenditure. In 2014, it was given to poor students while in 2015 it has been extended to include poor and almost poor students. This program gives benefits not only for poor students within the school system but also school-age children outside the system. The program has been renamed, "Program Indonesia Pintar" (PIP).
Remove formal education from the negative investment list.	No notification of action taken.
Encourage tertiary education financing through student loans.	No notification of action taken.
Create a national training fund to consolidate resources allocated to training and direct them to their most cost efficient use.	No notification of action taken.
Clarify government responsibility in the delivery of support to small firms. Regularly assess the efficiency of existing programmes, phase out inefficient measures, and redirect resource to the most cost effective schemes.	Regular assessments of the efficiency of government activities are conducted with the aim of reducing inefficiencies so that the budget is used on target. Steps to be done are to provide incentives for employees based on performance and improve the empowerment schemes for SME and co-operatives.
Re-examine the effectiveness of policies to encourage the formation of clusters, to reserve certain industries for small firms alone, and to require foreign direct investors to partner with local SMEs.	Various improvements on institutional, business, and financing are continuing to be implemented in co-operatives. In the future, co-operative empowerment is directed to co-operative located in the area of agriculture, fishery, marine, and SME to support the government's vision and mission.

Thematic chapters

Chapter 1

Policies for inclusive and sustainable growth

Indonesia has a very good record of poverty reduction, having halved its incidence over the past two decades. Nevertheless, almost 30 million people still live below the national poverty line, mostly in rural areas and in certain provinces. In order to make further progress in lifting these people out of poverty and economic vulnerability, policy needs to focus on generating strong, inclusive and sustainable growth. Pro-poor growth can assist in the process of economic convergence by facilitating the migration of workers out of the low-productivity agricultural sector into the industry and services sectors. By putting in place the right fundamentals, such as a well-designed and inclusive education system, efficient infrastructure and a stable macroeconomic environment, Indonesia will have decades of strong growth ahead by virtue of economic convergence with frontier countries. This has the potential to lift millions more out of poverty without exacerbating income inequality. Moreover, it will set Indonesia up for the next phase of innovation-driven growth that will propel it into the ranks of high income countries. While existing poverty-reduction programmes have become increasingly effective, more resources are required, and efficiency could be further enhanced, especially through better targeting. The distribution of income has become markedly more unequal over the past decade and needs to be kept in mind when formulating growth policies.

Introduction

With per capita income of around USD 9 300, Indonesia has barely exited the ranks of the low middle-income cohort of countries. By continuing to put in place the right policies, it can enjoy many more years of rapid per capita growth by virtue of economic convergence. This catch-up process happens as economic factors (labour, in particular) move from low-productivity largely informal sectors (like agriculture) to higher-productivity sectors, and as firms emulate their foreign counterparts by importing and adapting more advanced technologies and production processes. This transfer and diffusion of technology can be further facilitated by attracting foreign direct investment (FDI).

Part of Indonesia's challenge in sustaining convergence is to manage the "curse" of its generous endowment of natural resources (Chapter 2). While its comparative advantage in natural resources cannot be denied, it should not be allowed to distort the reallocation of resources into other productive sectors, and rent seeking should be minimised by ensuring that the dividends flowing from it are utilised for the long-term economic betterment of all Indonesians. However, this needs to be managed very carefully so as not to discourage further development in the commodities sector.

Another challenge for Indonesia is to make growth inclusive, that is, to ensure that its fruits are shared equitably and that social cohesion and poverty reduction remain high on the policy agenda. Indeed, over recent decades poverty in Indonesia has fallen significantly, thanks to strong and steady economic growth, declining joblessness, rising incomes and poverty-alleviation programmes that have become increasing affective. However, despite this impressive performance, Indonesia has a long way to go in further lowering the incidence of poverty, which remains widespread. Indeed, compared to the group of countries clustered around Indonesia's per capita income level, its poverty rate is relatively high. While an efficient, responsive and well-targeted social safety net is extremely important, particularly for protecting economically vulnerable households, more fundamental reforms are also critical. The focus must be on the formulation and implementation of policies and strategies that enable the poor to participate in and benefit from economic growth.

Stable and sustainable growth

With its abundant natural resources and large and youthful population located in the most dynamic part of the world, Indonesia has plenty of scope for economic catch-up over the coming decades. By continuing to put in place the right fundamental policies that best harness its generous resource endowment, both natural and human, Indonesia should enjoy decades of strong growth that could lift it into the ranks of the upper-middle-income group of countries. Growth is a vital ingredient in tackling poverty, and with poverty still widespread, even when compared to other countries at similar levels of per capita income, sustained and robust growth will be needed to make inroads into poverty across the archipelago.

The challenge will be to sustain long periods of strong and stable growth that is inclusive and pro-poor. In this phase of Indonesia's development, a critical element for reducing poverty is growth that is jobs-rich – particularly in the employment of unskilled labour. In the long run, the main requirement for both growth and poverty reduction is undoubtedly education. However, the temptation for quick fixes and moving too quickly needs to be avoided. Policies that ignore the country's comparative advantages and advocate a "great leap forward" in industrial development are misguided. Only by putting in place a fundamental basis for economic development and transformation will the economy progress. Industrial policies, in the absence of the prerequisite and complementary human capital and infrastructure, will not generate the desired results. Policy reforms need to be focused on equipping the economy for the next phase of development – by boosting the human capital of all Indonesians and increasing investment in infrastructure throughout the country. In this way growth will be both sustainable and inclusive.

Macroeconomic stability is paramount for poverty reduction, given that output declines caused by economic crises are the biggest source of long-lasting welfare losses among developing countries. On average, it takes 6-12 years for per capita GDP to return to pre-crisis levels after an initial output drop (IMF, 2012). With a large share of Indonesians clustered around the poverty line, many are vulnerable to economic shocks that can tip them into poverty. It is critical that Indonesia continues to build policy frameworks that minimise the frequency and amplitude of economic cycles by avoiding home-made crises and by strengthening the economy's resilience in the face of external shocks. The large deterioration in the current account balance starting in mid-2011 was a case in point. That episode threatened to plunge Indonesia into crisis, and this uncertainty precipitated volatile capital outflows, a very large depreciation in the currency and a sense of vulnerability among policy makers that led to a number of unwise policy choices. In the end, in the most important domains the right choices were made: the currency was allowed to depreciate, helping to address international competitiveness issues; and interest rates were increased to tackle the imported inflation and to dampen import demand.

Economic convergence and the "middle income trap"

The idea that the country is confronting a so-called "middle-income trap" has gained currency among some Indonesian politicians and policymakers. On this view at a certain threshold level of per capita income countries encounter a barrier and growth stagnates, preventing progress to high-income status. In a recent study Shekhar et al. (2013) show that growth-slowdown episodes are disproportionately likely to occur in middle-income countries. Eichengreen et al. (2013) find two "traps", one at the USD 10 000 to USD 11 000 per capita income range and another at USD 15 000 to USD 16 000, both far higher than Indonesia's current level. These thresholds are in PPP constant 2005 USD. By this measure, in 2011 Indonesia was at 4 300 USD per capita; a considerable distance from these thresholds.

Figure 1.1, which plots five-year average growth rates against levels of real per capita GDP for the 164 countries in the *Penn World Tables Database*, confirms the existence of an apparent threshold at just below USD 15 000 after which growth tends to slow down. However, there does not seem to be any evidence of a cluster or logjam of countries "trapped" below this threshold. Growth slows down, that is clear, but countries typically continue to progress, albeit more slowly, up the rungs of the income ladder.

Figure 1.1. **Per capita GDP growth and levels**

Level of real per capita GDP PPP (2005 international prices, USD), 5-year average growth

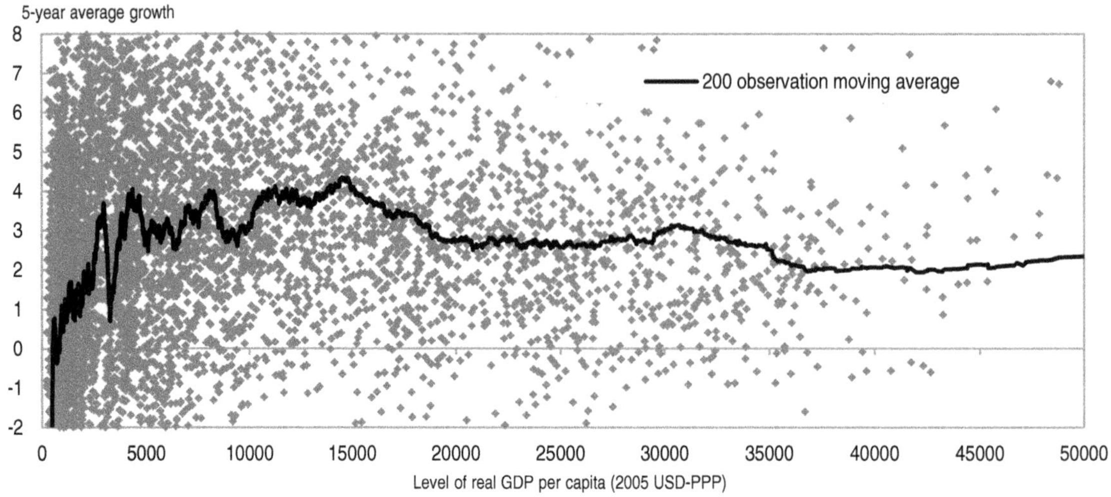

Source: Penn World Tables 8.0 and OECD calculations.

StatLink http://dx.doi.org/10.1787/888933200142

In a similar vein, Rodrik (2011) argues that economic convergence is not preordained and depends on sustaining rapid structural change in the direction of tradables such as manufacturing and modern services. He finds that low-productivity countries tend to enjoy faster productivity growth in the industrial sector while catching up with frontier countries. Importantly, he finds that this catch-up is not conditional on country characteristics – the industry sector in any country enjoys this catch-up regardless of the particular features of that country; that is to say, industrial-sector convergence is unconditional. Eichengreen et al. (2013) find that slowdowns are less likely in countries where the population has a relatively high level of secondary and tertiary education and where high-technology products account for a relatively large share of exports. Shekhar et al. (2013) try to identify the determinants of growth slowdowns for middle-income countries, showing that factors such as institutions, demography, infrastructure, macroeconomic environment and policies, economic and trade structure all have some influence on the probability of a slowdown.

In contrast, the World Bank's (1993) report *The East Asian Miracle* analysed the East Asian Tigers' catch-up growth (economic convergence), and some of its conclusions are relevant to the "middle-income trap". Contrary to the emphasis some put on policies to foster high-tech manufacturing, the Bank stressed the need to "get the basics right": macroeconomic stability, relatively low distortions to domestic competition, openness to external trade, broad-based and effective education, flexible labour markets and adequate investment in tangible infrastructure. The report argued that these fundamental "horizontal", economy-wide policies are far more important than "vertical" industrial policies that promote favoured sectors and national champions. It accepted that convergence is conditional on country fundamentals, and putting these fundamentals in place allows growth convergence to higher income levels by allowing the maximum mobilisation of capital and labour inputs, and large productivity gains from efficient resource reallocation. For middle-income countries, additional reforms are advocated that go beyond liberalisation of product markets to encompass deregulation of factor markets, opening up of services sectors, upgrading "soft infrastructure" (such as higher education and skills) and improving the quality of public administration, regulatory agencies and judicial systems. These lift the convergence frontier even further and pave the way for the subsequent mode of catch-up – namely productivity – and innovation-based growth.

Overlaying these arguments is the idea that countries should focus economic resources in sectors where they have a comparative advantage. In the case of a commodity-rich country like Indonesia, this would be mining, forestry and agriculture. The argument here is that policies that direct resources away from sectors in which the country enjoys a comparative advantage can have a large opportunity cost and will lower national welfare. And, indeed, industry policies that promote certain favoured sectors, before the economic prerequisites, like skills and infrastructure, are in place are inefficient and wasteful. Instead, efforts should be focused on fundamental "horizontal", economy-wide policies that improve the general efficiency of the economy, including the sector in which there is a comparative advantage.

However, this static policy proscription seems unfair in the opinion of many developing-country policy makers. For example, Chang (2002) argues that the principle of comparative advantage may have helped developed countries maintain relatively advanced technology and industry compared to developing countries. The author argues that all major developed countries used interventionist and protectionist economic policies in order to get rich, and these countries now try to dissuade other countries from following the same pattern of development. This leaves developing countries lagging behind, and polarisation of wealth becomes entrenched. Chang asserts that premature free trade has been one of the fundamental obstacles to the alleviation of poverty in the developing world.

The fundamental question is whether comparative advantage is immutable, and, if not, to what extent is trying to manipulate comparative advantage distortionary and wasteful. Many economists, such as Chang (2002) and Rodrik (2011) believe that the only way to escape the "middle income trap" is with policies that actively promote sectors higher up the technology scale and in which the local value-added component is larger. However, while "getting the prices wrong" (interventionist) policies (Amsden, 1989; Wade, 1990; Rodrick, 1995) might be the way to go, without the accompanying fundamental reforms, these are likely to be very costly, both fiscally and in terms of opportunity cost. A successful, self-sustaining, export-focused manufacturing sector will not succeed without an efficient and well-functioning economic foundation upon which to build. This includes a well-educated workforce, well-functioning legal and economic institutions, minimum corruption, good transport and other infrastructure, and an efficient business service sector.

Global value chains (GVCs) build on the idea of comparative advantage. Close integration into GVCs allows countries to specialise in particular segments of global manufacturing chains and thereby reap a share of the value added embodied in these manufactured goods (OECD, 2013b). This very much works to the advantage of countries that in the past would have missed out on the benefits and their associated positive externalities, because developing domestic manufacturing would have involved co-locating many of the contiguous links in the chain locally. But many developing countries are unable to do this due to a lack of the prerequisite skills or infrastructure. Integration into GVCs gives countries a foothold in global manufacturing best practice, starting with those links in the chains for which they have a comparative advantage. But, once again, in order in integrate into GVCs it is critical to have the right fundamentals in place. These include minimal trade distortions, policies to promote innovation, skills and infrastructure, and a flexible service sector that facilitates co-ordination of GVC manufacturing links and processes. Indonesia's integration into GVCs is discussed in more detail below.

Economic convergence and structural change

It is clear that economic convergence involves structural change. The significance of the agricultural sector shrinks dramatically as productivity rises and resources shift to manufacturing and especially services. After about USD 10 000 per capita (PPP constant 2011 USD), very few countries have an agricultural sector larger than 15% of total value added. On average, the share of manufacturing plateaus at around 20% of total value added – poorer countries do indeed have smaller manufacturing sectors, but it's share peaks at income levels of around USD 9 000 per capita (Figure 1.2, Panel A). Moreover, a large manufacturing sector is not associated with higher per capita growth. The feature of sectoral shares that is unequivocally associated with higher GDP per capita is the services sector (Panel B) – the share of services in total value added keeps increasing with respect to GDP per capita. Indeed, since 1960 no country (except Equatorial Guinea) has exceeded USD 30 000 per capita GDP without a services sector accounting for more than 55% of total value added. Indonesia's services share of just 38% in 2012 lags most other countries in its per capita GDP cohort. In contrast, its manufacturing share of around 24% is just above the average for its per capita GDP cohort.

Figure 1.2. **Sectoral shares and real GDP per capita**[1]

Per cent of total value added and GDP per capita PPP 2011 USD

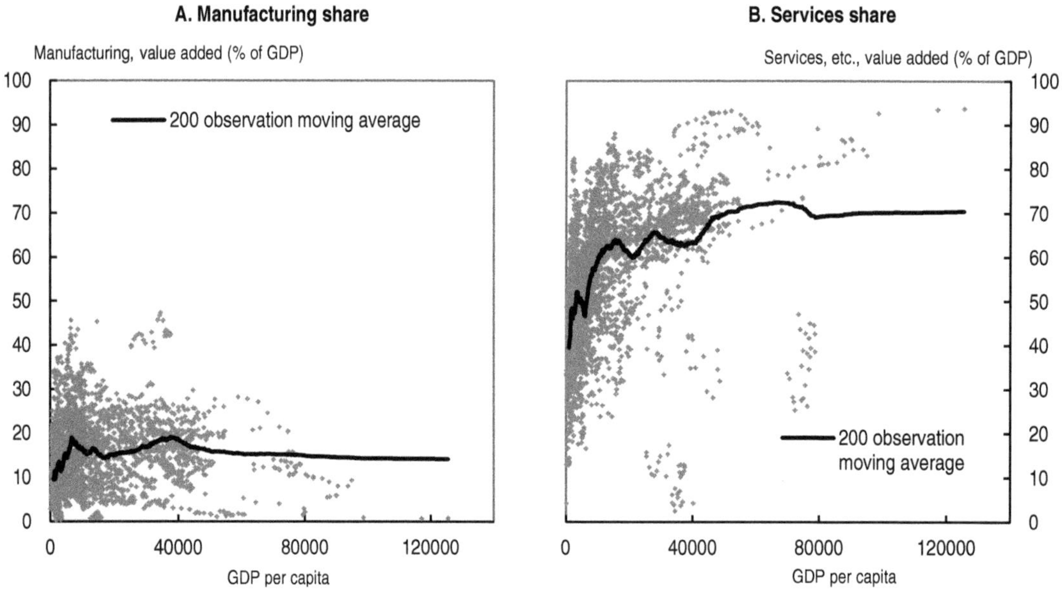

1. Sample between 1960 and 2012, for all 214 countries in the *World Bank WDI Database* except major oil exporters.
Source: World Bank, *World Development Indicators.*

StatLink http://dx.doi.org/10.1787/888933200157

The current structure of the Indonesian economy reflects its comparative advantage in agriculture and natural resources. Agriculture's share of output has declined from around 45% in 1970 to around 14% in 2012, still large by comparison with other comparable countries (Table 1.1), although in line with its level of GDP per capita (Figure 1.3, Panel A).

Table 1.1. **Economic structure for selected countries**

1970 and 2012

		Agriculture	Industry (less manufacturing)	Manufacturing	Services
Indonesia	**1970**	**44.9**	**8.4**	**10.3**	**36.4**
	2012	**14.4**	**23.0**	**23.9**	**38.6**
Brazil	1970	12.3	9.0	29.3	49.4
	2012	5.2	13.0	13.3	68.5
Chile	1970	6.9	16.1	25.9	51.1
	2012	3.6	24.5	11.0	60.9
China	1970	35.2	6.7	33.7	24.3
	2012	10.1	14.3	32.5	43.2
India	1970	42.0	6.8	13.7	37.6
	2012	17.4	12.2	13.5	56.9
Korea, Republic	1970	29.3	8.2	17.8	44.7
	2012	2.6	8.1	31.1	58.2
Malaysia	1970	29.4	15.0	12.4	43.2
	2012	10.1	16.6	24.2	49.1
Philippines	1970	29.5	7.0	24.9	38.6
	2012	11.8	10.5	20.5	57.1
Thailand	1970	25.9	9.4	15.9	48.8
	2012	12.3	9.6	34.0	44.2

Source: World Bank, *World Development Indicators.*

Figure 1.3. **Shares of total valued added**

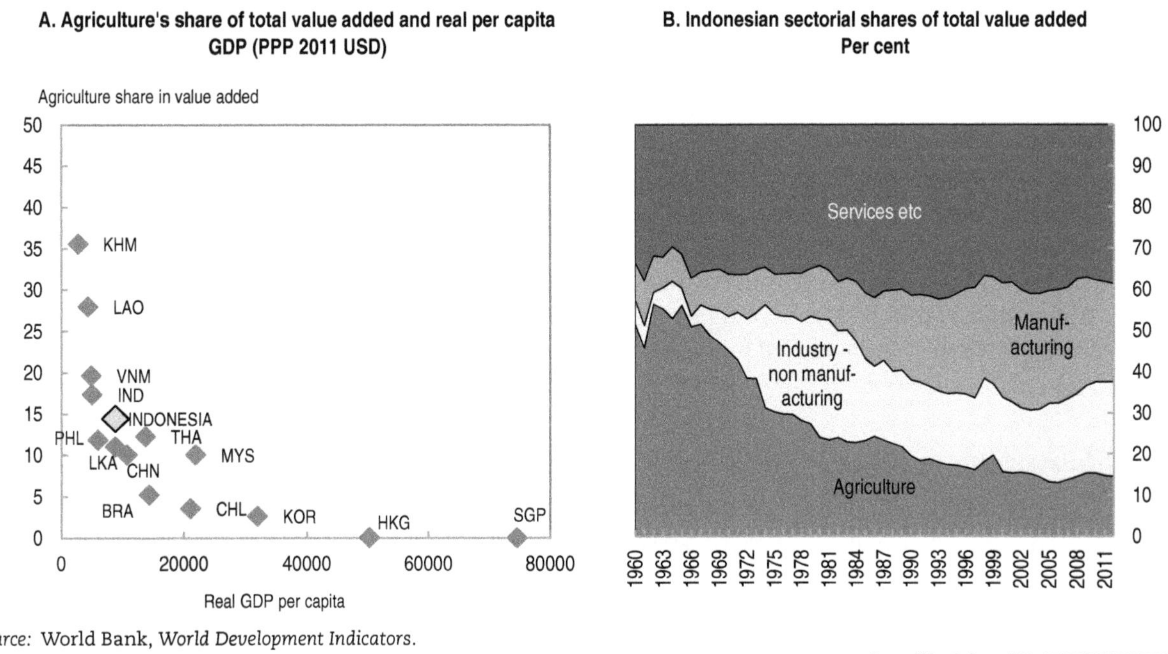

Source: World Bank, *World Development Indicators.*

StatLink http://dx.doi.org/10.1787/888933200168

Its share of total employment, at around 36%, is even larger, reflecting the sector's low productivity. Similarly, non-manufacturing industry's share of GDP is relatively large and has increased over the past 40 years, which, as in Chile, reflects the growth of the mining sector. Indonesia has also had a significant increase in the share of manufacturing, especially from the mid-1980s. However, since the turn of the century manufacturing's share has started to decline as a result of the growing dominance of the mining sector. The services sector on the other hand has been stagnant in terms of its share of GDP over the past four decades (Panel B).

The services sector is also expected to expand as the middle class grows, boosting demand for social services, like health and education, and as the retail sector grows and the economy becomes more formalised. Continued urbanisation will also drive this process. Tourism is a service sector in which Indonesia has a strong comparative advantage and which has the potential to generate strong jobs growth (Box 1.1). Putting in place policies that facilitate this transformation and avoiding those that hinder it needs to continue. The first half of this chapter goes through a number of areas that deserve particular attention from Indonesian policymakers if the process of economic convergence is to continue to drive sustainable and inclusive growth.

Box 1.1. **Tourism in Indonesia**

In 2012, the tourism sector contributed 3.9% to the national economy. After about 10 years of stagnation, international tourism has been growing quickly and continuously since the mid-2000s. In 2013, the number of foreign tourist arrivals increased by 9.4% to 8.8 million but was accompanied by a slight decline in the average length of stay. Nevertheless, the contribution of foreign tourists to Indonesia's foreign exchange earnings has increased steadily to reach USD 9.1 billion in 2012. Indeed, tourism is the country's fifth largest foreign currency earner.

Domestic tourism is also increasing. In 2012, the number of domestic tourist trips was estimated at 245.3 million, with average expenditure of IDR 700 000 (USD 62) per trip. This growth is being driven by rising household incomes and the promotional campaign "Know and Love Your Country", as well as the growing number of national tourism attractions and events. The 2012 budget for the Ministry of Tourism and Creative Economy was IDR 2 730 billion (USD 242 million), a 62.5% increase on 2010.

Despite having the potential to be a major tourist destination for the rapidly growing Asian middle class, there are obstacles to further growth, such as poor infrastructure, lack of tourist facilities and concerns about safety. In its 2013 travel and tourism competitiveness index, which ranks nations according to their ability to develop their tourism industries, the World Economic Forum ranked Indonesia 70th out of 140 countries (OECD, 2014c).

Infrastructure

Good-quality infrastructure is a key ingredient for inclusive and sustainable economic growth. The *2010 Survey* (OECD, 2010b) highlighted the urgent need to step up infrastructure investment. In the three years immediately prior to the Asian Crisis infrastructure spending averaged around 9% of GDP, but since 1999 the average has only been around 4% (World Bank, 2012c). The lack of infrastructure, and the poor quality thereof, has long been seen as the biggest hindrance to continued economic development. Intercity road transport is overburdened, and traffic jams in the major cities, particularly in Jakarta, are major impediments to doing business. Air pollution is also a serious health issue. Furthermore, both road and rail networks are considerably smaller than what Indonesia's population density would call for compared to other emerging economies (Figure 1.4). However, this comparison may not be fair given that Indonesia is a scattered

Figure 1.4. **Rail and road networks relative to population density**

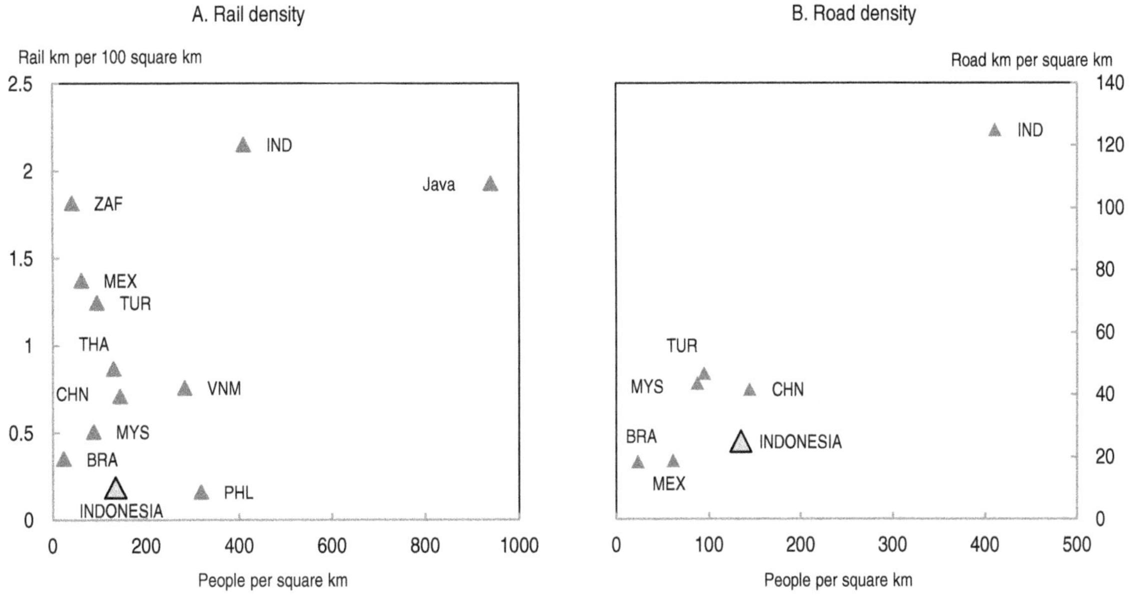

Source: World Bank, *World Development Indicators*; PT Kereta Api Indonesia (Indonesian Railway).

StatLink http://dx.doi.org/10.1787/888933200178

archipelago, and population densities vary greatly across the islands. Indeed, around three-quarters of the country's total rail track length is located in the most densely populated island, Java. Only 10% of railway lines are electrified. Local governments play an important role with regards to roads, with around 80% of the network's total length presently under their responsibility. Furthermore, the provision of infrastructure is a major factor in improving health and tackling poverty and deprivation, including through the provision of drinking water and modern sanitation.

A lack of power generating capacity is also inhibiting capital investment, and delays at the country's outdated airports and ports are increasing the cost of international trade. Given the opportunities offered by integration into GVCs, both in terms of generating well-paid jobs and boosting high-valued added exports, efficient communication and logistics are extremely important. Indeed, the situation in ports is deteriorating, with average import container dwell time at Tanjung Priok Port in Jakarta, which handles two-thirds of Indonesia's international trade, increasing from 4.8 days in 2010 to 6.4 days in 2013 (World Bank, 2014a). Moreover, the two main container terminals in Tanjung Priok, which together account for 70% of all Indonesian container traffic, are both operated by the same joint venture. This means that there is virtually no intra-port competition (OECD, 2014b). This leads to high logistics costs for firms, which are then passed onto consumers and businesses in higher prices. The World Bank (2013) estimates that logistics costs across Indonesia account for some 24% of GDP – an enormous tax on Indonesia's economic growth – while LPEM (2005) estimates that logistics account for 14% of total production costs, significantly higher than Japan's 5%. The World Bank's 2014 Logistics Performance Indicator (LPI) report ranks Indonesia 53th out of 160 countries, well behind other middle-income countries in the region. Indeed Indonesia ranks lowest in all sub-components of the LPI, when compared to Malaysia, Singapore, Thailand, China, Chinese Taipei and Vietnam; and particularly poorly in international shipments.

Numerous studies show the importance of infrastructure in spurring growth, and especially in the manufacturing sector. Moreover, as world-wide manufacturing moves to exploiting GVCs, connectedness is becoming increasingly important. Day and Ellis (2013) show that in Indonesia manufacturing firms benefit from localisation economies and that the "economic distance" between firms is extremely important for fostering growth in this sector. Interestingly, urbanisation itself does not seem to be a positive impetus to growth in this sector.

The recently established Infrastructure Prioritising Body (KP2IP) is welcome. It will assess and prioritise project proposals, and allocate them for implementation to line agencies, state-owned enterprises or the PPP centre in the Ministry of Finance. It will also provide guidance on how each project can be appropriately financed. Key challenges to improve the business environment and encourage good decision-making are to ensure that its deliberations and decisions are transparent and that it succeeds in improving co-ordination among infrastructure-related government agencies. As the government alone does not have the resources to meet all of the country's infrastructure needs, the private sector, both domestic and foreign, is expected to play an important role. However, there remain major impediments to expanding the private sector's role. For instance, Blundell-Wignall and Roulet (2015) show that in the sample of 56 countries Indonesia is the 2nd least open to portfolios flows (after only Argentina) and that this has a significant negative impact on both infrastructure and non-infrastructure business investment across countries. Greater efforts will need to be made to better channel available funds from both public and private sources towards more productive infrastructure investments. Creating more transparent regulatory frameworks, improving accessibility to capital through more supportive financial markets and increasing the capacity to absorb capital flows are all issues that need to be addressed.

The new government has chosen maritime connectivity as one of its major policy focuses. This includes enhancing inter-island links and upgrading port infrastructure. Many of the ports are in poor shape and impede the country's internal and external maritime commerce. The plan is to significantly expand maritime infrastructure to reduce logistics costs, boost economic growth and reduce inequality between Indonesia's more remote eastern islands and the demographic concentrations of the western part of the country. The plan includes the establishment of a minimum of 10 new deep-water ports to connect the far reaches of the archipelago to the rest of the country and the world. In addition to maritime connectivity the new government's other immediate focus will be on irrigation (including dam building), water supply and energy. Funding for these projects would be public, utilising the fiscal space created by the recent cut in fuel subsidies. Giving state-owned enterprises direct access to Official Development Assistance (ODA) funds, under the supervision of the Ministry of Finance, is also being considered.

One positive development in removing barriers to investment in infrastructure was the 2011 Land Procurement for Development in the Public Interest Act ("Land Acquisition Act"). Prior to its enactment, the long process of land acquisition inhibited investment in infrastructure and other business-related fixed investment. The new law allows the government to acquire private land for public works projects and sets out a fair and transparent framework for compensating landowners, including spelling out a simplified and accelerated appeals procedure using prescribed time frames for each stage of the process.

The government is strongly promoting the use of public-private partnerships (PPPs) to deliver infrastructure investment. A Presidential Regulation provides the legal framework for PPPs to deliver roads (including toll roads and bridges), irrigation systems, drinking water, waste management, telecommunications, power and oil and gas infrastructure. Indonesia's National Development Planning Agency (BAPPENAS) recently released its latest PPP Book which identified 27 projects worth USD 47.3 billion to be made available to investors from 2014. While progress has been made in establishing the legal framework for PPPs, to date no PPP financing has yet been closed.

As part of the Regulatory Reform Review of Indonesia (2012) the OECD assessed the framework for developing, procuring and managing PPPs. Indonesia thus participated in a peer review process in the OECD Network of Senior PPP Officials based on the Principles for Public Governance of PPPs (2012). The recently established PPP centre within the Ministry of Finance is a timely step. This will focus on developing a pipeline of bankable government-supported infrastructure projects. Likewise, the recently instituted Infrastructure Prioritising Body (KP2IP) is welcome. It will assess and prioritise project proposals, and allocate them for implementation to line agencies, state-owned enterprises or the PPP centre in the Ministry of Finance. It will also provide guidance on how each project can be appropriately financed. Given the complexities, including dealing with regional governments, a central co-ordinating entity is needed to help champion and shepherd PPP projects, including offering direct assistance to private firms tendering for these projects, but it remains unclear as to whether the new bodies will play this role. Despite these initiatives, as of October 2013, of the 21 PPPs that have been tendered since 2009, only seven had reached the final stage of negotiations (BAPPENAS, 2013).

Infrastructure bonds are another avenue that could be pursued. Indonesia could learn from countries like China and Malaysia, which have successfully accelerated the development of infrastructure by issuing bonds, both those issued directly by the government or through state-owned enterprises. In Malaysia they accounted for about 35% of Malaysia's corporate bond issuance in 2006-10, amounting to an average of USD 6 billion per year over this period. Infrastructure bonds are typically long-dated and match the bond's maturity with the lifetime of the infrastructure project. The bonds can be conventional or Islamic, and their principal and coupons can be secured by the assets and cash flow of the infrastructure project. Typically, infrastructure bonds are structured similarly to project finance loans. There are designated accounts to ring-fence the project's cash flow and assets so that they can be used to meet debt-servicing requirements. Although government guarantees are not involved, infrastructure projects are usually backed by concession agreements (for example, for toll roads) or power purchase agreements. The ratings and pricing of the infrastructure bond take into account factors including the concession/purchase agreement, the strength of the issuer and the integrity of the financing structure.

Urbanisation

Urbanisation has been and will remain a powerful driver of growth and social change in Indonesia. While agglomeration economies can have positive effects, rapid urbanisation is challenging the capacity of governments and private-sector entities to provide infrastructure and job opportunities. Indonesia has urbanised more quickly than most of its neighbours, and with over 70% of the population expected to live in urban areas by 2050 – up from around 50% currently (Figure 1.5) – inefficiencies and bottlenecks in cities will become increasingly

Figure 1.5. **Urbanisation projections**

Per cent of total population

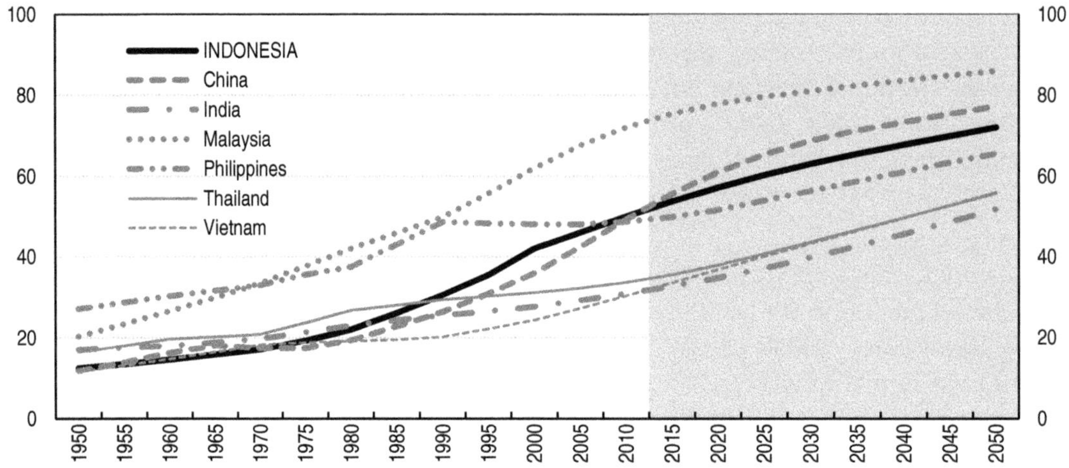

Source: United Nations, Department of Economic and Social Affairs, Population Division (2012), *World Urbanization Prospects: The 2011 Revision*, CD-ROM Edition.

StatLink http://dx.doi.org/10.1787/888933200183

serious impediments to economic development. Indeed, urbanisation is associated closely with the process relocating out of agriculture into higher-productivity sectors, and urban concentration delivers the benefits of clusters and agglomeration. For example, in Jakarta wages are higher, economic growth is stronger and, while unemployment is not notably lower than other regions, the city continues to draw migrants from rural areas in search of work. Urbanisation is also associated with improving living standards and migration of underemployed farmers to urban areas; their remittances help to lift per capita income in rural areas, helping to limit the rural-urban income gap.

The two largest cities in Indonesia are Jakarta and Surabaya. Jakarta has grown from 2.7 million residents in 1960 to 9.8 million in 2011 (United Nations, 2012), with a density of more than 14 400 people per square kilometre. Surabaya's population was around 2.5 million in 2011, with around 12 500 people per square kilometre. The agglomerations are of course much larger and have been growing much more quickly. Indeed, in the case of Jakarta, the population of the core of the city has actually been shrinking over the past decade due to suburbanisation, while that of the entire Jakarta agglomeration, encompassing Bogor, Tangerang, Depok and Bekasi (abbreviated as Botadebek), has continued to increase rapidly – from 17 million in 1996 to 27 million in 2007. Part of the reason for suburbanisation is that moderate and high-income families have been moving out of the central city to the Botadebek, where amenities are of higher quality (World Bank, 2012a). In addition, poorer Jakartans are relocating to the fringe areas because commercial expansion in the central city has increased rents and reduced space dramatically.

While urbanisation brings considerable benefits, it also has costs. In a number of big cities, and most particularly in Jakarta, traffic congestion is a major headache for citizens and businesses, and periodic flooding plagues the city, causing major disruptions. The new satellite towns have grown rapidly, but road infrastructure has not kept pace, causing massive traffic jams and long commutes for residents. Only now is there some progress in building new metro and elevated roads within Jakarta and adding toll roads that connect the city's suburbs. Large-scale investment in infrastructure is required to facilitate intra-urban links between core and periphery. The new Land Acquisition Act should remove one of the major impediments to building infrastructure. International connectivity also needs to be improved with better ports and airports. Consideration should be given to creating manufacturing estates so as to avoid industrial sprawl. Improvement is needed in the co-ordination across districts and with central government regarding planning and prioritising investments. For Jakarta, expanding the city limits, so as to bring under one political administration many of the urban areas adjoining the city, would help with integrated planning.

Improving human capital formation

In 2011, the Indonesian government spent around 15% of its total expenditures on education (excluding social assistance schemes). This is a decline over recent years and well below the official 20% floor set in 2002. Nevertheless, the current share of education spending is on a par with many OECD countries, but a little lower than many other emerging economies. As a share of GDP spending on education is only 2.8%. This is low even by developing-country standards (Figure 1.6) but has increased substantially from around 1% in 1990 and has plateaued over the last decade. Enrolment rates in Indonesia are high at the primary level but drop off at the secondary and particularly the tertiary levels (Figure 1.7). While these enrolment rates are roughly on a par with other countries at similar per capita income levels, the emphasis should remain on doing as much as possible to promote access to higher education for all young Indonesians. A particular problem is not the drop-out rates within the three levels of non-tertiary education, but rather at the interface between them, specifically at the ages of 12 and 15. Increasing the resources directed at building human capital should be a top priority for Indonesia, especially if it wants to best utilise its abundant supply of labour. Currently Indonesia is being out-performed by countries like Vietnam, China and Thailand in accumulating the human capital needed to facilitate the further emergence of industries that rely on a skilled labour force. The OECD Education Policy Review of Indonesia (OECD, 2015) goes into these issues in more detail, including expanding vocational schemes aimed at promoting youth employment.

Figure 1.6. **Spending on education in selected emerging economies, 2012**

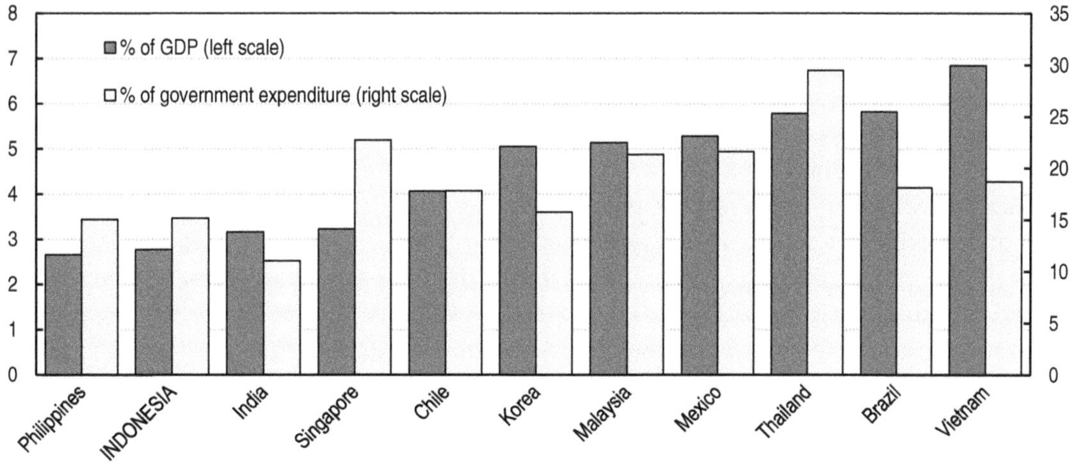

Source: World Bank, *World Development Indicators.*

StatLink http://dx.doi.org/10.1787/888933200190

Figure 1.7. **Enrolment rates in selected emerging economies**[1]

Per cent of respective school-age populations

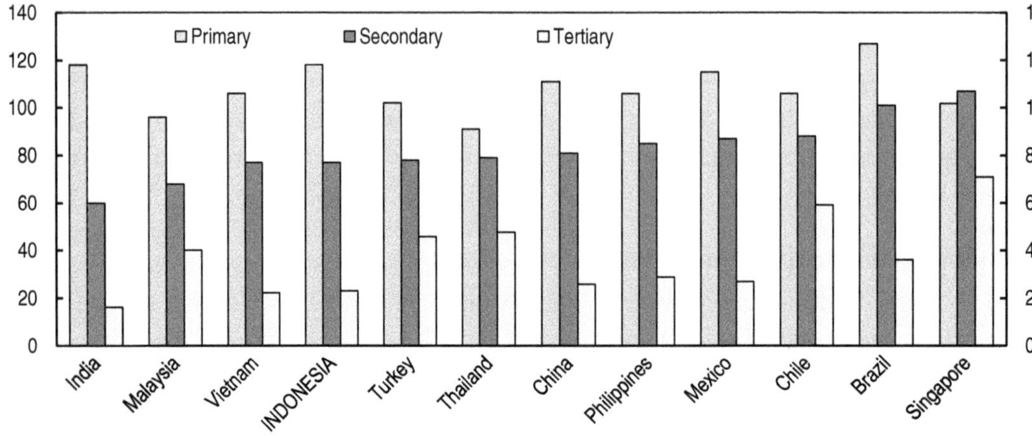

1. Gross enrolment rates are calculated on the basis of standard school-age age cohorts. Enrolment rates over 100 per cent occur because students outside the standard age cohorts may be enrolled at that level of education.

Source: United Nations, *International Human Development Indicators 2013.*

StatLink http://dx.doi.org/10.1787/888933200207

According to the 2012 Programme for International Student Assessment (PISA), 15 year-old Indonesian students score poorly by international standards in mathematics, science and reading. While there has been some improvement over time, Indonesia is ranked second last among the 65 countries that participated, ahead only of Peru. That said, when adjusted for GDP per capita, Indonesia's performance is not out of line with other countries at similar levels of development. Moreover, when accounting for the share of students from disadvantaged backgrounds, Indonesia's performance does not look so bad by international comparison, even though a number of neighbouring countries such as Vietnam and Thailand significantly outperform it in this regard. Another positive feature of Indonesia's PISA 2012 performance is the gender equality in outcomes.

PISA tests 15 year-olds in school, and Indonesia's low enrolment rates at this age are likely to mean that the academic capacity of the whole age cohort might actually be well below that suggested by PISA. However, in this regard Indonesia performs on a par with peer countries. Enrolment rates at the primary levels are around 120% of the age cohort, and the secondary enrolment rate of around 80% is only a little lower than other countries at a similar level of economic development. Likewise, tertiary enrolment, while low by OECD standards, at around 20% of the age cohort, is also comparable to other emerging economies like India, China, Vietnam and the Philippines. One interesting feature of tertiary enrolment in Indonesia is the relatively low share of Type-B or vocational tertiary enrolment, which is considerably lower than most OECD countries and also much lower than all the other emerging economies for which data are available. Given the success of vocational training in providing a smooth school-to-work transition for non-academic students in many OECD countries, consideration should be given to boosting the vocational share in tertiary education. These are also skills that are highly valued in the growing industrial and manufacturing sectors.

Quality of learning remains a concern in Indonesia, with around one in ten children having to repeat their first year of primary study to attain the required standards (UNICEF, 2012). While class sizes tend to be large compared to OECD countries (OECD, 2012b), increasing the quality of teaching is often a more efficient policy lever to improve student performance than reducing class size. Even though class size may affect how much time and attention a teacher can give to individual students, as well as the social dynamics among students, PISA results suggest that systems prioritising higher teacher quality over smaller classes tend to perform better. This confirms other research that shows that raising teacher quality is a more effective measure to improve student outcomes. For example, while in Japan and Korea, both of which perform strongly in PISA testing, school systems spend comparatively heavily on education, they tend to prioritise teachers' salaries over class size.

Improving the quality of teaching should go hand in hand with regular teacher assessments and increasing teacher salaries. Baedhowi (2009) estimates that around one-third of all elementary school teachers have not undertaken any professional teacher training beyond a high-school diploma, and 76% do not possess an undergraduate degree. Training and retraining is particularly important with the introduction of the *Curriculum 2013* reform, which shifts the emphasis to a "thematic and integrated" approach. The Teacher Law 2005 sets the target that teachers have at least a 4-year Bachelor degree and teaching certificates. Teachers with a Bachelor degree and teaching experience of at least 10 years may apply for teaching certificates by submitting a portfolio of documents to be assessed by a university panel. If the portfolio is assessed to meet the requirements, teachers are awarded a teaching certificate, and receive salary increases. Otherwise teachers are required to take 90 hours of training and then written and performance tests. If teachers pass these tests, they are then awarded teaching certificates; otherwise they are required to repeat the examination. These retraining and certification programmes should be expanded to all 2.8 million Indonesian teachers. Continuous professional development programmes should also be further developed and linked to salary increments and promotion opportunities. Local administrations should also be obliged to better monitor the quality of instruction.

While direct comparison with peer countries is difficult, teacher salaries in Indonesia are comparatively low in relation to average per capita incomes, even compared to low-income OECD countries (OECD, 2012b). Moreover, teachers' educational attainment is not positively correlated to their earnings. Teachers with relatively low educational levels are comparatively overpaid, and those with relatively higher educational levels are underpaid compared to other occupations. This implies weak incentives for teachers to upgrade their academic qualifications. In addition, according to a World Bank (2008) study, compared to other occupations with an equivalent education level, teachers earn relatively low incomes. Perhaps related to low pay, teacher absenteeism remains a problem, and anecdotal evidence suggests that many teachers are forced to supplement their incomes by working in two or more schools or even at other part-time jobs. This undoubtedly affects teacher commitment and performance. Another problem is that because most teachers are paid by the central government, districts tend to over-recruit; this should be addressed, as recommended in the previous *Survey* (OECD, 2012a).

While professional development opportunities are important for teachers in Indonesia, this is equally true for workers in all other sectors. Opportunities for workers, including in the informal sector, to do on-the-job training is an important avenue through which overall productivity can be improved. However, Indonesia has a particularly poor record in this regard, with only around 5% of all firms offering training to their employees (Figure 1.8), considerably fewer than in many other comparable countries.

Figure 1.8. **Firms offering formal training to their employees**

Per cent of firms

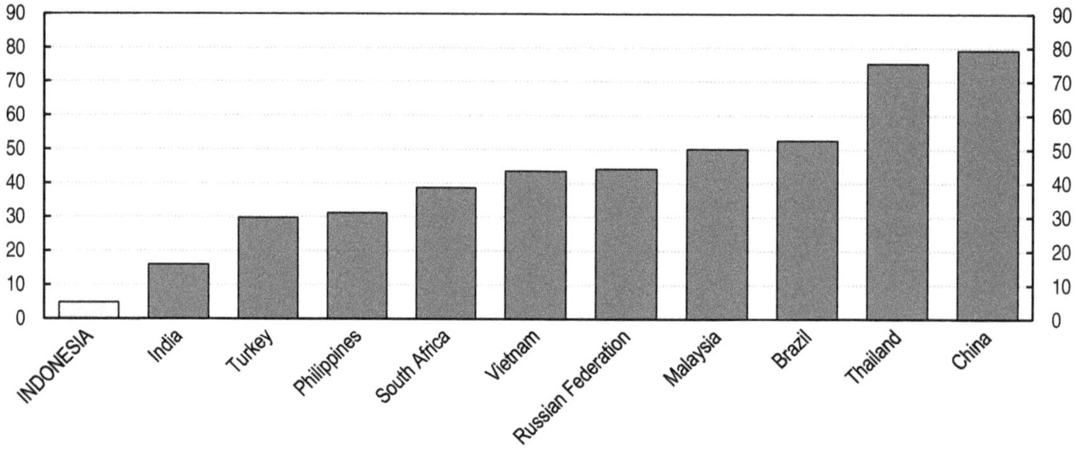

Source: World Bank, *World Development Indicators.*

StatLink http://dx.doi.org/10.1787/888933200215

Making taxes and expenditure more growth friendly

The *2012 Survey* made a number of recommendations to improve Indonesia's tax system. The principle motivation was to increase the amount of revenue raised and to improve efficiency, and in this way create the fiscal space to fund much needed increases in spending on education, infrastructure and social services. The recommendations included broadening the tax base by bringing the self-employed into the tax net and reducing exemptions to the value-added tax. Recommendations also focused on promoting longer-term growth, including the use of broad-based investment credits (in place of tax holidays), and introducing a simplified tax regime for small- to medium-size enterprises. It was also recommended that the taxation of the resources sector be rationalised so that rents are captured in a more comprehensive and less distortionary way. Chapter 2of this *Survey* looks at this issue more closely.

Integrating into global value chains

For low- and low-to-middle income countries like Indonesia, there are large pay-offs to successfully inserting themselves into GVCs. This offers them the opportunity to leverage their comparative advantage through deeper specialisation (Baldwin and Lopez-Gonzalez, 2013). Moreover, integration into GVCs facilitates the importing of technology, capital and know-how. Indonesia's current position in GVCs – that is, manufacturing and assembly – reflects its comparative advantage in basic commodities, other upstream inputs and labour. In the longer term, the challenge for countries like Indonesia is to move to higher value-added production and to capture the longest possible portion of the value chain (Figure 1.9). However, at its current stage of development Indonesia's focus should also be on competing with other similarly endowed countries for a greater share of the lower valued-added labour-intensive manufacturing and assembly links in the global production process, thereby drawing labour away from its low-productivity sectors and towards more productive and dynamic activities, which provide well-paid and secure jobs in the formal sector. While Indonesia currently does reasonably well in creating or capturing value added in GVCs, it may be falling behind relative to competitors. China's GVC income increased by a factor of five between 1995 and 2009, and in India it tripled, while

Figure 1.9. **Valued added in the global value chain process**

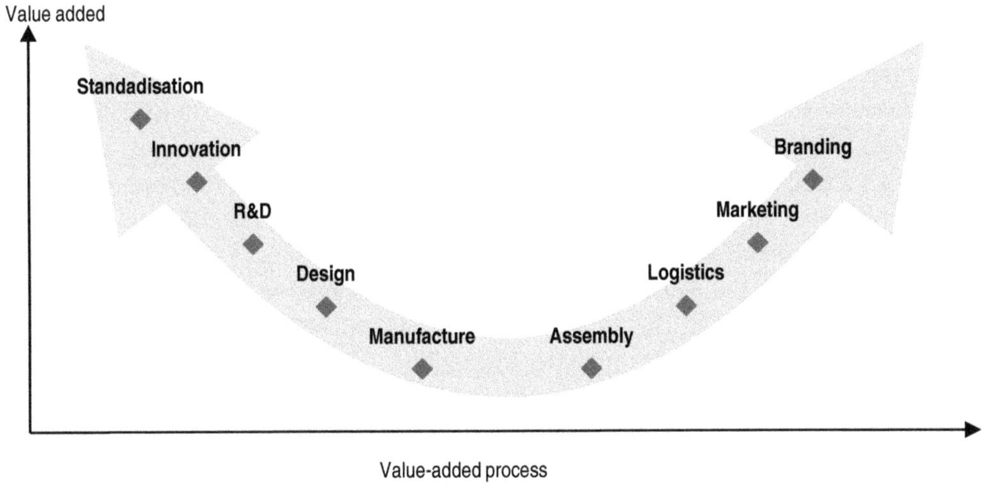

Source: Business Week International Extra Online, 16 May 2005.

Indonesia's only doubled to around USD 170 billion (OECD, 2013). Furthermore, the length of its value chains in the manufacturing sector is relatively short (Figure 1.10). According to the *World Investment Report* (UNCTAD, 2013), Indonesia, with a GVC participation rate of 44% (the share of a country's exports that is part of a multi-stage trade process), ranks lower than its neighbours, including Singapore (82%), Malaysia (68%), the Philippines (56%), Thailand (52%) and Vietnam (48%).

Figure 1.10. **Production stages in the manufacturing sector for selected emerging economies**

Index of production stages[1]

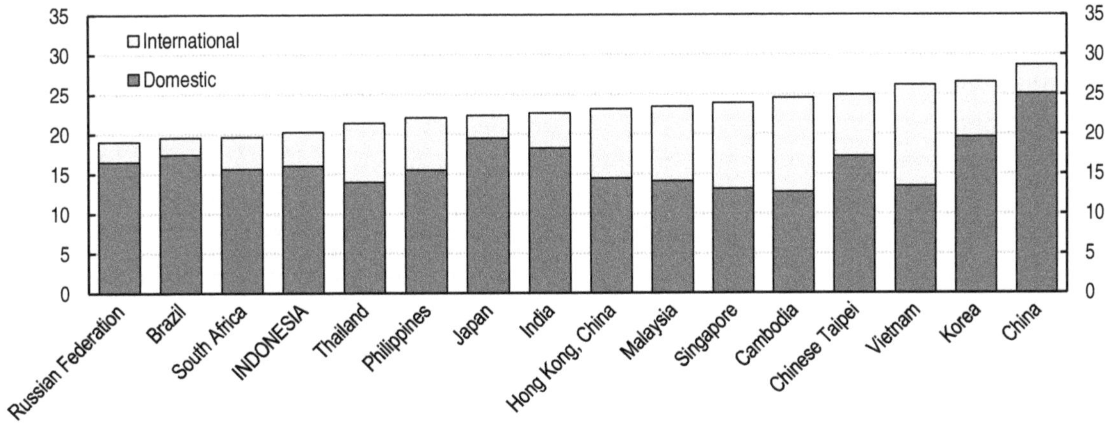

1. Index measuring the number of production stages required to realise a product or provide a service in a given final industry. In other words it measures the length of GVCs in each industry. The index takes the value of 1 if there is a single production stage in the final industry and its value increases when intermediate inputs from the same industry or other industries are used in the production of the final good or service. This indicator is decomposed to reflect domestic production stages and foreign production stages. Details on the index calculation can be found in the OECD *Trade Policy Paper*, No. 159.

Source: OECD, *Global Value Chain Indicators*, May 2013.

StatLink http://dx.doi.org/10.1787/888933200227

One critical element in facilitating integration into GVCs is an efficient services sector that provides firms with access to competitive business services, such as finance, engineering, transport and logistics, and telecommunications. Moreover, the growth of the middle class will continue to increase demands for nearly all types of services, but particularly more sophisticated services in health, education and communications (Ghani, 2011). At around 38% of GDP Indonesia has a relatively small services sector, and services' share of foreign trade, at around 12%, is also small. While this share has increased steadily for most countries, Indonesia's services share has stagnated for the past 30 years. Its services sectors tend to be heavily regulated and market access for foreign services providers highly restricted. For example, in the business services sector, Indonesia ranks third from the bottom out of the 59 countries in the OECD FDI regulatory restrictiveness database, while in distribution it ranks the lowest.

Another critical element for closer integration into GVCs is openness to trade. Lower barriers to trade mean that intermediate goods from previous links in the chain can enter the country at a lower cost, ready for value to be added domestically before being re-exported to the next link. Import tariffs and export duties are examples of such impediments to trade, but there are other aspects that are equally important such as the efficiency of trade procedures. According to the OECD Services Trade Restrictiveness Index (STRI) Indonesia scores below the average of peer countries (Brazil, Chile, China, India, Mexico, Russian Federation, South Africa, Turkey) in 16 of the 18 service sectors included. Indeed, in the logistics sectors (road freight transport and distribution services) Indonesia's settings are comparatively the most restrictive. In 2012, average most favoured nation (MFN) tariff rates in Indonesia were 7.8%, down from 9.5% in 2006 (WTO, 2013). This compares with 9.9 for China, 13.5 for Brazil, 13.7 for India, 6.5 for Malaysia and 6.2 for the Philippines. However, overall, Indonesia's tariff rates show positive escalation, implying higher rates of effective protection. While the simple average applied tariff on goods at the first stage of processing is 5%, it is 6.2% for semi-processed goods and 9% for fully processed goods. Indonesia also imposes various export taxes, but these are principally on raw commodities, including palm oil, raw cocoa, and mineral ore exports (see Chapter 2 for further details). According to the *OECD Trade Facilitation Indicators*, Indonesia performs better than the averages of Asian and lower-middle income countries in the areas of fees and charges, harmonisation and simplification of documents, automation and internal border agency co-operation (Figure 1.11). However, its performance in the areas of information availability and streamlining of procedures is below average.

Another important element in integrating into GVCs is openness to foreign investment. Protectionist sentiment has long been evident in policy making in Indonesia. This sentiment comes from the arguments that recent policy measures introduced by the Government are aimed at increasing value-added to some of its strategic commodities, reaching self-sufficiency, and climbing up its value chain in order to deepen the economy and create jobs as (mandated by its Constitution). Having said this, Indonesia has taken concrete steps to liberalise trade, both unilaterally and through regional free trade agreements (ASEAN, and ASEAN + Japan, China, Australia and New Zealand). These trade agreements account for a large proportion of Indonesia's traded goods and to some extent render unilateral protectionist policies ineffective. Moreover, self-sufficiency does not necessarily mean protectionism. In some contexts, self-sufficiency can be directed towards enhancing production efficiency, sustainability and environmentally friendliness. Many sectors of the economy are protected from foreign investment and competition. For

Figure 1.11. **Trade facilitation indicators for Indonesia**

Index, 2 = best performance

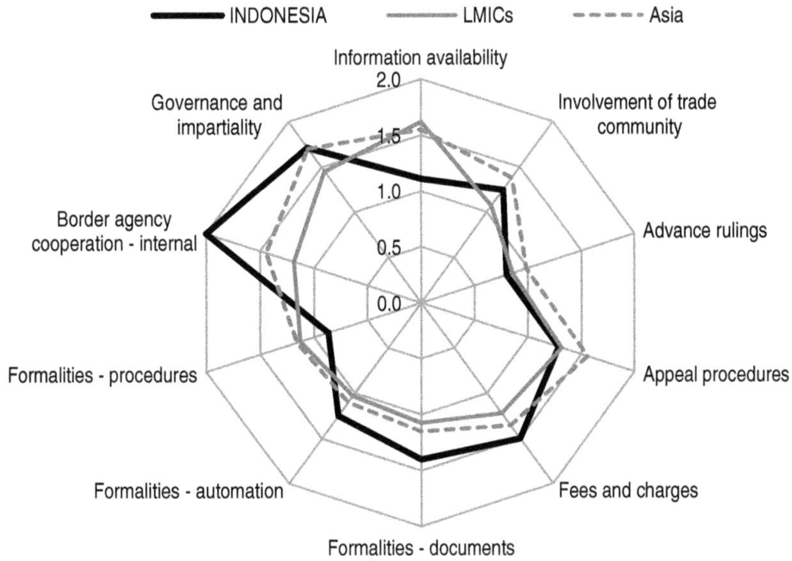

Note: LMICs: Lower middle income countries (World Bank classification). Analysis is based on latest available data as of January 2013 and the set of TFIs as constructed in "Trade Facilitation Indicators: The Potential Impact of Trade Facilitation on Developing Countries' Trade" (OECD, *Trade Policy Paper*, No. 144) for 107 countries outside the OECD area.

StatLink http://dx.doi.org/10.1787/888933200238

example, limits on the foreign ownership of mines have hampered investment in the sector (see Chapter 2). The inauguration of the ASEAN Economic Community (AEC) free trade area in 2015 has prompted some changes, including a revision of the Negative Investment List (NIL), which sets out sectors of the economy that are either wholly closed to foreign direct investment or in which foreign direct investment is limited to a certain share. In May 2014 changes to the NIL reflected both national development priorities and AEC obligations. Restrictions on foreign investment in some infrastructure sectors such as ports, electricity generation and waste treatment were relaxed, and special provisions were made for ASEAN investors. However, the May 2014 revision of the NIL also included tightening of restrictions in other sectors, including in the oil industry and in logistics.

Indonesia is one of the most restrictive countries in terms of FDI as measured in the OECD FDI regulatory restrictiveness index (Figure 1.12, Panel A). While there have been big improvements over the past three decades, much remains to be done to open the economy to foreign investment. Even in important sectors like mining, Indonesia's rules relating to FDI are considerably more restrictive than many other commodity-based economies', like South Africa, Malaysia and Chile, which compete directly with Indonesia to attract mining FDI. That said, FDI flows into Indonesia have been strong in recent years, particularly in manufacturing, which between 2010 and 2014 attracted around 42% of all FDI inflows (32% in services and 23% in natural resources) (Panel B).

Managing natural resources

Managing Indonesia's reliance on commodities is another major challenge. Chapter 2 of this *Survey* discusses issues related to managing Indonesia's rich natural resource endowment in a sustainable and efficient manner, to the benefit of all Indonesians. Its comparative advantage in commodities cannot be denied, but they should be utilised as a

Figure 1.12. **FDI restrictiveness and flows**

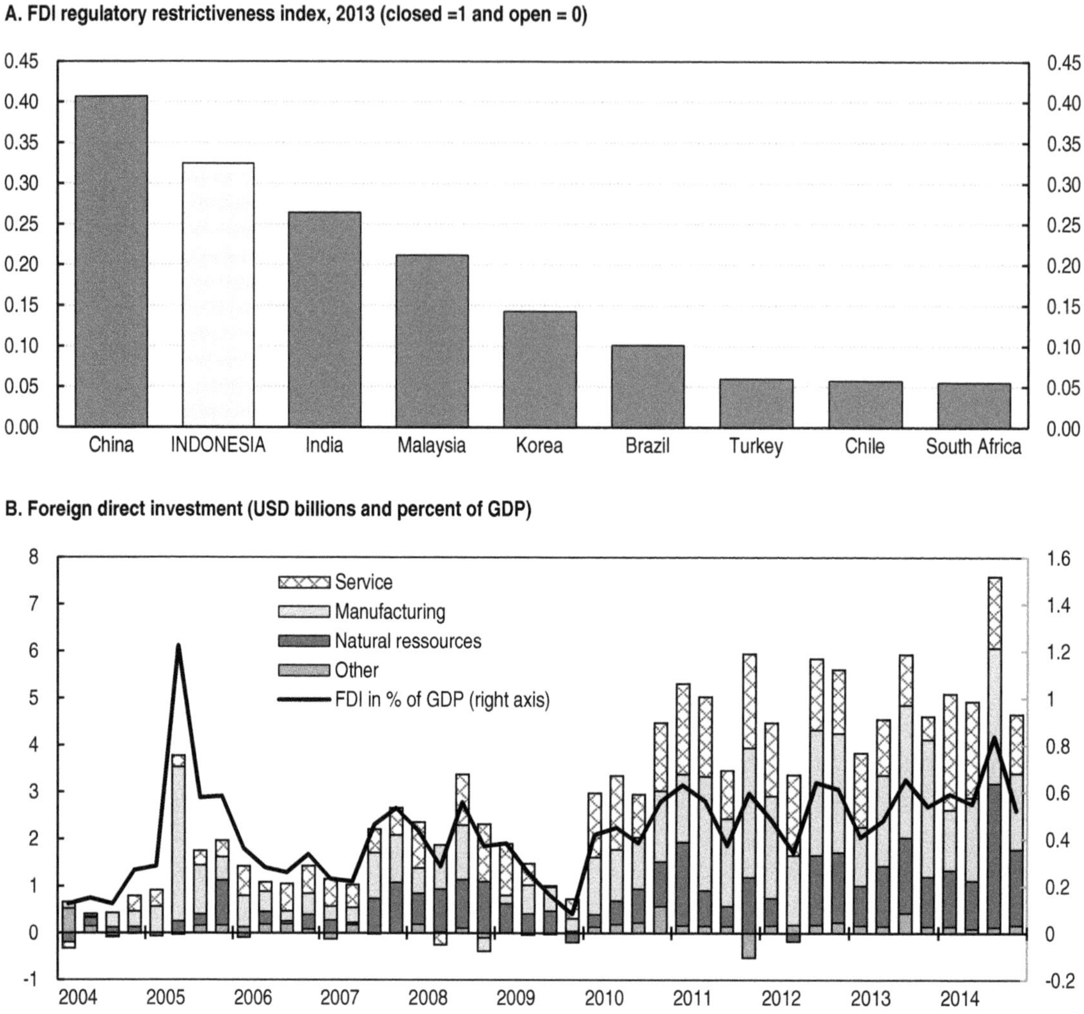

Note: The FDI Regulatory Restrictiveness Index measures statutory restrictions on foreign direct investment.
Sources: OECD; Bank Indonesia.

StatLink http://dx.doi.org/10.1787/888933200246

resource for broader national development. The benefits of the exploitation of these resources in the form of either employment or royalties are not equally distributed. Indeed, while the commodities super cycle has now ended, one troubling feature of Indonesia's management of its natural resources is the lack of any substantial fiscal dividend through its duration. Many other resource exporters around the world, such as Norway, Chile and Botswana, benefited noticeably during the boom, recording fiscal surpluses, paying off debt, investing heavily and building up sovereign wealth funds. But Indonesia has failed to capture many resource rents, pointing to the need to rethink that aspect of its fiscal framework. In this regard, Botswana and Chile provide excellent models from which Indonesia can draw lessons (Korinek, 2013 and 2014).

More fundamentally, a dependence on commodities may distort the process of economic convergence. McMillan and Rodrik (2011) argue that dependence on commodity exports and specialisation in a few highly profitable primary activities tend not to generate much productive employment, even when they spur growth. And, indeed, they may distort the process of convergence by inhibiting the transfer of factors towards high-productivity sectors. Moreover, they encourage rent seeking. This can be thought of as another variant of the natural resource curse. It is then the role of government to extract resource rents on behalf of citizens and to use these revenues to advance broader national development priorities, like education and infrastructure. But in doing this the government should be aware that with the end of the commodities super-cycle, international competitive pressures among suppliers are likely to mount in this sector, so strategies for extracting rent on behalf of the citizenry should be considered carefully so as not to inhibit future exploration and investment, particularly from foreign companies. Further consideration should then be given to measures such as a resource rent tax (also discussed in Chapter 2 and in the previous *Survey*), which would be less distortionary than export taxes and ore export bans. There is an extensive literature on how to implement such a tax in the face of a number of specific sector characteristics, including significant uncertainty, high sunk costs, long payback periods and high output price volatility (Daniel et al., 2009).

Recommendations for promoting sustainable and inclusive long-term growth

- Create fiscal space so that more public resources can be directed at improving education access and outcomes, and improving infrastructure. Revenues could be boosted by better enforcing the taxation of small firms and the self-employed, improving enforcement of personal income tax and removing VAT exemptions.
- Raise public spending on infrastructure. Focus on transportation and logistics to support industry, as well as natural disaster prevention and water treatment.
- Continue promoting PPP investments. However, the framework is too complicated. The effectiveness of the new co-ordinating entities should be monitored.
- Re-examine the option of issuing infrastructure bonds.
- Move forward with plans that will allow state-owned enterprises to borrow directly from Overseas Development Assistance sources, under the supervision of the Ministry of Finance.
- Accommodate the process of urbanisation through better planning and co-ordination between city, local and national authorities. In the same vein, expand the Jakarta administrative area to encompass the surrounding agglomerations.
- Direct more public resources to improving education access and outcomes. Accelerate the existing programme of regular teacher assessments and professional development. Link teacher salaries more closely to qualifications and performance.
- Develop programmes that focus on reducing drop-out rates between primary and middle school (at age 12), and middle and high school (at age 15).
- Facilitate trade so as to foster more integration into global value chains. This includes removing logistics bottlenecks in ports.
- Avoid protectionist measures that inhibit openness to trade and foreign investment with uncertain development payoff. Further relax foreign direct investment rules. This includes further paring down the "negative investment list".
- Remove barriers to the development of a vibrant services sector including over-regulation of the sector.

Recommendations for promoting sustainable and inclusive long-term growth *(cont.)*

- Relax employment protection legislation so as to encourage more employment in the formal sector.
- Re-examine ways to efficiently tax resources, including through a resource rent tax.

Poverty, inequality and inclusiveness

On 11 October 2012, Indonesia's former President, Susilo Bambang Yudhoyono, declared that the reduction of poverty would be the government's top priority. He went on to state that poverty could be reduced through sustainable economic growth, recognising its importance in creating jobs and fulfilling the basic needs of the nation's people. Indonesia's National Long-Term Development Plan 2005-25 sets out the country's key aims in terms of poverty reduction and development:

- Achieving equitable development that gives greater attention to those who are disadvantaged, including poor communities in remote or disaster-prone areas.
- Increasing national food security and self-reliance based on local diversified food resources.
- Developing rural areas through the promotion of agricultural production and the agro-food industry, by building capacity, developing infrastructure and enhancing access to information, markets and financial services.

The previous government also articulated a National Medium-Term Development Plan (RPJMN) for 2010-14, which included poverty reduction as one of its 11 national priorities and set a target of lowering poverty (national measure) to 8-10%. The new Widodo government released its five-year National Medium-Term Development Plan in January 2015, which includes a target absolute poverty rate of 7-8% by 2019. The absolute poverty rate was 11% in September 2014, before the reductions in fuel subsidies. Currently, Indonesia spends around 1.2% of GDP on social assistance, of which around a third is on poverty-related social assistance and the remainder on social insurance – principally on civil servants' pensions and health insurance. Of this only 0.5% of GDP is spent on targeted social assistance, compared to a regional average of 1%, and 1.5% for all developing countries.

Growth should be at the heart of policies aimed at alleviating poverty. As long as the proceeds of growth are to some extent shared across the income distribution and the purchasing power of the increase in income is not eroded by faster increases in the cost of living, then poverty will diminish (Kaary, 2004). However, while absolute poverty responds to sustained periods of growth, the impact on relative poverty is ambiguous. Cross-country evidence suggests that there is no systematic relationship between sustained periods of per capita income growth and the concentration of income (Figure 1.13, Panel B); De Silva and Sumarto (2014) find the same result looking just at time-series data for Indonesia. It is also evident that the relationship between growth and poverty reduction is not a simple one: the growth elasticity of poverty is not the same across countries. In Vietnam, Indonesia, Mexico, Brazil and several other countries the reductions in poverty for any given rate of income growth have been larger than for China, India, Malaysia and Turkey (Panel A). Clearly there are other factors at play in addition to just growth. Indeed, some countries have recorded sustained per capita GDP growth but have seen very small

Figure 1.13. **GDP growth, poverty reduction and the change in the GINI coefficient**

Per cent, percentage points, and change in GINI coefficient

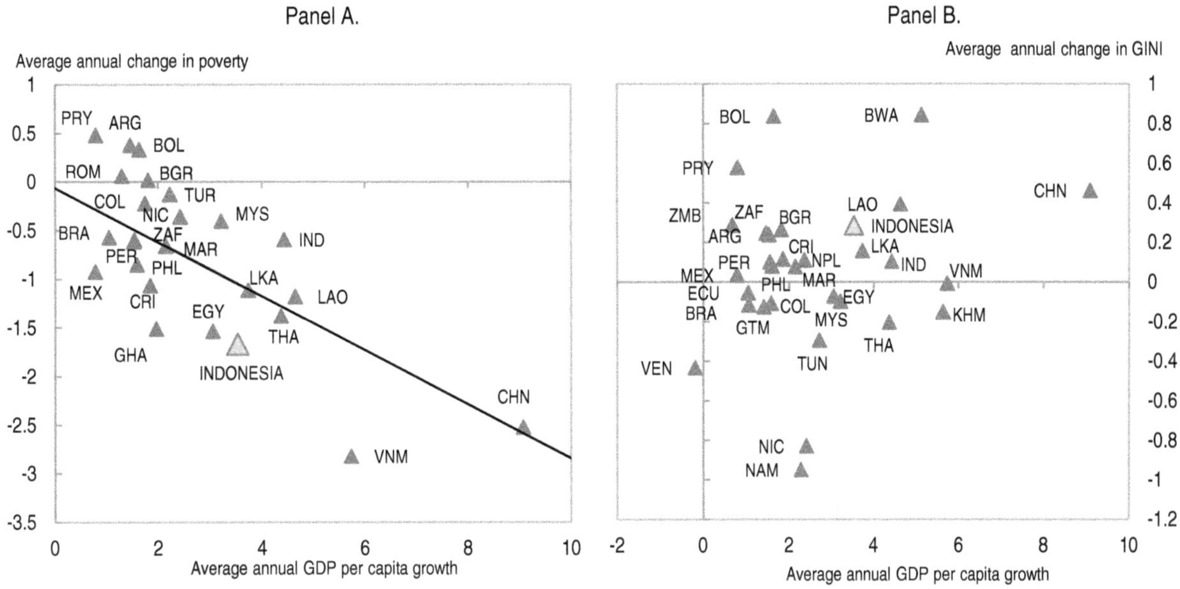

Note: GDP is GDP per capita, PPP (constant 2005 international dollars) and poverty is the poverty headcount ratio at USD 2 a day (PPP) (% of population). Varying periods starting from 1981 to 1993 and ending from 2006 to 2011.

Source: World Bank, *World Development Indicators*.

StatLink http://dx.doi.org/10.1787/888933200256

declines or indeed even increases in poverty. The literature suggests that growth appears to be a necessary but not a sufficient condition for reducing poverty. In addition to the unique features of each country, including demographic and economic structure, poverty reduction policies and programmes are also likely to play a crucial role.

Like China and Vietnam, Indonesia has performed admirably in reducing absolute poverty. Over the past three decades, per capita GDP growth has averaged around 3.5% annually, and this, in combination with poverty-reduction programmes, has been sufficient to make very impressive inroads into poverty. The USD 2 per day poverty headcount halved from around 85% of the population to 43% (Figure 1.14, Panel A). However, income alone is not the sole measure of the well-being of the poor; there are other figures that cannot be overlooked: for example, less than half of the rural poor have access to clean water, only three-quarters of all Indonesians have access to electricity (IEA, 2013), and only 55% of poor Indonesian children complete junior high school.

The government has two official poverty lines for each province, reflecting the different cost of living in rural and urban areas in each province. As of September 2014, the average rural poverty line was IDR 297 000 per capita per month (around USD 24) and the urban poverty line was IDR 327 000 (around USD 26). These poverty lines are determined by a complex function taking into account what the poor spend on food to reach 2 100 calories per day, as well as costs associated with dozens of non-food items, including housing, clothing, education and health care. According to these definitions, in September 2014 there were 10.4 million urban poor and 17.3 million rural poor, comprising 8.2% of the urban population and 13.8% of the rural population, down sharply from 13.6% and 20.2% a decade ago.

Indonesia's record concerning income distribution has been less impressive, particularly over the past decade, which saw a notable increase in the Gini coefficient

Figure 1.14. **Poverty headcount ratio and GINI coefficient**

Per cent of population and index

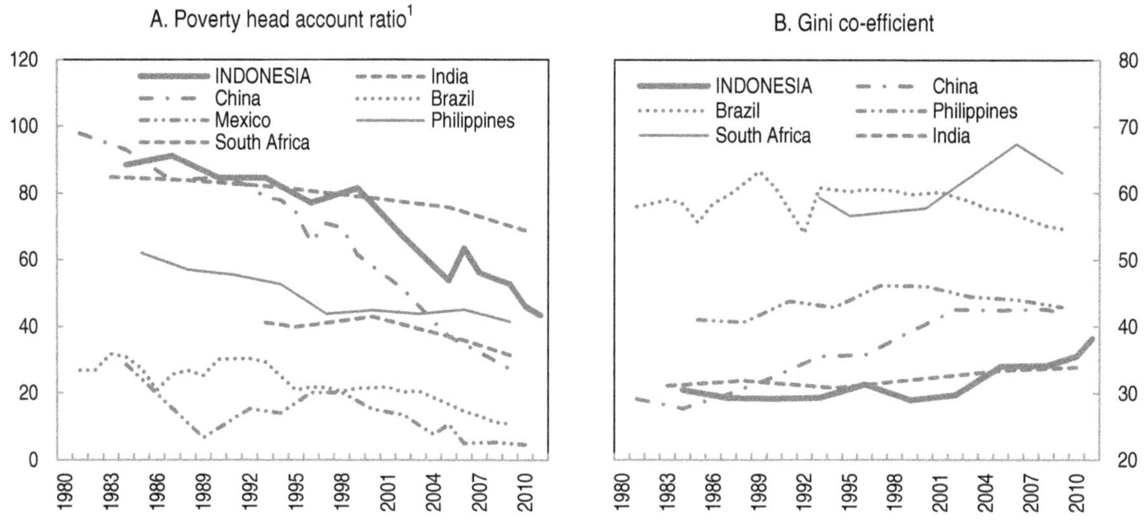

1. At USD 2 a day (PPP).

Source: World Bank, *World Development Indicators.*

StatLink http://dx.doi.org/10.1787/888933200268

(Figure 1.14, Panel B). Since the 1997-98 Asian financial crisis, the gap between rich and poor has widened. However, despite this increase, in comparison to many other developing countries, income inequality in Indonesia remains low. Of the 154 countries for which World Bank data are available, Indonesia ranks 74th in terms of income inequality: lower than China, the Philippines, Malaysia, Singapore and Thailand but above India. There was a sharp rise in top income shares in Indonesia during the late 1990s, coinciding with the 1997-98 economic crisis (Leigh and van der Eng, 2009), and they remain generally higher than elsewhere. The 0.1% top income earners in Indonesia tend to be wealthier than those in other countries, although the income share of the top 10% seems to be on par with other countries in the region. A number of reasons have been put forward to explain the recent deterioration in consumption equality in Indonesia. First, the rents from the booming mining and other commodity industries are likely to be concentrated at the top income levels (Yusef et al., 2013). Also the real price of rice increased substantially in the mid-2000s, eroding the purchasing power of poorer household in which rice makes up a large part of the consumption bundle, and this may account for the spike in inequality seen over that period (Yusef, 2014). Labour market developments, including increases in severance payments, rising minimum wages, slower growth in manufacturing employment and greater informality, are all likely have resulted in less low-wage jobs growth. Finally, the regressivity of fuel subsidies may also have played a role in increasing inequality (Agustina et al., 2013).

Vulnerability

The falling absolute poverty rate, however, partially masks a high degree of vulnerability: much of Indonesia's population is clustered just above the poverty line. Around 21% of Indonesians live below or close to the official poverty line (with consumption of less than 1.2 times the poverty line), while 34% of the population live below 1.5 times the poverty line and is almost equally vulnerable (Figure 1.15). The World Bank (2012) estimates that 40% of Indonesians are highly vulnerable to poverty. Turnover

Figure 1.15. **Distribution of per capita consumption, 2012**

Thousands of people

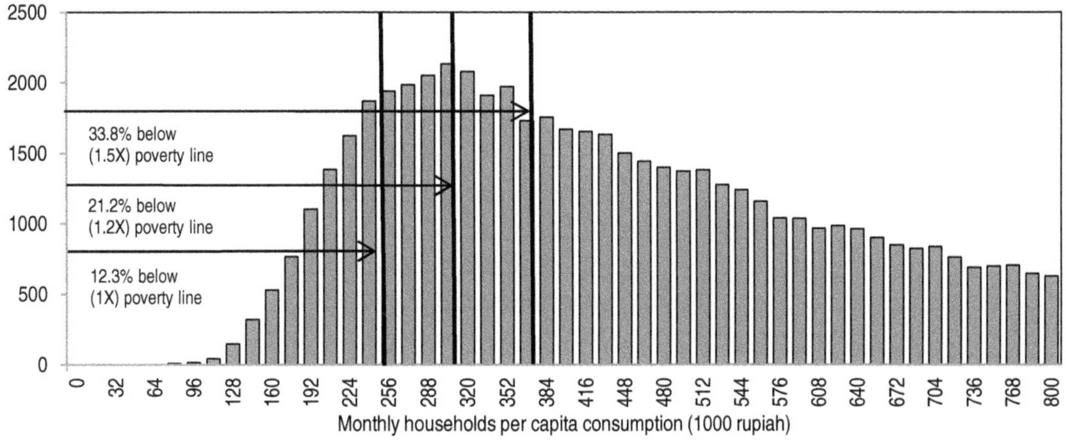

Source: World Bank, SUSENAS and OECD calculations.

StatLink http://dx.doi.org/10.1787/888933200278

among the poor is considerable: Sumarto (2014) estimates that of the 30 million poor in 2010, 55% were not classified as poor the previous year, even though the absolute level of poverty did not increase over those two years. Even relatively small shocks to these vulnerable households can be enough to push them into poverty. Indeed, the poor are particularly affected by food prices, with up to three quarters of expenditure going on food. In addition to lifting families out of poverty, social assistance programmes need to be responsive enough so as to provide an effective social safety net so households close to the poverty threshold do not slip back into poverty in the event spikes in food prices or natural disasters, such as earthquakes, to which the country is prone.

Astuti et al. (2012) estimate that the following factors are the strongest indicators of vulnerability to falling into poverty in Indonesia: young households; female-headed (rural areas only); low education; working in agriculture; high dependency ratio; larger households; and living in Nusa Tenggara (urban) and Papua (rural). More work needs to be done on identifying risk factors for households falling into poverty, and programmes should be fine-tuned to earmark them for early assistance.

Rural poverty

For Indonesia, poverty is mostly, but not exclusively a rural and agricultural phenomenon. Approximately half of the population lives in such areas, and, as mentioned previously, in 2012 around 14.3% of the rural population were below the rural poverty line, compared to around 8.4% of the urban population. Poverty is most severe in the remote eastern islands of Indonesia, where up to 95% of people in rural communities can be poor. These provinces are home to many indigenous peoples, who are often on the margins of development processes and programmes. Most of their inhabitants are small close-to-subsistence farmers, farm workers and fishers who are unable to take advantage of the opportunities offered by economic growth. They are often geographically isolated and lack access to social services, including health and education, as well as markets and financial services.

In addition to gender, age, family size, and landholding condition of the household head, the level of education of the head of the household is a critical determinant of poverty in Indonesia (Hondai, 2005). Families whose household head has at least finished junior high school have a far smaller-than-average incidence of poverty. This suggests that providing more education is an essential element in reducing poverty. Estimates of the rate of increase in household expenditure associated with an additional year of education by area and by industry show that increases are almost zero in the agricultural and manufacturing sectors in rural areas. Even if a rural household head completes more education than junior high school, the household may not be able to raise its expenditure as long as s/he stays in one of these two sectors. To enjoy greater benefits from higher educational attainment, s/he has to find work in other sectors. This implies that education alone will not solve the poverty problem in rural areas. Effective poverty alleviation there requires other measures. Such measures would include: i) improving rural employment opportunities; ii) expanding rural non-farm activity, and iii) encouraging migration out of rural areas.

Pro-poor growth should focus on rural areas, improved incomes and productivity in agriculture and must make intensive use of available labour. Indonesia's geographical diversity, including its many islands and mountainous topography, makes the provision of social services to the rural poor particularly challenging and costly, and development and assistance programmes need to be adapted to this (Box 1.2). Certain innovation policies can help play a role in promoting inclusiveness. For instance, the National Community Empowerment Program (PNPM) provides communities with block grants for spending on projects (related to infrastructure, education, etc.) developed through a participatory, bottom-up planning process, which is facilitated by social and technical specialists who provide advice to communities.

Box 1.2. **Existing social assistance programmes**

Social assistance programmes first emerged in Indonesia during the 1997-98 Asian financial crisis, with the government introducing a number of temporary measures aimed at assisting the most affected households. These programmes were supplemented in 2005 with measures designed to help low-income households to cope with price increases associated with a reduction of fuel subsides. More recently conditional cash transfer (CCT) schemes have been rolled out, focusing on promoting school attendance and the use of health services.

The Bantuan Langsung Tunai (BLT) programme is one of the largest targeted cash transfer programmes in the developing world. It was established in 2005 – initially called the Fuel Subsidy Reduction Compensation Fund (PKPS-BBM) – as a timely and fungible one-off assistance programme to compensate the poor for reductions in fuel subsidies. It was used again in 2008 and 2013 for the same reason. It provides transfers of about USD 10 per month to about 19 million households below and near the poverty line.

On 1 January 2014, Indonesia introduced a new national heath scheme, the National Health Insurance Program (JKN). It is being phased in to replace Jamkesmas (Jaminan Kesehatan Masyarakat or Health Insurance for the Poor). The plan is to roll out medical coverage under the new scheme for all of the country's 247 million people by 2019. For the first phase of the rollout, the participants are principally civil servants and military personnel and their families. The government pays the premiums of the poor, but others have a choice of three levels of cover. The existing programme, Jamkesmas, which covers around one-third of the population, was designed to mitigate health shocks and, like BLT, started as a scheme to help cushion the impact of reducing fuel subsidies in 2005. It is a free health-care programme, aimed at making basic health services available to beneficiary

Box 1.2. **Existing social assistance programmes** *(cont.)*

households. These households are given health cards entitling them to free health care at local clinics and in-patient treatment, as well as obstetric services, mobile health services, immunisations and medicines. It is financed by the central government without any insurance contributions or cost-sharing on the part of beneficiaries or local governments and accounts for about a quarter of the central government's annual health budget.

The RASKIN (Rice for Poor Families) programme was implemented during the 1997-98 crisis to alleviate poverty through the distribution of a regular ration of subsidised rice to vulnerable households. About one-third of the population benefitted from the programme at the time of the crisis. Under its current version, the National Logistics Agency (Bulog) purchases rice from wholesalers using a subsidy from the government. This rice is distributed to villages, where eligible households can buy up to a set quantity of rice at considerably less than market price. RASKIN currently distributes rice to around 17.5 million families across the country. It was also used as an additional compensatory mechanism for offsetting the impact of fuel price hikes on the poor in 2002-03 and 2005. However, administrative costs of this programme have been estimated to be as high as 30% (McCulloch, 2005).

The BSM (Beasiswa untuk Siswa Miskin) programme is a mix of several independent initiatives designed to help children to stay in school. It includes bursaries and scholarships, providing transfers directly to students or the schools that they attend, contingent on enrolment, attendance and other criteria. Currently, around 4.6 million students are covered. The amount of the transfers provided rises with the level of education, from IDR 360 000 annually for primary school to approximately IDR 1.2 million at the tertiary level, and includes vocational education. The individual initiatives within the BSM are independently administered and budgeted, with little co-ordination between them, even those run from within the same institution.

The Community Cash Transfer (PNPM Generasi) and Conditional Cash Transfer (PKH, Program Keluarga Harapan) programmes were launched as pilots in 2007. PNPM is a block grant to communities, giving them autonomy in designing and managing their own activities in pursuit of programme objectives of providing better community health and education services. PKH is a quarterly cash transfer targeting poor households, conditional on participation in health and education services, ranging from IDR 600 000 to IDR 2.2 million per year (depending on the number of qualifying dependents in the household). The direct household payments are contingent on verified pre- and post-natal check-ups, a professionally attended birth, new-born and infant weighing and health checks, and good school attendance records. In 2010, PKH reached 816 000 very poor households, with plans to expand to 3 million households nationally by 2014.

There are also a number of smaller programmes that provide cash and services aimed at assisting particular disadvantaged groups including vulnerable children (PKSA), the severely disabled (JSPACA) and vulnerable elderly (JSLU).

Conditional cash transfer schemes

Indonesia currently operates two large conditional cash transfer (CCT) schemes: BSM focusing on education and PKH on both health and education (Box 1.2). CCT schemes have a number of advantages. First, they typically focus on expanding investment in the human capital (education, nutrition and health) of children from households in extreme poverty. They therefore help reduce the intergenerational transmission of poverty and improve efficiency and productivity on a much larger scale. Second, they are typically well targeted as they are by definition designed to provide resources to those most in need. Verification of need can therefore often be built into the scheme.

Brazil has successfully used CCT schemes to combat poverty. In 2003, the *Bolsa Família* programme was established as a single national cash transfer, consolidating four existing CCTs. The reform aimed to make efficient use of public resources, improve targeting, jointly promote education and health incentives, strengthen monitoring and evaluation and systematise complementarities between national and sub-national social safety net programmes. A consolidated single registry database, which enables beneficiaries to access additional programmes and services, is credited as being the single most important management tool available to *Bolsa Família*. It serves as a targeting and monitoring instrument to reduce both duplicate registrations and administrative costs, monitor eligibility requirements, improve efficiency and ensure horizontal co-ordination between social policies. The scheme costs only 0.4% of GDP, and covers more beneficiaries than other Brazilian social assistance programmes.

The newly-elected government expects existing poverty-alleviation programmes, as well has the accelerated rollout of the Indonesia Health Card (KIS), the Indonesia Smart Card (KIP) and the Prosperous Family Card (KKS), to lower the absolute poverty rate to 7-8% by 2019. The KKS card was used to facilitate monthly cash transfers to low-income household of 400 000 rupiah (approximately USD 31) in compensation for the November 2014 cut in fuel subsidies. As of December 2014, only 1 million household have been issued with the KKS card, but the aim is to distribute 15.5 million cards by end of 2015. The government has announced plans to combine these three social welfare cards into one by the end of 2016.

Improving targeting of social assistance programmes

Most OECD countries rely heavily on the tax system for targeting, verification of eligibility and, in many cases, delivery of social assistance. In Indonesia, as in most other developing countries, this is difficult due to widespread labour-market informality (see below) and low tax compliance, particularly among very low income earners in isolated rural areas. Non-universal social assistance programmes, which try to target poor and near-poor households, will always need to identify which households qualify for assistance. Assessment of the entire population is expensive, so other data collection methods must be utilised to keep down costs and to reduce delays – especially when assistance might be urgently required. The lack of reliable information about individual household incomes and the costs in both time and money in gathering it means that there is a trade-off from greater efforts to reduce mis-targeting. This challenge is particularly acute in Indonesia, with its very large and dispersed population, preponderance of informality, decentralisation of much budgetary and operational governance, and frequent household turnover into and out of poverty. In additional to identifying target households, conditional programmes, such as school and health care attendance, add complexity.

A number of strategies can be employed to improve targeting. Geographic targeting or poverty mapping can help to identify areas for attention. Pre-nomination by local community members including community leaders and self-nomination can be used to build lists for further assessment and verification. However, relying on community leaders risks elite capture and nepotism, and they may use different criteria than the programme intends in identifying the needy. In poor communities the direct observation of income or consumption levels can be impossible, in which case methods such as proxy-means testing (PMT) can be employed. PMT indirectly measures household income using statistical techniques based on a set of easily observable and difficult to manipulate household characteristics. These include: housing, assets, household composition, head of household education and occupation, and village characteristics. This has the advantage of being relatively accurate, repeatable, verifiable, and difficult to manipulate if properly designed. On the other hand, it is better for identifying long-term poor rather than newly poor, does not allow for flexibility in assessing households and requires relatively high administrative capacity.

The BLT programme uses community-based nomination to identify candidate households before verification by PMT. If a poor household is not nominated, they are not assessed, and so they miss out on the programme. BLT is aimed at the poorest 30% of Indonesian households, but just 46% of these households actually received transfers (World Bank, 2012b). At the same time, many better-off households are included and account for half of all benefits distributed. However, pure PMT identification outperforms alternative targeting strategies such as community and hybrid identification schemes (Alatas et al., 2012). The Rice for Poor Families (RASKIN) programme, which delivers subsidised rice to around half of all Indonesian households, also suffers from a degree of mis-targeting but in this case related to its implementation. According to National Socioeconomic Survey (SUSENAS) data, targeting of RASKIN is relatively poor with a significant share of the benefits goes to the higher income deciles (Figure 1.16). Over half of RASKIN rice goes to families above the target three poorest deciles. Distribution of subsidised rice is handled by village and community leaders, but often, for cultural and political reasons, leaders often choose to distribute the rice equally to the entire community, rather than just those in particular need. RASKIN also suffers from high administrative costs and its exclusive focus on rice distorts the market, including because of corrupt practices. The option of converting RASKIN into a food voucher programme (or cash transfer) that includes other foodstuffs beyond just rice should be considered. This would diversify the diets of the poor and reduce operational costs.

Figure 1.16. **Coverage of social security programmes**

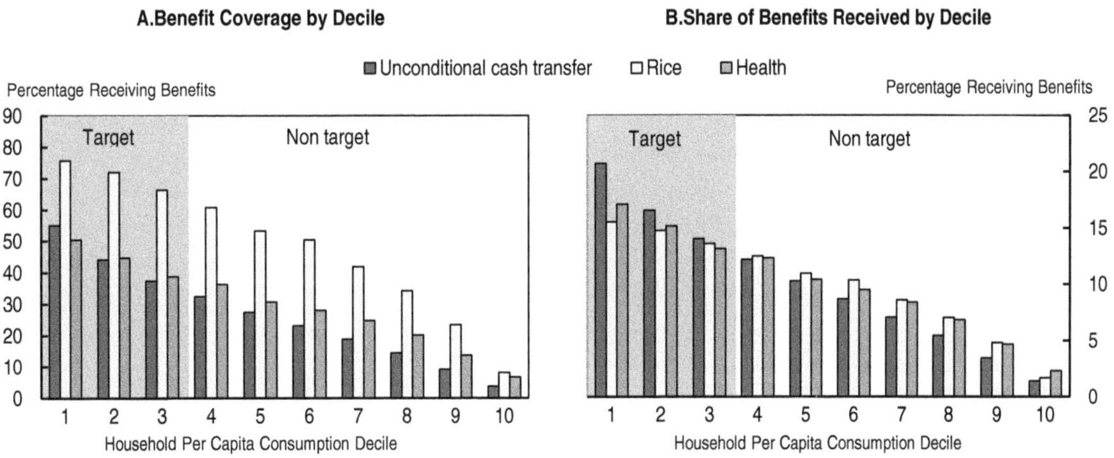

Source: Sumarto (2014).

StatLink http://dx.doi.org/10.1787/888933200283

Compiling and maintaining a comprehensive unified census-based database of all households and their incomes would be expensive. Instead, a national targeting system (NTS) that includes a single registry of vulnerable households would result in reasonably accurate and cost-effective targeting and greater programme effectiveness. In 2011, a further step in this direction was taken when the National Team for Accelerating Poverty Reduction (TNP2K) in the Vice President's office and Statistics Indonesia (BPS) spent considerable resources updating the existing list of Indonesia's poor. This project, called PPLS11, had the objective of including in the database 40% of the poorest Indonesians. This update, which increased the number of households surveyed from around 19 million in 2008 to 25 million, covering up to 40% of the country, could serve as the basis for a unified registry. In addition to increasing the number of households surveyed, a broader range of demographic data are being collected as well, which can be used as targeting criteria for different programmes, and the additional indicators being collected could serve to improve targeting by PMT scoring. Moreover, moving towards a NTS, if sufficiently comprehensive, would help in the implementation of the whole array of social assistance measures envisioned by the government, including health-care coverage and unemployment insurance.

Another impediment to the efficient delivery of social assistance in Indonesia is the very low rates of financial inclusion, even relative to other countries with similar income per capita levels. For example, only around 20% of Indonesians above the age of 15 hold an account in a formal financial institution, and for households in the bottom two income quintiles the rate is less than half that. (Demirguc-Kunt and Klapper, 2013). These are among the lowest financial inclusion rates for countries in the region. By eliminating the need for costly branch infrastructure, branchless banking could foster financial inclusion by making serving poor and isolated, unbanked households and businesses profitable (World Bank, 2014c). Improving the financial inclusion of the poor would help with moves towards digitising social assistance payments which in turn would help to lower delivery costs and barriers (World Bank, 2014a). In addition, branchless banking can be used by the government for tax collection for unbanked segments of the population. Governments in a number of emerging-market economies are moving forward with plans to improve this situation. For example, in August 2014, the Indian government introduced the Jan Dhan Yojana scheme, which aims at opening 75 million bank accounts by end-January 2015. Opening an account through the scheme will entitle a holder to an accidental insurance cover and, after six months of operations, to an overdraft facility. To enhance financial inclusion, more attention could be given to less costly methods of service provision such as mobile phone banking. This has been a success in countries like Kenya and the Philippines (World Bank, 2012d, and BBVA, 2015). Financial services could also be offered through local gas stations or shops, as in Mexico or Brazil. In Mexico, new regulations enabling the use of nonbank correspondents (also known as banking agents) make it possible for financial institutions to increase their reach at lower costs both for banks and potential customers. BI recently conducted a pilot in some provinces (Stapleton, 2013), and if it is judged successful, branchless banking should extended.

Schooling for poor families

As in most developing countries, Indonesian children from poor families tend to get less schooling. The inability of poor families to finance their children's education has long been recognised as a key factor perpetuating poverty across generations. Families often cannot afford to keep their children in school for long and thus miss out on the higher returns to education that could accrue in the next generation with each year of schooling. Lower education levels reduce the earnings potential and mobility of labour. Education also affects health, child mortality and household size. De Silva and Sumarto (2014) find that education is the single largest determinant of inequality in Indonesia. Policies that can promote the extended schooling of children from poor families are important for improving both equity and efficiency, and allow poor people to escape from a self-perpetuating poverty trap. Moreover, there is solid evidence that social policies targeted at reducing poverty and promoting human development can have a powerful impact. For example, CCT programmes in Brazil and Mexico were responsible for about 20% of the decline in inequality over a ten-year period (IMF, 2012). As already mentioned (Box 1.1), the two large Indonesian CCT schemes that focus on education (BSM and PKH) function well, although coverage and targeting are issues for both. The expansion of the PPLS11 database should improve their effectiveness. The section above on sustainable growth and human capital makes several recommendations aimed at improving the performance of the education system more generally.

Health services for the poor

Indonesia has made steady and significant progress on several key population health outcomes over the past 50 years. Life expectancy has increased steadily from about 45 years in 1960 to almost 70 years in 2011. The under-five mortality rate has declined from 216 per 1 000 live births in 1960 to 31 in 2012 (UN IGME Childinfo, 2014). However, infant and child mortality remain higher than for comparable countries, and for the lowest wealth quintile in Indonesia it is over three times that of the highest quintile (OECD, 2014a). Moreover, 36% of all children were stunted in 2010 because of a lack of proper nutrition (UNICEF, 2013), and 9% of the population suffered from undernourishment (FAO, 2013). Total spending on health care as a share of GDP is low, as is the physicians share of the population (Figure 1.17). Indeed, by the time China had reached Indonesia's current GDP per capita (in 2005), it was spending almost double the share of GDP on health care. Moreover, the Philippines, India and Vietnam, all of which are currently at a lower level of GDP per capita, all spend a greater share. Indonesia needs to spend significantly more on the health care of its population through some combination of expanded private insurance schemes and direct government expenditures.

While health insurance coverage has increased significantly over the past decade, almost 60% of the population remains uncovered, and out-of-pocket expenses remain high, even for those with coverage. The prevalence of the informal sector makes expanding coverage especially challenging. At the beginning of 2014, Indonesia implemented a new universal social security system that will put Indonesian employees and residents under a single health-care regime by 2019 (Box 1.3). While some formal employees may see automatic deductions from their salaries for the health-insurance plan, non-salaried or informal workers will be given three options with different monthly fees – IDR 25 500 for third-class wards, IDR 42 500 for second-class and IDR 59 500 for first-class. However, there remains a serious question mark as to whether the level of these premiums will be sufficient to provide an adequate quality of medical services without drawing too heavily on governments resources.

Out of pocket expenses are very high, even for those with insurance. About 45% of total health expenditure in 2012 came from out-of-pocket spending, up from 43% in 2009, with the majority for hospital care; for example 77% of all expenditure on out-patient care

Figure 1.17. **Total health expenditure and the number of physicians in emerging economies**

% of GDP and per 1 000 inhabitants, 2011 or nearest year

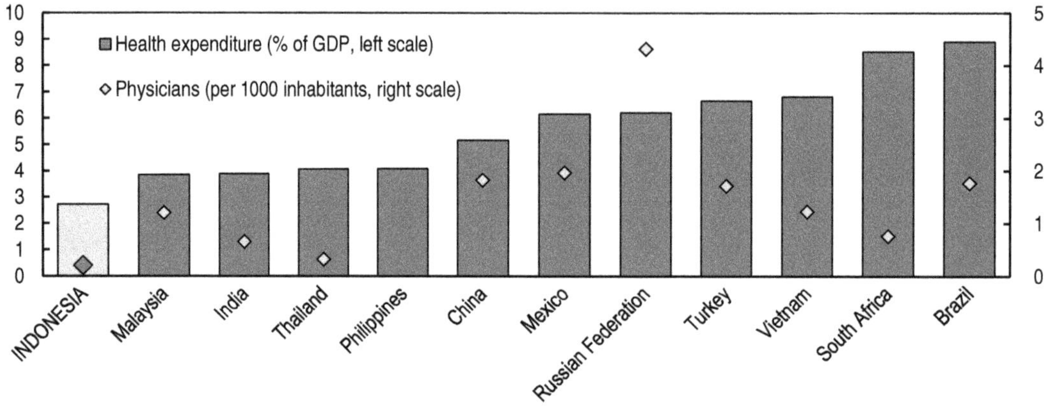

Source: OECD *Health Data 2013* and World Bank, *World Development Indicators.*

StatLink http://dx.doi.org/10.1787/888933200295

Box 1.3. **India's health insurance scheme for the poor**

In 2008, India created a health insurance scheme, the Rashtriya Swasthya Bima Yojana (RSBY), which provides hospitalisation coverage for the poor and informal sector workers. As of February 2014, the RSBY operated in 512 districts across 28 states and union territories (out of 35) and covered 37 million families, out of the 69 million below-the-poverty-line families in India (RSBY, 2014), totalling 120 million people.

Currently, the scheme reimburses spending up to Rs. 30 000 (USD 485) for a family per year. A small annual premium of Rs. 30 (USD 0.7) is paid by each family and the remainder is financed for by the government. The central government funds 75% of premiums under the RSBY, and states contribute the balance. The programme itself is operated by private insurance companies which tender for operating within regions. With the premium paid for each household enrolled, insurers have an incentive to enrol as many households as possible from the beneficiary list.

It gives users a choice across private and public hospitals, creates incentives for public providers to increase volumes of care and for private insurers to extend coverage rapidly.

In order to best suit the poor in India, the scheme was designed to be a cashless and paperless way of claiming benefits (lowering the risk of abuse and corruption) and to cater for migration across regions. The principle way these objectives have been achieved is through the introduction of a biometric-enabled smart card. The RSBY smart card, which is linked to a central database but also provides offline capabilities for use in remote unconnected locations. The card is increasingly being used as a platform for the distribution of other social benefits, with pilot schemes for some subsidies launched in some areas to minimise leakages; for example, the National Social Assistance Programme in Jharkhand, and the food and kerosene subsidy in Chhattisgarh where in some cases it has largely eliminated fraud, which was involved in up to 70% of disbursements.

The RSBY operates accredited hospitals, public or private, across the country – 6823 private hospitals and 4 064 public as of February 2014. The RSBY thus introduces some level of competition among providers. With hospitals paid on a per case basis, the RSBY also creates incentives to increase the volume of activity.

Box 1.3. **India's health insurance scheme for the poor** *(cont.)*

Targeting remains an issue with RSBY. The initial beneficiaries were identified from a scored-based census that is conducted once every 10 years, with some inter-period updating. While RSBY enrolment includes some verification, this only disqualifies non-poor families and does not add new poor to the list. With plans to broaden eligibility, targeting should become less of a problem.

comes from household out-of-pocket spending (Soewondo et al., 2011). While the new health-insurance scheme is welcome, it needs to be monitored closely to ensure that it properly protects households (including those that have children, elderly, non-salaried and informal workers) from catastrophic payments for illnesses and ensures good accessibility to health-care services at a low cost.

Land tenure and titles

The poor often do not have access to credit markets and lack land title or other collateral; hence, potential investments lie dormant. Access to credit is critical to managing household consumption, particularly insofar as the poor are concerned, because it affords them the means to smooth their incomes in the event of unfavourable shocks, such as a failed harvest or natural disaster. Moreover, without adequate insurance and credit markets, poor households face higher risks of investment and so underinvest compared with households with more diversified income sources or access to funds to tide them over following shocks. Since 2007, agrarian reform has been a priority for the government, and part of this has involved clearing up the legal title of land. This follows the ideas of Peruvian economist Hernando de Soto (1986) that the solution to rural poverty lies in providing secure property rights to the poor, and integrating their land assets into the market system. The policy tool to achieve this is a massive government land registration and titling effort.

The land tenure legal system in Indonesia is administered under the Basic Agrarian Law No. 5 Year 1960. Land tenures and titles are the jurisdiction of The National Land Agency ("Badan Pertanahan Nasional" or "BPN"), a government body that manages all grants, extensions, renewals of certified titles as well as running the land registration system. Land ownership titles in Indonesia are divided into two broad categories: customary traditional land title ("adat" land rights), and certified titles. Traditional land is usually owned by inheritance and is not registered in the BPN, although land plots containing such "adat" title can be converted into certified titles and registered in the BPN. Buying land with traditional title is always riskier than with certified title. Certified land titles are registered at the local BPN office and can take a number of forms that confer on the holder of the title the right to utilise the land in various ways. These include freehold, the right to use, the right to build and the right to exploit resources located on the land.

BPN has dramatically increased the rate at which it registers land title since 2007, although the original agrarian reform goal of redistributing land to the poor seems to have been forgotten. The argument in favour of land titling is that "legalising" individual titles makes land easier for small land holders to sell or to mortgage their property – especially if they lack capital or other resources to efficiently use the land, and thereby makes the land more valuable to those who do have access to these resources. However, without accompanying agrarian reforms that help small farmers become more productive, titling results in farmers selling their land more quickly so that the distribution of land becomes more unequal.

Infrastructure

Infrastructure is important for pro-poor growth. Without infrastructure and human capital, poor regions cannot attract investments from outside, and people living in those regions face even greater obstacles to seeking opportunities elsewhere. A number of studies have concluded that infrastructure spending is one of the most powerful instruments that can be used to promote economic growth and poverty reduction (OECD, 2006). Infrastructure supports pro-poor growth by: i) enhancing economic activity by reducing production and transaction costs, increasing private investment and raising productivity; ii) removing bottlenecks in the economy, which hurt poor people by impeding asset accumulation, lowering asset values and imposing high transactions costs; iii) generating distributional effects on growth and poverty reduction through poor people's increased participation in the growth process by increasing their access to factor and product markets, and reducing risk and vulnerability. The section above on sustainable growth and infrastructure looks at impediments to infrastructure investment in Indonesia and makes several recommendations as to how it can be boosted.

The tax and transfer system

The previous *Survey* (OECD, 2012a) examined Indonesia's tax system and found that while improvements have been made in raising revenues and improving efficiency, the tax take was still low, especially in light of Indonesia's public infrastructure, social protection, health and education needs. Indonesia's tax-to-GDP ratio of around 12% in 2012 is low even by the standards of other countries at similar GDP per capita levels. The Ministry of Finance estimates that 70% of all income tax revenues come from just the top 5% of income earners, principally because of poor enforcement. Moreover, the tax wedge on labour income is very low, even by standards of other emerging-market economies (Figure 1.18). One consistent recommendation across all three *Surveys* to date has been the need to increase fiscal space to make room for increased public expenditures on infrastructure, social protection, health and education. As we have seen in terms of tackling poverty, all these issues are important. The new Medium Term National Plan aims to lift the tax-to-GDP ratio to 16% by 2019 (BAPPENAS, 2015).

In addition to the public provision of goods and services that both directly and indirectly target poverty, the tax and transfer system can also directly impact on the livelihoods of the poor. To the extent that workers are in the formal sector and therefore within the tax system, the progressivity of personal income tax and the deductions and transfers integrated within the tax system can have a direct and immediate impact. However, with over 60% of the labour force outside the formal sector (see below), and a much greater share of the poor, the reach of the tax and transfer system is likely to be limited in so far as addressing poverty is concerned. So a first step in addressing the effectiveness of the tax and transfer system as a tool for poverty alleviation is to take measures to promote formalisation of the workforce.

Figure 1.18. **Average tax wedge on labour**

At 100% of average worker earnings, couple with two children[1]

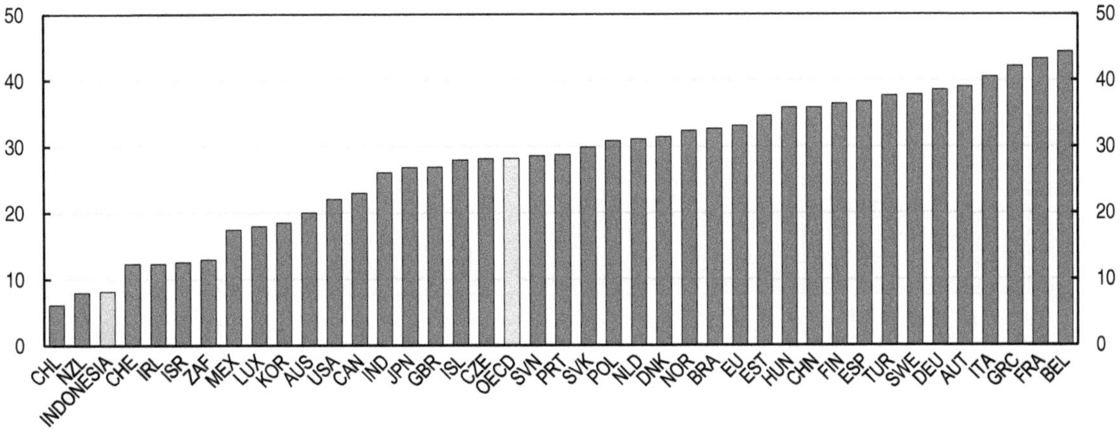

1. Couple with two children, at 100% of average worker earnings for the first earner. Average of three situations regarding the wage of the second earner (0%, 33% and 67% of average worker earnings).

Source: OECD (2013), *Taxing Wages Database*; For BIICS countries, data represent the latest figures based on the methodology described in: L. Gandullia et al. (2012), "Modelling the Tax Burden on Labour Income in Brazil, China, India, Indonesia and South Africa", *OECD Taxation Working Papers*, No. 14.

StatLink http://dx.doi.org/10.1787/888933200305

The minimum wage

Imposing a minimum wage can be one way to alleviate poverty. Minimum wages are stipulated under Articles 88, 89 and 90 of Act 13 of Indonesia's Labour Law (2003), which allows for district and provincial governments to set minimum wage levels. There is no nationwide minimum wage. The governor of each province, or mayor of each district/city, decides the minimum wage rates in their jurisdiction based on recommendations and advice from district- and provincial-level wage councils. The wage councils typically include representatives of governmental officials, entrepreneurs and various labour unions. The law allows for employers to apply to be exempted from the minimum wage if they can prove that increases would hurt them financially. To obtain this exemption, the company must provide the Ministry of Industry and Trade access to its accounts covering the previous two fiscal years to prove that its profits would be seriously affected. In addition, the business needs to obtain written consent from its employees. According to the Ministry of Manpower, 941 firms have applied for this exemption to date, but only 47 applications have been approved.

Minimum wages have risen considerably in recent years; indeed, between 2011 and 2013, while the national economy was slowing and unemployment flat, the average increase across all provinces was around 25%, but ranging from 8% to over 60% (Figure 1.19). These increases seem to be uncorrelated with any features of provincial economies or labour markets more specifically. (see the previous *Survey*), In 2013 the minimum wage itself ranged from IDR 1.2 million to 2.1 million per month. In terms of the ratio to the average wage, Jakarta was highest at 0.97, a very high level by any standard. According to ILO data, the national average ratio of the minimum to average wage was 0.63 in 2010, which is also very high by international standards (Figure 1.20).

High minimum wages can help to alleviate poverty, but only for insiders, that is, those with jobs, and, in Indonesia's case, only those with jobs in the formal sector where the minimum wage is enforced. To the extent that it reduces employment (Neumark et al.,

Figure 1.19. **Provincial minimum wage as a ratio of provincial average wage, 2013**

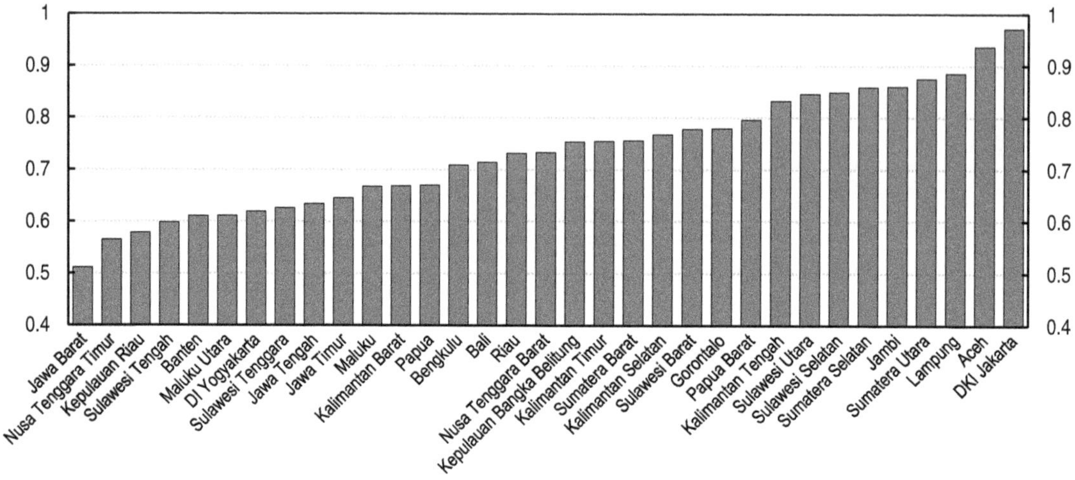

Source: Statistics Indonesia (BPS).

StatLink http://dx.doi.org/10.1787/888933200314

Figure 1.20. **Ratio of minimum to average wage for selected countries, 2011**

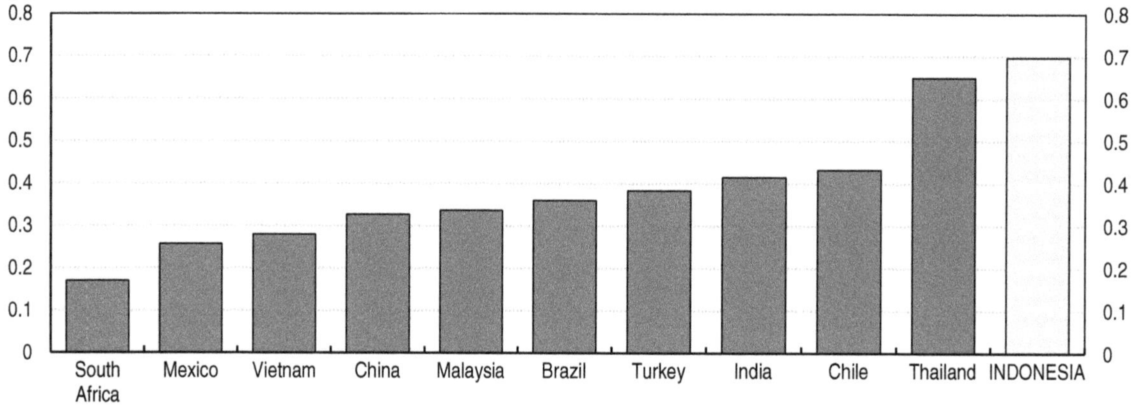

Source: ILO, *Global Wage Database 2012.*

StatLink http://dx.doi.org/10.1787/888933200326

2013; Sabia, 2013), especially of low-skilled and young workers (at least in the formal sector), a higher minimum wage may in fact not be as effective as might be expected in reducing poverty across the population. For Indonesia, a low-cost manufacturing exporter that is competing directly with other such countries like Vietnam and China, increases in the minimum wage that exceed productivity growth in these sectors may bite more deeply.

The minimum wage is used as a reference in wage negotiations, meaning that the large increases in the minimum wage have propagated across the wage structure. This has resulted in a rapid increase in unit labour costs, which is likely to have hurt international competitiveness, especially relative to countries in the region like Vietnam where, in the manufacturing sector, wage growth has been slower, productivity growth has been higher, and the absolute level of the average wage in US dollars has been around 25% lower than in Indonesia in recent years.

The authorities should carefully consider the consequences of raising minimum wages. More fundamentally, the degree to which minimum wages spill over to the wage structure would be reduced if firm-level collective bargaining were strengthened so that wage increases better reflect firm-level productivity, and not a provincial minimum wage. The government is currently preparing a wages policy in a draft government regulation (RPP), and this should include reforms that delink wages higher up the pay structure from the minimum wage.

Labour market informality

Indonesia needs to generate more good jobs to fully share the benefits of sustained economic growth with all workers. Labour is one of the few assets that the poor possess, and if they are to earn their way out of poverty, they need good jobs. In particular, policies that foster job growth in the formal, non-agricultural sector are a priority, both in terms of poverty reduction as well as sustaining development and growth. The Indonesian labour market is characterised by a rigid formal sector and a very large unregulated informal sector. These jobs are outside the formal structures that govern taxes, wages, workplace regulations and social protection schemes, and consequently workers in the informal sector are often exploited. This can perpetuate poverty. The International Labour Organisation (ILO) estimates that around 60% of all non-agricultural jobs in Indonesia are in the informal sector and over 90% in the construction and trade sectors (ILO, 2012). While this aggregate figure is lower than in India (68%) and the Philippines (73%), it is higher than in China (33%) and Vietnam (44%).

There are several causes of informality in Indonesia. The *first* is the long-standing prevalence of unregistered micro-enterprises that are not tied into the formal structures of the labour market and tax and social security systems. *Second*, it might be that formal regulations have mostly been designed for larger enterprises and are therefore often inappropriate for the needs and conditions of micro-firms. Related to this is the rigidity of hiring and firing rules that apply in the formal sector. These increase the cost to employers of engaging workers in the formal sector. Employment protection legislation is particularly strident in Indonesia (Figure 1.21). *Third*, employers may try to make formal workers informal as part of a strategy to lower labour costs and deal with competition. Given the relatively high minimum wage, as discussed above, this is likely to be an important factor in the case of Indonesia. This can hurt particularly young and low-skilled workers, given that high minimum wages truncate the distribution of wages in the low-skilled low-earners segment of the labour market (Kantor et al., 2006). *Fourth*, the strong growth in the

Figure 1.21. **Employment protection legislation, 2012**

Index scale of 0-6 from least to most restrictive

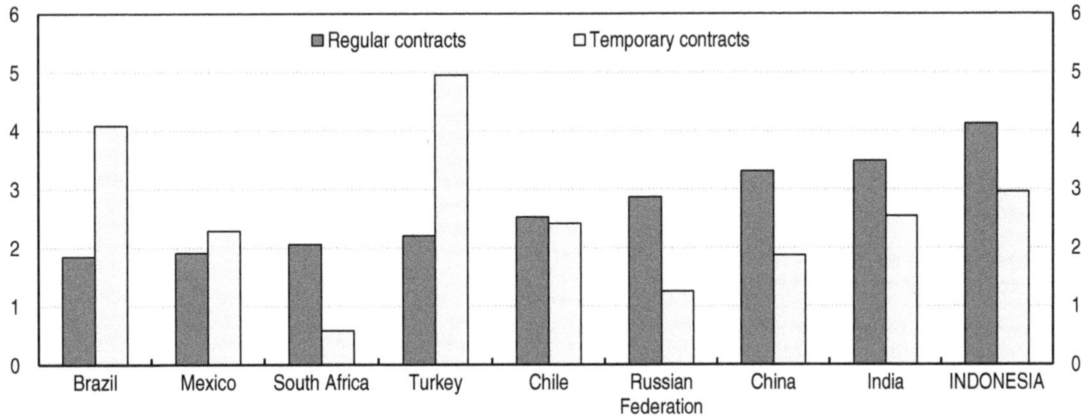

Source: OECD (2014), *Going for Growth Interim Report*.

StatLink http://dx.doi.org/10.1787/888933200333

minimum wage may have contributed to informality – or at least slower than otherwise formalisation of employment. Comola and de Mello (2011) show that high minimum wages have curtailed the creation of formal relative to informal jobs in Indonesia.

While it is preferable to move workers out of the informal sector and into formal employment, not least as a means of addressing poverty, policies aimed at achieving this may in fact be at the cost of these jobs themselves and thereby exacerbate poverty. Rather than reducing poverty, policies aimed at formalisation, such as stricter enforcement of laws and regulations, may contribute to increasing poverty and vulnerability by pushing already vulnerable groups of people into even more difficult situations. With this in mind, a three-pronged approach should be pursued:

- Working informally is often the only way for the poor to participate in the labour market. Policies should consequently try to free these people from their low-productivity activities, enable them to be more productive and provide them with economic opportunities on fair terms. Specific recommendations include expanding active labour market policies, such as vocational training and skill-development programmes, aimed specifically at workers in informal jobs; and improving credit, business development services, technology and market access and knowledge for those who operate informal enterprises.
- To the extent that informal employment is a deliberate choice to avoid taxes or administrative burdens, the government should create structures that encourage workers and micro-enterprises to join the formal sector, including flexible and simple business registration and tax regimes, and credible enforcement mechanisms.
- To the extent that informal employment is a consequence of insufficient job creation in the formal economy, pro-poor growth that generates employment in the formal sector should be pursued. This means policies that facilitate migration of labour away from low-productivity informal sectors to higher-productivity jobs in the formal sector.

Recommendations for tackling poverty

- Increase, and further improve targeting of, spending on poverty alleviation, health and education.
- Make poverty alleviation programmes more responsive to the needs of households vulnerable to slipping into poverty due to misfortune and economic shocks. Part of this work should be to further develop measures that help to earmark vulnerable households for rapid assistance.
- Continue progress towards a single registry of vulnerable households which would result in accurate and cost-effective targeting outcomes and greater effectiveness of poverty-alleviation programmes.
- Expand the use of conditional cash transfers (CCTs) so as to motivate families to keep children in school and encourage the regular use of health-care services – particularly maternity clinics.
- Consider converting RASKIN into a food voucher programme that includes other foodstuffs beyond just rice.
- Maintain the focus on increasing access to education, especially for students from remote regions and disadvantaged backgrounds. Focus on keeping children at school beyond the primary level. The current CCT programmes that are conditional on school attendance could be refined to focus more on facilitating access and improving targeting.

Recommendations for tackling poverty *(cont.)*

- Increase spending on health care significantly. Carefully monitor and assess the adequacy of the new health insurance scheme.
- Maintain the programme of land titling, but combine it with agrarian reforms that ensure that titling land does not lead to its more unequal distribution.
- Improve the minimum-wage-setting mechanism, so that the process is more transparent and predictable and better reflects firm-level productivity.
- Improve the effectiveness of the tax and transfer system as a tool for poverty alleviation by promoting formalisation of the workforce.
- Tackle informality in the labour market by:
  - Improving opportunities for informal workers to join the formal sector through schemes to improve their productivity, including active labour market programmes and vocational training;
  - Creating structures that encourage workers and micro-enterprises to join the formal sector, including flexible and simple business registration and tax regimes.

Bibliography

Aiyar, S., R. Duval, D. Puy, Y. Wu and L. Zhang (2013), "Growth Slowdowns and the Middle-Income Trap", *IMF Working Paper*, WP/13/71, March.

Alatas, V., A. Banerjee, R. Hanna, B. Olken and J. Tobias (2012), "Targeting the Poor: Evidence from a Field Experiment in Indonesia", *American Economic Review*, Vol. 102, No. 4, pp. 1206-40.

Amiti, M. and J. Konings (2007), "Trade Liberalisation, Intermediate Inputs and Productivity: Evidence from Indonesia", *American Economic Review*, Vol. 97, No. 5, pp. 1611-38.

Amsden, A. (1989), *Asia's Next Giant: South Korea and Late Industrialization*, Oxford University Press, New York.

Astuti, A., A. Asra and A. Illma (2012), "Poverty Dynamics in Indonesia, 2008-2010", *Review of Business and Economics in Indonesia* (RIEBS), Vol. 3, No. 1, June.

Agustina, C., W. Fengler and G. Schulze (2012), "The Regional Effects of Indonesia's Oil and Gas Policy: Options for Reform", *Bulletin of Indonesian Economic Studies*, Vol. 48, No. 3, pp. 369-97.

Baedhowi (2009), "Tantangan Profesionalisme Guru Pada Era Sertifikasi", *unpublished Pidato Pengukuhan Guru Besar*, Universitas Sebelas Maret, Solo.

Baldwin, R. and J. Lopez-Gonzalez (2013), "Supply-Chain Trade: A Portrait of Global Patterns and Several Testable Hypotheses", *NBER Working Paper*, No. 18957.

BAPPENAS (2013), *Public-Private Partnerships: Infrastructure Projects Plan in Indonesia 2013*, Badan Perencanaan Pembangunan Nasional (Bappenas), *http://pkps.bappenas.go.id/attachments/article/1154/PPP%20BOOK%202013.pdf*.

BAPPENAS (2015), *Medium Term National Development Plan (RPJMN) 2015-2019*.

Blundell-Wignall, A. and C. Roulet (2015), "Infrastructure Versus Other Investments in the Global Economy and Stagnation Hypotheses: What Do Company Data Tell Us?", *OECD Journal: Financial Market Trends*, Vol. 2014, Iss. 2, January.

BBVA (2015), *Mexico Banking Outlook*, January 2015, *www.bbvaresearch.com/wp-content/uploads/2015/02/1501_MexicoBankingOutlook_Jan15.pdf*.

Cameron, L. (2002), "Did Social Safety Net Scholarships Reduce Drop-Out Rates During the Indonesian Economic Crisis?", *Policy Research Working Paper*, No. 2800, World Bank.

Comola, M. and L. de Mello (2011), "How Does Decentralized Minimum Wage Setting Affect Employment and Informality? The Case of Indonesia", *Review of Income and Wealth*, Vol. 57, pp. S79-S99.

Daniel, P., M. Keen and C. McPherson (eds.) (2009), *The Taxation of Petroleum and Minerals: Principles, Problems and Practice*, Routledge, New York.

Day, J. and P. Ellis (2013), "Growth in Indonesia's Manufacturing Sectors: Urban and Localization Contributions", *Regional Science Policy & Practice*, Vol. 5, Iss. 3, pp. 343-68, August.

Demirguc-Kunt, A. and L. Klapper (2013), "Measuring Financial Inclusion – Explaining Variation Across and Within Countries", *www.brookings.edu/~/media/Projects/BPEA/Spring-2013/2013a_klapper.pdf?la=en.*

De Silva, I. and S. Sumarto (2014), "Does Economic Growth Really Benefit the Poor? Income Distribution Dynamics and Pro-Poor Growth in Indonesia", *Bulletin of Indonesian Economic Studies*, Vol. 5, No. 2, pp. 227-42.

De Soto, H. (1986). *The Other Path: The Invisible Revolution in the Third World*, Harpercollins.

Eichengreen, B., D. Park and K. Shin (2011), "When Fast Growing Economies Slow Down: International Evidence and Implications for China", *NBER Working Paper*, No. 16919, March.

Eichengreen, B., D. Park and K. Shin (2013), "Growth Slowdowns Redux: New Evidence on the Middle-Income Trap", *NBER Working Paper*, No. 18673, January.

FAO (2013), *The State of Food Insecurity in the World 2013*, Food and Agriculture Organization of the United Nations.

Hondai, S. (2005), "Profile of Poverty and Probability of Being Poor in Rural Indonesia", International Centre for Study of East Asian Development, *Working Paper Series*, Vol. 2005-16, October.

IEA (2013), *World Energy Outlook 2013*, Paris.

ILO (2012), "Statistical Update on Employment in the Informal Economy", ILO Department of Statistics, Geneva, June.

IMF (2012), *World Economic Outlook 2012*, International Monetary Fund, October.

Jalal, F., M. Samani, M. Chang, R. Stevenson, A. Ragatz and S. Negara (2009), "Teacher Certification in Indonesia: A Strategy for Teacher Quality Improvement", World Bank, April.

Kantor, P., U. Rani and J. Unni (2006), "Decent Work Deficits in the Informal Economy: The Case of Surat", *Economic and Political Weekly*, 27 May.

Korinek, J. (2013), "Mineral Resource Trade in Chile: Contribution to Development and Policy Implications", *OECD Trade Policy Papers*, No. 145, OECD Publishing.

Korinek, J. (2014), "Export Restrictions on Raw Materials: Experience with Alternative Policies in Botswana", *OECD Trade Policy Papers*, No. 163, OECD Publishing.

Kaary, A. (2004), "When Is Growth Pro-Poor? Cross-Country Evidence", *IMF Working Paper*, WP/04/47.

Leigh, A. and P. van der Eng (2009), "Inequality in Indonesia: What Can We Learn from Top Incomes?", *Journal of Public Economics*, Vol. 93, Iss. 1-2, pp. 209-12, February.

LPEM (2005), "Inefficiencies in the Logistics of Export Industries: The Case of Indonesia", *Report* in collaboration with Japan Bank for International Co-operation (JBIC), Lembaga Penyelidikan Ekonomi dan Masyarakat, Jakarta.

Mankiw, G., D. Romer and D. Weil (1992), "A Contribution to the Empirics of Economic Growth", *Quarterly Journal of Economics*, Vol. 107, No. 2, pp. 407-37, May.

McCulloch, N. (2005), "Raskin Program: A Note", The World Bank, Jakarta.

McMillan, M., and D. Rodrik (2011), "Globalization, Structural Change and Productivity Growth", *NBER Working Paper*, No. 17143, June.

Miranti, R., Y. Vidyattama, E. Hansnata, R. Cassells and A. Duncan (2013), "Trends in Poverty and Inequality in Decentralising Indonesia", *OECD Social, Employment and Migration Working Papers*, No. 148, OECD Publishing.

Neumark, D., I. Salas and W. Wascher (2013), "Revisiting the Minimum Wage-Employment Debate: An Evaluation of New Evidence (Or, Be Careful Not to Throw the Baby Out with the Bathwater)", *NBER Working Paper*, No. 18681.

OECD (2006), "Promoting Pro-Poor Growth: Infrastructure", extract from the publication "Promoting Pro-Poor Growth: Guidelines for Donors", *www.oecd.org/dataoecd/9/60/37922155.pdf*.

OECD (2008), *OECD Economic Surveys: Indonesia Economic Assessment*, OECD Publishing.

OECD (2010a), *OECD Investment Policy Reviews: Indonesia*, OECD Publishing.

OECD (2010b), *OECD Economic Surveys: Indonesia*, OECD Publishing.

OECD (2012a), *OECD Economic Surveys: Indonesia*, OECD Publishing.

OECD (2012b), *Education at a Glance 2012: OECD Indicators*. OECD Publishing.

OECD (2013), *Interconnected Economies: Benefiting from Global Value Chains*, OECD Publishing.

OECD (2014a), *Health at a Glance 2014: Asia/Pacific 2014*. OECD Publishing.

OECD (2014b), *The Competitiveness of Global Port-Cities*, OECD Publishing.

OECD (2014c), *OECD Tourism Trends and Policies 2014*, OECD Publishing.

OECD (2015), *Education Policy Review of Indonesia 2015*, OECD Publishing.

Osorio, C., D. Abriningrum, E. Armas and M. Firdaus (2011), "Who Is Benefiting from Fertilizer Subsidies in Indonesia?", *World Bank Policy Research Working Paper*, No. 5758, August.

Perry, G., O. Arias, J. Lopez, W. Maloney and L. Serven (2006), *Poverty Reduction and Growth: Virtuous and Vicious Circles*, World Bank Latin American and Caribbean Studies, Washington, DC.

Ravallion, M. (2013), "The Idea of Antipoverty Policy", *NBER Working Paper*, No. 19210.

Rodrik, D. (1995), "Getting Interventions Right: How South Korea and Taiwan Grew Rich", *Economic Policy*, Vol. 20, pp. 55-107, April.

Rodrik, D. (2011), "The Future of Economic Convergence", *NBER Working Paper*, No. 17400.

Sabia, J. (2013), "Minimum Wages and the Business Cycle: Does a Wage Hike Hurt More in a Weak Economy?", Employment Policies Institute, January.

Soewondo, P., M. Nadjib, K. Sari, Y. Afdhila, and N. Afdhila (2011), "SHA-Based Health Accounts in the Asia-Pacific Region: Indonesia 2005-2009", *SHA Technical Paper*, No. 15, OECD-Korea Policy Center, Seoul, Korea.

Stapleton, T. (2013), "Unlocking the Transformative Potential of Branchless Banking in Indonesia", *Bulletin of Indonesian Economic Studies*, Vol. 49, No. 3, pp. 55-80.

Suryahadi, A., G. Hadiwidjajaa and S. Sumartoa (2012), "Economic Growth and Poverty Reduction in Indonesia Before and After the Asian Financial Crisis", *Bulletin of Indonesian Economic Studies*, Vol. 48, Iss. 2.

Sumarto, S. (2014), "Social Protection Policies Responding to Threats to Food Insecurity", Presentation to *OECD Study on Transitory Food Insecurity* in Indonesia, Bogor, 26 February.

United Nations (2012), *World Urbanization Prospects: The 2011 Revision*, Department of Economic and Social Affairs, Population Division.

UN Inter-agency Group for Child Mortality Estimation (IGME) Childinfo (2014), "Childinfo: Monitoring the Situation of Children and Women".

UNICEF (2012), *Indonesia: Annual Report 2012*.

UNICEF (2013), *Improving Child Nutrition: The Achievable Imperative for Global Progress*, United Nations Children's Fund (UNICEF), April.

UNCTAD (2013), *World Investment Report 2013: Global Value Chains: Investment and Trade for Development*. United Nations Conference on Trade and Development, Geneva.

Vujanovic, P. (2014) "Indonesia's 2011-14 Current Account Crisis: Causes and Solutions", forthcoming.

Wade, R. (1990), *Governing the Market: Economic Theory and the Role of the Government in East Asian Industrialization*, Princeton University Press, Princeton, NJ.

World Bank (1993), "The East Asian Miracle: Economic Growth and Public Policy", *World Bank Policy Research Report*, Oxford University Press.

World Bank (2004), *Education in Indonesia: Managing the Transition to Decentralisation*, Jakarta.

World Bank (2008), *Teacher Employment and Deployment in Indonesia: Opportunities for Equity, Efficiency and Quality Improvement*, Jakarta.

World Bank (2012a), *Indonesia – The Rise of Metropolitan Regions: Towards Inclusive and Sustainable Regional Development*, Jakarta.

World Bank (2012b), "Targeting Poor and Vulnerable Households in Indonesia", *Public Expenditure Review* (PER), Washington, DC.

World Bank (2012c), *Indonesia Economic Quarterly: Pressures Mounting*, Jakarta.

World Bank (2012d), *India Economic Update*, September, Washington, DC.

World Bank (2013), *Press Release*, *www.worldbank.org/en/news/press-release/2013/11/12/world-bank-study-to-support-connectivity-agenda-in-indonesia*.

World Bank (2014a), "The Opportunities of Digitizing Payments: How Digitization of Payments, Transfers, and Remittances Contributes to the G20 Goals of Broad-Based Economic Growth, Financial Inclusion, and Women's Economic Empowerment", Prepared by the World Bank Development Research Group for the G20 Australian Presidency.

World Bank (2014b), "Investment in Flux", *Indonesian Economic Quarterly*, March, Washington, DC.

World Bank (2014c), "The Opportunities of Digitizing Payments: How Digitization of Payments, Transfers, and Remittances Contributes to the G20 Goals of Broad-Based Economic Growth, Financial Inclusion, and Women's Economic Empowerment", World Bank Development Research Group.

World Bank (2014d), "Why Is Reducing Energy Subsidies a Prudent, Fair, and Transformative Policy for Indonesia?", *Economic Premise*, No. 136, Washington, DC.

WTO (2013), "Trade Policy Review: Indonesia", WT/TPR/S/278, World Trade Organisation, Geneva.

Young, A. (1992) "A Tale of Two Cities: Factor Accumulation and Technical Change in Hong Kong and Singapore", *NBER Macroeconomics Annual* 1992, Vol. 7, pp. 13-64.

Yusuf, A., A. Komarulzaman, M. Purnagunawan and B. Resosudarmo (2013), "Growth, Poverty and Labor Market Rigidity in Indonesia: A General Equilibrium Investigation", *Working Papers in Economics and Development Studies* (WoPEDS) 201304, Department of Economics, Padjadjaran University, revised January 2013.

Yusuf, A., A. Sumner and I. Rum (2014), "Twenty Years of Expenditure Inequality in Indonesia, 1993-2013", *Bulletin of Indonesian Economic Studies*, Vol. 50, No. 2, pp. 243-54.

Chapter 2

Making the most of natural resources

Indonesia abounds with natural resources. But the unique nature of its geography, coupled with the lack of transport infrastructure, makes their exploitation challenging. Moreover, a lack of investment, protectionism and an unwieldy regulatory environment are all inhibiting the sector from reaching its full potential. Agriculture has been held back by low productivity, under-investment, unclear property rights on land, ill-advised trade regulations, misplaced support for staples and restrictions on foreign ownership. By pursuing crop diversification, encouraging co-operation between smallholders and large estates and easing constraints on foreign investment, Indonesia could raise its farmers' productivity. Fossil fuels have become central to Indonesia's energy policy and its main source of export revenues. Growing environmental concerns, both domestically and internationally, combined with subsiding coal prices and the on-going shale gas revolution, call into question the sustainability of such a strategy. Indonesia should increase its energy efficiency and further develop gas to plug the gap until sufficient renewable energy, especially geothermal, comes on line. Government control over the oil industry via state-owned Pertamina should be gradually reduced. Clarifying, streamlining and publicising simple regulations in energy and minerals, especially regarding land rights and on-shore processing, and removing foreign-ownership restrictions will help bring much needed investment. The pressure on the environment that natural resource exploitation is creating should be addressed by increasing the share of gas and renewables in the energy mix, properly defining property rights and regulations regarding forest land, and implementing a positive implicit carbon price. More resources should be devoted to combating widespread illegal mining and deforestation.

Indonesia abounds with natural resources. It is the world's largest exporter of steam coal, refined tin and (until the enforcement of the export ban earlier this year) nickel ore. It is also a leading exporter of gold, bauxite, lead, zinc and copper. Its potential in renewable resources is also huge. It has become the world's number one palm oil producer and exporter. In addition, it is the second-largest producer of rubber, robusta coffee and fisheries products, and holds 40% of the world's geothermal energy reserves (IEA, 2008). Indonesia's top five exports are all commodities.

Commodities have served Indonesia well in the past decade and now represent more than half of its exports (Figure 2.1, Panel A). Natural resources still represents some 25% of GDP (Panel B).

Figure 2.1. **Natural resources in the Indonesian economy**

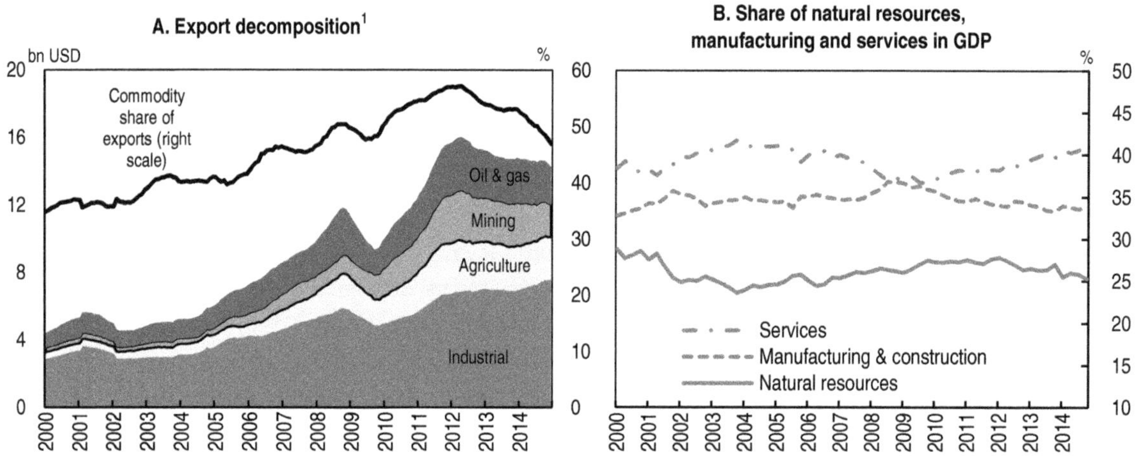

1. 12-month moving averages.
Source: CEIC.

StatLink http://dx.doi.org/10.1787/888933200340

Despite those achievements, the natural resources sector faces several challenges. First, the rising share of commodities in Indonesian exports coincides with the rapid increase in commodity prices that took place between 2003 and 2011 (Figure 2.2). Now that prices have fallen significantly, the sustainability of the expansion is in question. As prices rose, the supply of many commodities rose (e.g. steam coal output more than quadrupled between 2002 and 2012), but production of others, such as oil, fell. For some commodities, especially palm oil and coal, expansion raised environmental concerns. Finally, the effect of rising commodity exports on employment is limited. Being highly capital-intensive, the employment content of the mining and energy sectors is traditionally low (1.9 million

Figure 2.2. **Top exports and commodity prices**

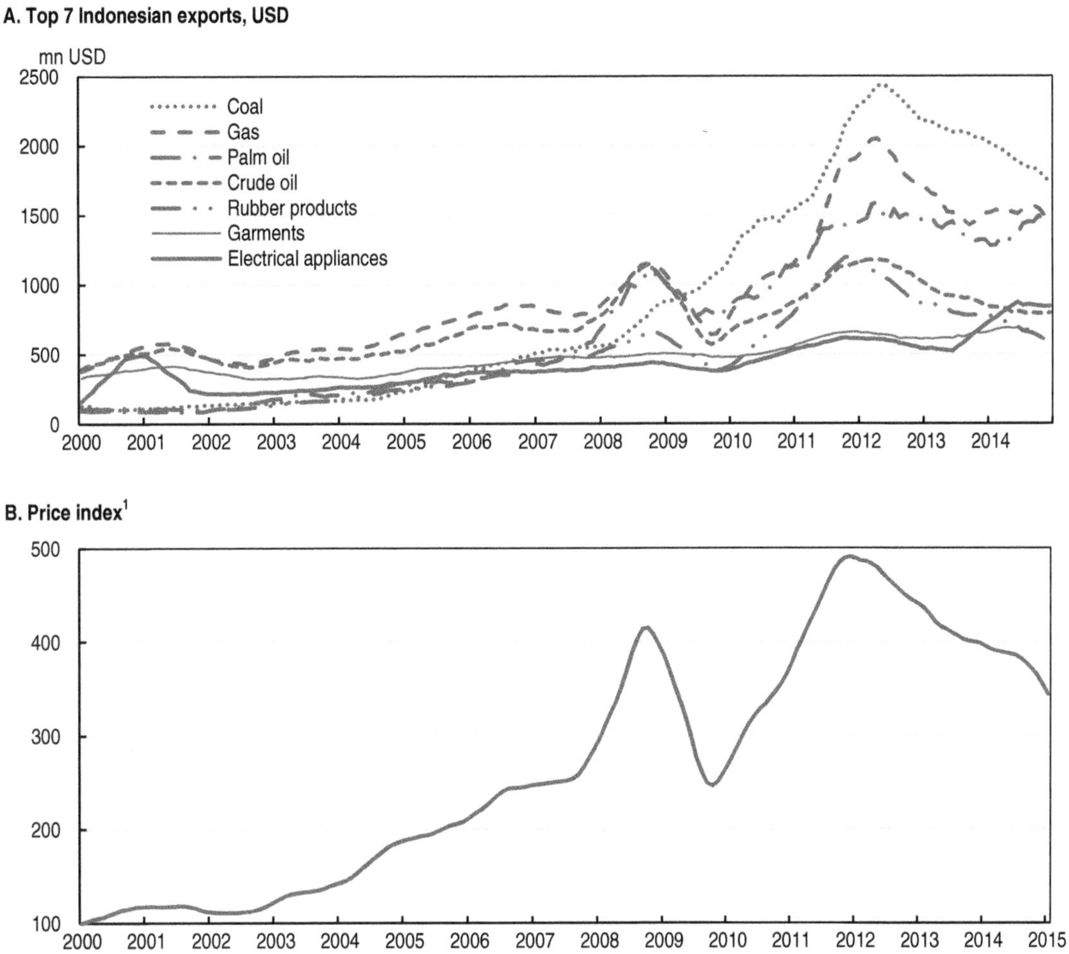

1. Unweighted price index (2000 = 100) of Indonesia's top 5 exports in value in 2012 (cf. Panel A).

Source: CEIC.

StatLink http://dx.doi.org/10.1787/888933200358

people work in these sectors in Indonesia, about 1.5% of the labour force). As for agriculture, it still employs a massive 42 million people (in part due to modest job creation in industry), and productivity is low. These numbers are to be compared with the 15.4 million people employed in manufacturing, for instance.

A second challenge is that Indonesia's natural resources are spread over a vast scattered country, making their exploitation and marketing difficult. Indonesia is an enormous archipelago, made up of about 17 500 islands, 6 000 of which are inhabited, extending over 5 120 kilometres from east to west and 1 760 kilometres from north to south, and covering a land area three times larger than France. It is populated by 242 million people, speaking 742 languages and dialects.

Third, Indonesia's natural resources sector faces a number of regulatory challenges. After years of stable mining legislation, Indonesia overhauled the legal framework with Law 4/2009 on Minerals and Coal Mining, replacing Law 11/1967 and its widely used Contract of Work (CoW) scheme. Among the most controversial aspects of this new mining law were divestment requirements for foreign firms, the replacement of CoWs with a dual exploration and exploitation license system and a mineral ore export ban coupled with a requirement for on-shore value added processing for most commodities. In agriculture, too, various trade restrictions and taxes have been implemented to foster onshore processing of raw commodities, while strict foreign ownership restrictions via Horticulture Law 17/2010 are hampering innovation and productivity growth. Both the law on Minerals and Coal Mining and the Horticulture Law came into force in 2014.

Finally, after decades of centralisation under Suharto's New Order, in the late 1990s Indonesia began a decentralisation process, giving the regions greater political autonomy and allowing resource-rich regions to retain a substantial share of the income generated. This increased the potential for inconsistent and incompatible regulations across levels of government and for associated corruption.

As a result the new regulatory environment for natural resources extraction is now less attractive to investors. In fact, under currently applicable Indonesian regulations, Indonesia's ranking in the Fraser Institute (2013) summary "Policy Potential" index is last out of 96 jurisdictions. On-going discussions regarding possible revisions to the legal framework and/or possible exemptions to the export ban are further increasing uncertainty for foreign investors. Yet, assuming industry best practises and no land-use restrictions, Indonesia would jump to 4th place in that ranking, ahead of Australia and Chile.

The next section describes Indonesia's resource endowment and assesses the role it plays in the economy. Then follows a discussion of ways by which productivity can be raised in agriculture and the benefits that may emerge from greater crop diversification, less focus on staple crops and self-sufficiency, and fewer trade restrictions. The next section assesses the challenges faced by Indonesia's fossil fuel industry and how that sector could benefit from a clearer, more streamlined regulatory environment. The final section discusses the environmental impact of natural resources exploitation and how a better utilisation of Indonesia's renewable energy potential could help it achieve its CO_2 and pollution reduction targets. Tourism and fisheries will also be briefly covered.

Natural resources in the Indonesian economy

A richly endowed country

Indonesia possesses vast reserves of coal, mostly steam coal of medium calorific value used for energy production (and some small amounts of lower-end coking coal products). It also possesses huge reservoirs of natural gas and oil, and was until 2009 the only Asian country in the Organisation of Petroleum Exporting Countries (OPEC). In terms of minerals, Indonesia is the world's largest exporter of refined tin and (until recently) nickel ore, and a leading exporter of bauxite, lead, gold and copper. The Grasberg mine in Papua has the world's third-largest copper reserves and the world's biggest gold reserves.

In terms of renewables, Indonesia has the world's third-largest forest coverage (944 320 km^2, 52% of the land area) located mainly in Sumatra, Kalimantan and Papua. Agricultural land covers 536 000 km^2 (29% of the land area). It consists of arable land (44%), permanent crops (35%) and permanent pasture and meadows (21%). Rice occupies the most land, followed by palm oil, maize and rubber (Figure 2.3). Indonesia's climate pattern allows for multiple cropping during the year, in particular in Java and Bali where good climate and soil allow for up to three crops per year. Arable land per farmer is at 1 000 square meters, however, which is half the world average.

Water is abundant in almost every region. Renewable water resources of 8 500 m^3/capita/year are slightly less than the United States, but four times more than in China and

Figure 2.3. **Harvested area, 1990 and 2012**

Hectares

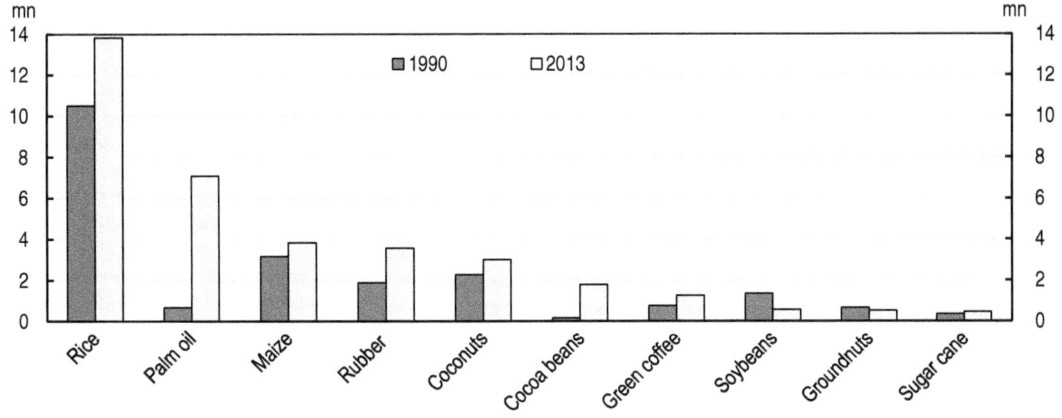

Source: FAOSTAT.

StatLink http://dx.doi.org/10.1787/888933200362

eight-fold more than in India. About 72 000 square kilometres, 17% of crop land, was irrigated in 2009. However, around half of all irrigation systems suffer to various degrees from a lack of maintenance. With agricultural activities responsible for 82% of all water withdrawals, urban and rural areas experience substantial constraints on the quality and quantity of water available for domestic and industrial use (Amin, 2011).

The regional distribution of natural resources is not uniform. At one extreme is Jakarta, whose economy is based almost entirely on manufacturing and services, and at the other is East Kalimantan, some 75% of whose GDP is derived from direct exploitation of natural resources, especially coal. Both regions enjoy the nation's highest standards of living (Figure 2.4). If one adds tourism to the picture, some provinces, such as Bali, generate substantial revenues from their natural beauty. The government, aware of each region's potential and comparative advantages, has put connectivity and specialisation at the heart of the Master Plan for Acceleration and Expansion of Indonesia's Economic Development 2011-25 (Box 2.1).

The benefits and risks of natural resource exploitation

Natural resources are particularly important in developing economies, accounting for an estimated 26% of total wealth in low-income countries, compared to 13% in middle-income countries and only 2% in advanced countries (OECD, 2009). When benefits flow to the community, the exploitation of natural resources provides a road out of poverty, as the revenues generated in the primary sector flow into the economy, increasing the fiscal take for the government. With the right policies, those revenues can help transform natural capital into physical, social and human capital. Chile and Botswana are recent examples of countries that have successfully harnessed their mineral wealth. Growth in agriculture too can help to reduce poverty by creating jobs often in poor and remote locations. According to the three most recent decennial agricultural censuses, incomes per rural Indonesian household increased by 56% in real terms during 1993-2003, compared with just 17% during 1983-93.

But a number of risks are associated with natural resource exploitation. Some countries are richly endowed but remain amongst the poorest in the world. First, resource-

Figure 2.4. **Natural resources and regional economies**[1]

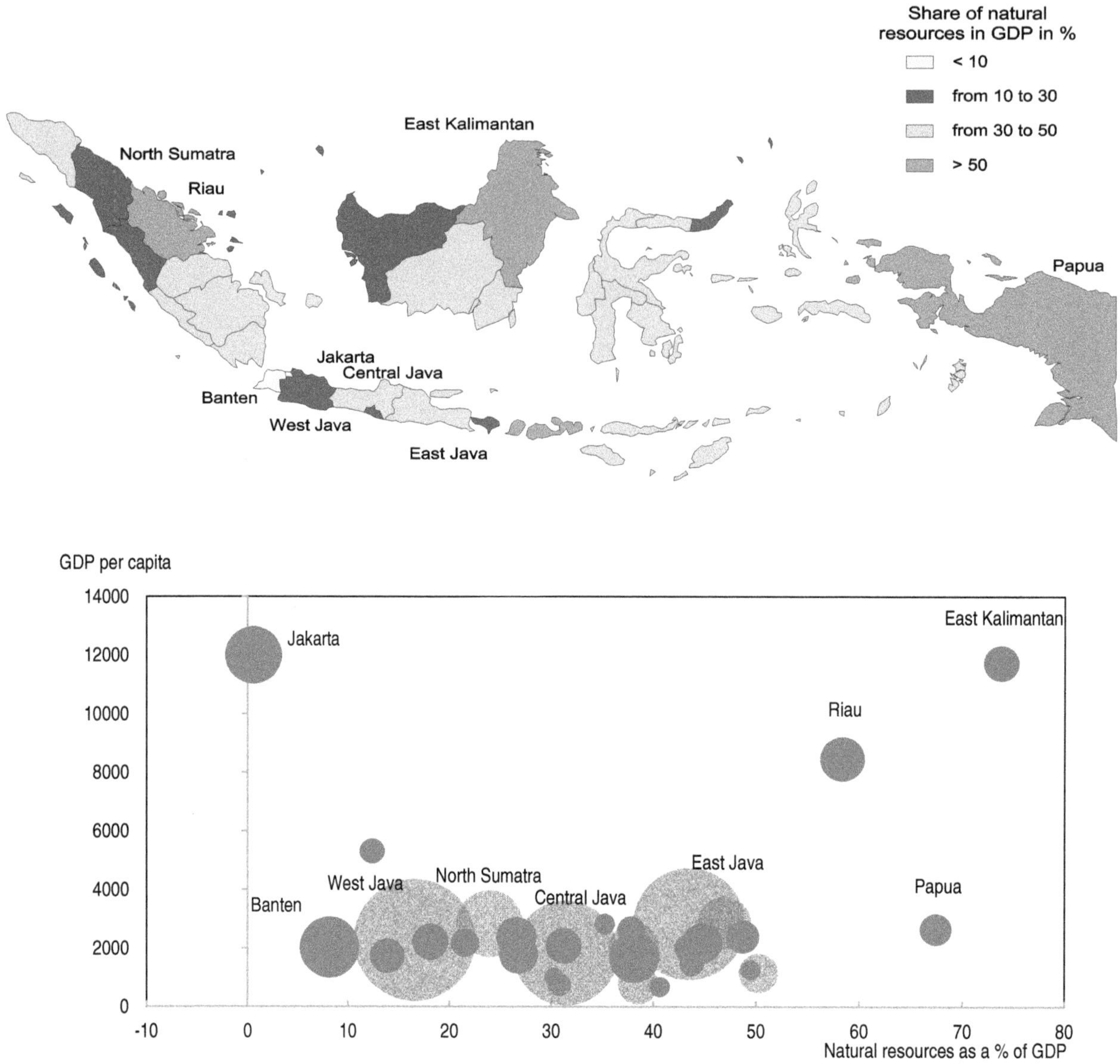

1. In the second panel, the size of each circle represents its share of total population.

Source: CEIC.

StatLink http://dx.doi.org/10.1787/888933200372

Box 2.1. **The Master Plan for the Acceleration and Expansion of Indonesia's Economic Development**

In 2011, the government announced a Master Plan for Acceleration and Expansion of Indonesia's Economic Development 2011-25 (MP3EI). The vision is for Indonesia to be one of the world's leading developed countries by 2025, taking GDP to USD 4.5 trillion and increasing per capita income from USD 3 000 to USD 15 000. The Master Plan aims at improving regional economic potential through the development of six economic corridors (Sumatra, Java, Kalimantan, Sulawesi, Bali-Nusa Tenggara and Papua-Kepulauan Maluku), optimising agglomeration advantages and strengthening national connectivity across those corridors. A subset of 22 economic activities will be promoted within each of the

Box 2.1. **The Master Plan for the Acceleration and Expansion of Indonesia's Economic Development** *(cont.)*

corridors. They were selected with reference to their natural advantages and to ensure development occurs across the archipelago.

Of these six corridors, all but Java have natural resources at the centre of their development strategy, illustrating the importance the government attaches to the sector. For instance, Kalimantan will become the "Center for Production and Processing of National Mining and Energy Reserves", while Bali-Nusa Tenggara will become a "Gateway for Tourism and National Food Support". Five of the 22 activities relate to agricultural production: palm oil, rubber, cocoa, food crops and animal husbandry. A common thread across the agricultural activities is to increase yields and stimulate further processing, e.g. increase planting with high-quality seeds, develop port capacity and establish research centres. With this plan, Indonesia aims to position itself as one of the world's main food suppliers, as a processing centre for agricultural, fishery and mineral resources and also a logistics hub.

The plan outlines IDR 4 000 trillion (USD 316 billion at the then current exchange rate) in investments to be made over the next 14 years, including in infrastructure. At the MP3EI launch, then-President Yudhoyono identified 17 strategic projects, such as hydroelectric and solar power plants, oil palm developments, a steel mill in East Java, new roads including toll motorways, mining projects, expansion of broadband internet, and nickel, cobalt and aluminium refineries. Mr. Yudhoyono also acknowledged that Indonesia must first overcome "five diseases that can make us fail", including slow bureaucratic processes, conflicting interests in regional government, obstructive regulations, broken promises to investors and "unhealthy" political factors.

In May 2014, the government claimed that IDR 838.7 trillion (about 20% of planned spending) had been spent, covering a total of 204 infrastructure and 174 other projects.

Source: BAPPENAS (2011), Master Plan for the Acceleration and Expansion of Indonesia's Economic Development 2011-25.

based economies are vulnerable to "boom and bust" (due to the low short-term price elasticity of supply for such products, while demand is relatively income elastic), which amplify their business cycles. Hence, when resource prices increase, typically the domestic currency appreciates to return to balance of payments equilibrium, which in turn crowds out other tradable sectors, an outcome known as "Dutch disease". In addition, extracting and selling raw commodities risks complacency, as it does not foster the development of high value-added industries. Possibly reflecting low levels of onshore processing, Indonesia has the world's second-highest domestic value added embodied in gross exports for both agricultural products and mining output (Figure 2.5). This suggests a lack of Indonesian involvement in global value chains in the resources sector.

Vast endowments of natural resources may also promote rent-seeking behaviour and corruption, rather than entrepreneurial and value-adding activities. The special characteristics of Indonesia's natural resources (such as unclear property rights, remote location and difficult access), in combination with weak institutions, give rise to special challenges, especially corruption of the agencies allocating property rights and licenses. Some other countries have managed to escape the curse, such as Botswana (Box 2.2). Furthermore, activities like mining can have a damaging impact on the environment via excessive water consumption, pollution, deforestation, subsidence and land alteration. In

Figure 2.5. **Domestic value added in gross exports of agricultural and mining products, 2009**

Per cent

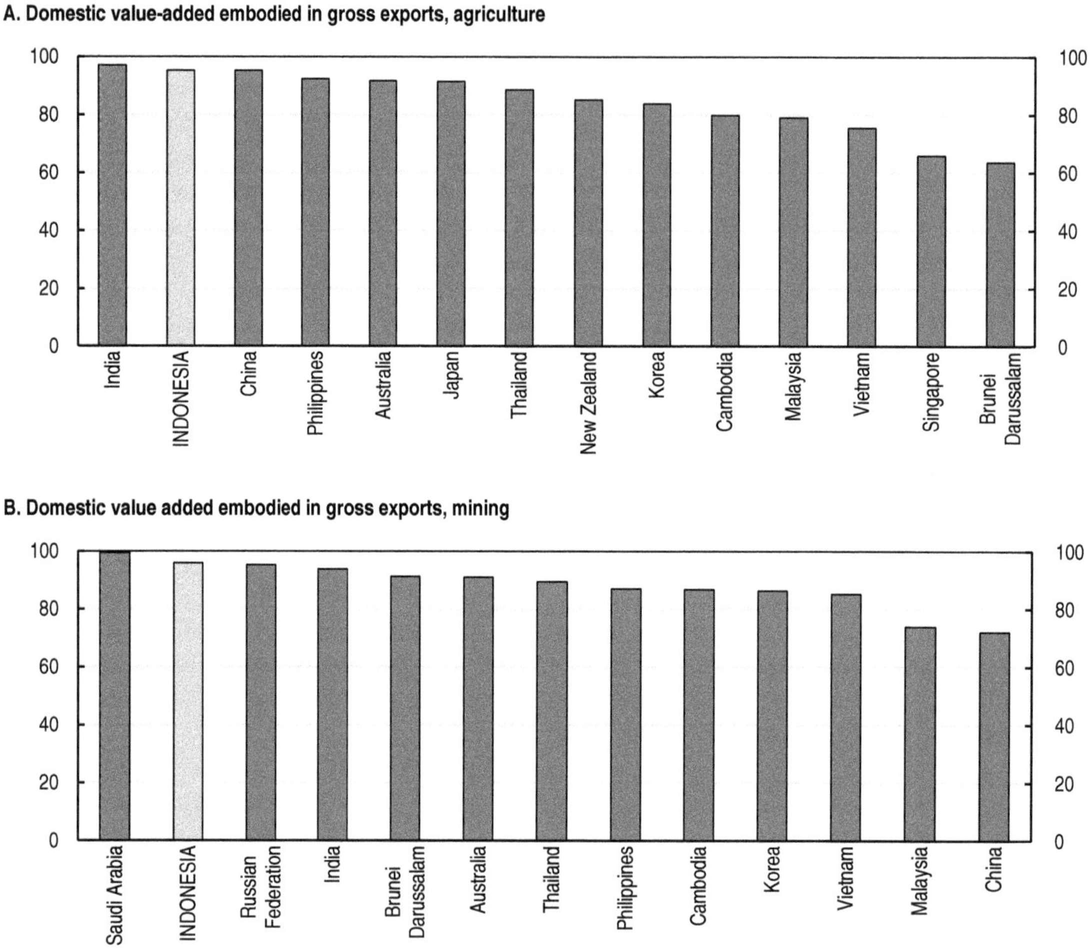

Source: OECD-WTO Trade in Value Added (Tiva).

StatLink http://dx.doi.org/10.1787/888933200384

Box 2.2. **Avoiding the "Resource Curse": The Case of Botswana**

Botswana is a sparsely populated, arid, landlocked country. At independence in 1966, it was one of the world's poorest countries, with per capita income of just USD 70 a year. In the first few years following independence, about 60% of current government expenditure consisted of international development assistance. There were only 12 kilometres of paved roads, and agriculture (mostly cattle farming for beef production) accounted for 40% of GDP. About 40 years later, in 2007, Botswana had 7 000 kilometres of paved roads, and per capita income had risen to about USD 6 100 (equivalent to USD 1 000 in 1966 prices and USD 12 000 at purchasing power parity), making Botswana an upper-middle-income country, comparable to Chile or Argentina.

Botswana's extraordinary growth was fuelled by minerals, particularly diamonds, but underpinned by good governance. The government established respect for property rights and the rule of law. It maintained a high degree of transparency, which was reinforced by continuing the Tswana tribal tradition of consultation. In addition, the first post-independence

Box 2.2. **Avoiding the "Resource Curse": the Case of Botswana** *(cont.)*

government made two key decisions: it passed a Mines and Minerals Act that gave all mineral rights to the state rather than to the tribal authorities and renegotiated a deal with the mining firm DeBeers in 1975, which allocated half of all net profits from diamond mining to the state. Also, Botswana did not adopt a policy of import substitution, nor did it expand the extent of state-owned producing entities.

The ensuing revenues for the government, primarily from diamond exports, were channelled into investments in education, health care and infrastructure, while tight fiscal control was maintained. A contributing factor has been the creation of a set of fiscal rules – a Sustainable Budget Index – to avoid deficits. In particular, government expenditure must stay in line with non-mineral fiscal revenues in order to make sure that key government functions can be kept up in case of a downturn in the commodity sector. A similar mechanism is in place in Chile.

Source: Lewin (2011), "Botswana's Success: Good Governance, Good Policies, and Good Luck", in *Yes Africa Can, Success Stories from a Dynamic Continent*, World Bank.

the end, good governance, strong institutions, effective regulation and rigorous environmental and social safeguards are needed to realise the potential contribution of natural wealth to growth and living standards.

Assessing the role of natural resources in Indonesian growth

The contribution of natural resources to Indonesian growth can be evaluated by incorporating the use of natural capital as a factor input into Indonesia's aggregate production function, alongside labour and produced capital. Such analysis, known as green growth accounting, also allows an assessment of the sustainability of natural resource development. Depleting natural capital can lead to higher growth for a while, but this can be sustained only if the revenues from resource extraction allow the accumulation of other assets, such as human and physical capital, to secure future economic growth when the possibility to use natural capital in production has been exhausted. Data on natural capital come from the World Bank (available until 2008). They are mainly focussed on sub-soil assets such as oil, gas, coal and various minerals. Some types of natural capital, such as water, soil or renewable resources (agriculture and fish in particular) are not included due to a lack of data. The methodology is detailed in Brandt et al. (2013) and covers the period from 1992 to 2008.

The results show that, except for the early 2000s, the net contribution of natural capital has been broadly positive but small (Figure 2.6). The negative contribution in the early years of the 2000s suggests overexploitation of natural resources as natural capital declined. This may be explained by dwindling oil and gas reserves. While exploitation of natural resources continued to increase in the second half of the decade, rapidly rising commodity prices helped bring the contribution of natural capital back into positive territory. Overall, the contribution is less than for countries like Chile, Canada, Australia and Norway (Brandt et al., 2013). Nevertheless, it is important to keep in mind that several natural resources are left out of the analysis, especially land (and thus agriculture), which represents a large share of the Indonesian economy.

Figure 2.6. **Growth accounting with natural capital for Indonesia**

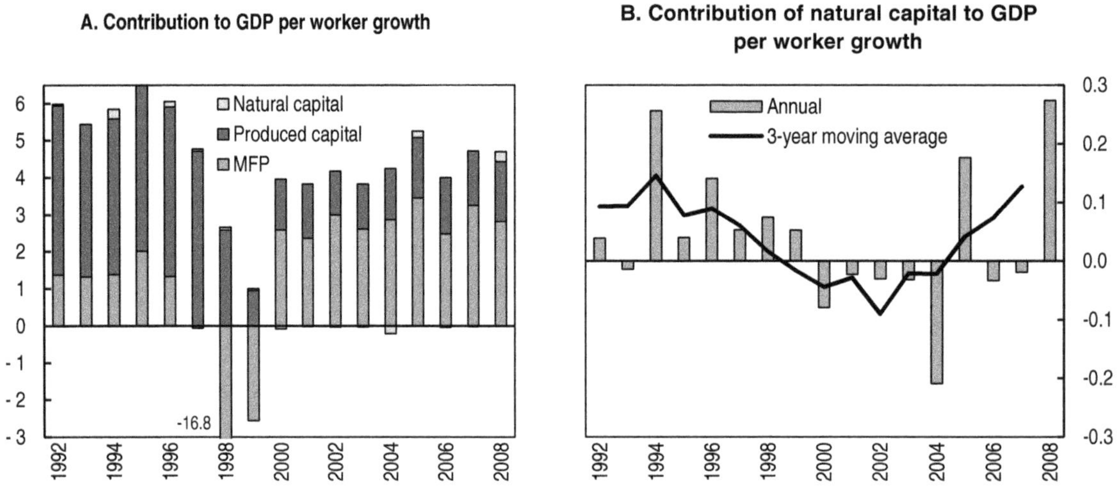

Source: *World Bank Database on Natural Capital* and OECD calculations.

StatLink http://dx.doi.org/10.1787/888933200396

Increasing productivity and crop diversification in agriculture

In 2012, of the world's 7.1 billion people, an estimated 1.3 billion (19%) were directly engaged in farming, yet agriculture represented just 2.8% of global income (Alston and Pardey, 2014). In Indonesia, agriculture accounted for around 12% of GDP in 2013, and employed about 42 million people, or 40% of the workforce (OECD, 2012b).

Since 2000, Indonesia has made some noticeable achievements by becoming a central player on the world stage for many key farm and food commodities. In addition to palm oil and rubber, the country is also the second-largest producer of fisheries products in the world after China (Box 2.3) and the third-largest rice and spices producer after China and India. Overall, it now ranks fifth, with 2.5% of the world's total agricultural output, after China (23%), the United States (10.1%), India (9.9%) and Brazil (6%) (FAOSTAT, 2015).

Box 2.3. **Fishing in Indonesia**

Indonesia is one of the largest fishing and aquaculture producers in the world. In 2011, total marine capture exceeded 5 million tonnes (the most valuable species being shrimp and lobsters), inland water catches were more than 347 000 tonnes, and aquaculture production was almost 7 million tonnes. The annual value of its aquaculture production alone is close to USD 7 billion; Indonesia has 8% of world aquaculture production, a distant second to China (61%).

A specific characteristic of the Indonesian fisheries is the importance of traditional management practices, which are based on unwritten agreements among coastal residents. These traditional management systems differ from one region and fishery to the next. Some include the closure of specific areas for one or two years, followed by limited fishing for a period of one or two weeks. Other traditional management measures include agreements on gear restrictions and fishing practices.

Traditional management measures are also applied to aquaculture. Pearl farms sometimes make informal arrangements with villages to lease a part of their fishing

Box 2.3. **Fishing in Indonesia** *(cont.)*

grounds. In Bali, plots of submerged land for seaweed culture are subject to informal administration and management systems.

Indonesia's fish stocks and aquatic habitats are in good condition. There is, however, little room for further expansion of the fishing fleet, since most stocks are fully or over exploited, especially in the West. Hence, further increases in production will be possible only after recovery of fish stocks through rationalisation of the fishing fleet.

Source: OECD (2013), *OECD Review of Fisheries, Policies and Summary Statistics*, OECD Publishing.

Given its vast endowments and strategic location, Indonesia could accelerate its transition to higher-productivity agriculture by encouraging investment and innovation, and pursuing consolidation and diversification into perennial and estate export-oriented crops. But Indonesian agriculture is being held back by issues such as poorly defined property rights, ill-advised trade restrictions, excessive focus on staple crops and self-sufficiency, and barriers to foreign ownership.

Increasing productivity in agriculture

Following a period of liberalisation, productivity growth in Indonesia's agriculture recovered significantly in the 2000s compared to its poor 1990s performance (Figure 2.7). Over 2000-06, multifactor productivity (MFP) growth in agriculture rose to rates as high as or higher than in the peak years of the 1968-92 "Green Revolution" (Table 2.1) and was even higher in agriculture than in the economy as a whole between 2001 and 2009-3.7% versus 2.1%. Adoption of improved technology and diversification into high-value commodities explain those results. Labour productivity gains in countries with the strongest growth, such as China in the 1990s and Malaysia in the 2000s, were due to both production increases and falling agricultural employment. This has not (yet) been the case in Indonesia where employment in agriculture has remained fairly constant. Raising productivity further will be crucial as Indonesia will find it increasingly difficult to expand agricultural land, given environmental concerns and increasing marginal costs of servicing

Figure 2.7. **Agriculture MFP growth in selected Asian countries**

Per cent

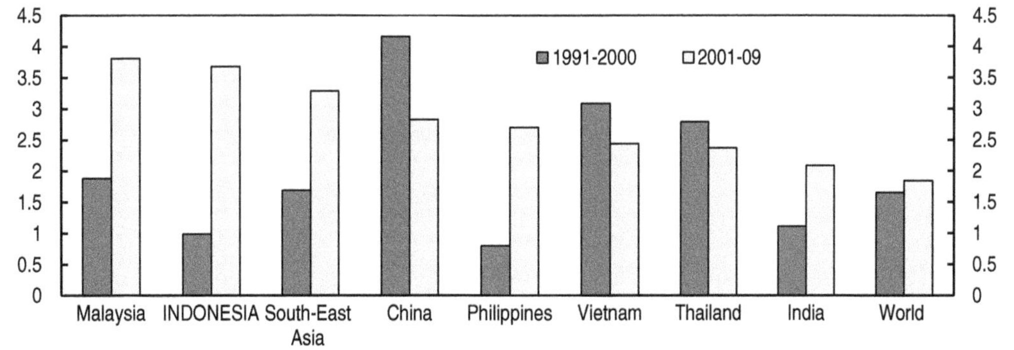

Source: Fuglie, K. (2012), "Productivity Growth and Technology Capital in the Global Agricultural Economy", in K. Fuglie et al. (eds.), *Productivity Growth in Agriculture: An International Perspective*, CAB International, Oxfordshire, UK.

StatLink http://dx.doi.org/10.1787/888933200408

Table 2.1. **Agriculture productivity growth decomposition**

	Output	Input	MFP
1961-1970	3.66	0.96	2.70
1971-1980	3.78	1.67	2.10
1981-1990	4.74	3.54	1.20
1991-2000	2.16	1.18	0.98
2001-2006	3.86	1.43	2.43

Source: Fuglie, K. (2010a), "Sources of Growth in Indonesian Agriculture", *Journal of Productivity Analysis*, Vol. 33, pp. 225-40.

land. Given the magnitude of agricultural employment, raising productivity in the sector is also key to reducing rural poverty. As of March 2013, rural poverty (defined by the government as less than IDR 253 000 per capita per month, around USD 20) was 14.3% (17.7 million) of the rural population, down from 20.2% a decade ago (see Chapter 1).

Progress in boosting agricultural yields has varied widely across crops (Figure 2.8). Rice yields, for instance, rose from 2.5 tonnes per ha in 1971 to 4.4 tonnes in 1991. Ten years later yields were still at 4.4 tonnes/ha before climbing to 5.15 tonnes/ha in 2013, which compares favourably with Thailand (3.1 tonnes/ha), India (3.7 tonnes/ha) and Malaysia (3.8 tonnes/ha), but not well with China (6.7 tonnes/ha) and Vietnam (5.5 tonnes/ha). On the other hand, crude palm oil yields have declined. Since land dedicated to palm oil production has risen considerably (Figure 2.3), this shows that the huge growth in that sector is primarily extensive. There is, however, significant potential to increase palm oil yields through fertilisers, high-yielding varieties and improved harvesting and management practices.

Figure 2.8. **Selected crop output per hectare**

2000 = 1

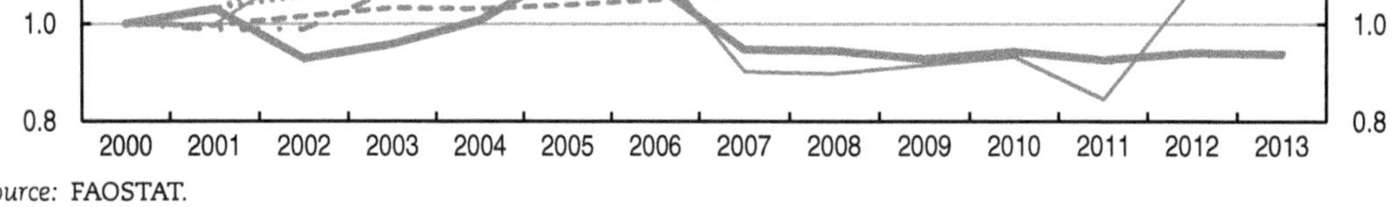

Source: FAOSTAT.

StatLink http://dx.doi.org/10.1787/888933200126

From a regional point of view, recent productivity growth has been concentrated in the western and northern parts of the country (especially Sumatra and Kalimantan), where export commodities like cocoa have been booming. In contrast, MFP growth has been low or stagnant in Java and the eastern provinces. This contrasts with the "Green Revolution" when productivity growth mainly benefitted irrigated rice production, which is especially important in Java (Fuglie, 2012).

Among the factors that are restraining agricultural productivity is the scarcity of available land, at just 2 300 square meters per capita, and the lack of scale economies. This is reflected in small average farm size, from 3 000 square meters in Java to 14 000 square meters for irrigated land outside of Java. Smallholders occupy 87% of cultivated land, produce 90% of total rice and maize output and hold 75% of the 180 000 square kilometres in estate cropland (Jeon, 2013). With production methods largely inherited from the past and based on the small family-farm model, modern productive technologies are only slowly being implemented. However, next to these small farms there are large state-owned farms in Kalimantan and Sumatra whose average size is 26 square kilometres. As noted in OECD (2012b), this dichotomy is especially apparent in the rubber and palm oil industry. While small farms are not a problem *per se*, that feature generates farmers' limited financial capacity to upgrade production methods, as many of them see farming as just another source of income besides other non-farming activities. Indonesia should develop a long-term strategy for farm restructuring that aims at boosting average farm size, increasing economies of scale.

One way to achieve this goal is to further develop partnership arrangements between estates and smallholders undertaken within so-called "nucleus plasma" schemes over the last 30 years. These have provided large companies (the nucleus), both private (such as Unilever) and state-owned, with subsidised capital and long-term leases for public lands for estate crop production, on condition that these companies provide technical and marketing services to neighbouring smallholders (the plasma). Such arrangements can be conducive to small farmers and boost productivity by providing training and technical assistance to (otherwise technology-poor) farmers on important inputs such as rice varieties, seeds, tools and machinery. Such partnerships have already contributed to bridge the yield gap between smallholders and large estates for palm oil, sugar cane and cocoa. The productivity gap remains large for tea and rubber, however. In the latter case, this may partly result from lower tree density per unit of land, as smallholders practice mixed cropping (which can have environmental advantages). This contrasts with monoculture-based cropping on large estates (Fuglie, 2010b).

As pointed out in OECD (2012b), the problem of small average farm size is exacerbated by the issue of land rights. Land rights in Indonesia are very complex with ample scope for drastic simplification. The Basic Agrarian Law of 1960 (BAL, 1960) required that all land rights be registered, but no time limit was given at the time of its promulgation. Land registration (titling) is still ongoing, and during the last four decades the National Land Agency (BPN) has managed to register only around one-third of privately owned plots. Thus, most rural households have unregistered land rights usually acquired through inheritance. Although Article 56 of the Law recognises the continuing validity of rights, the right of the new holder cannot be fully recognised by the State until a new certificate is issued confirming that the land is not State land (USAID, 2010). The slow progress in land registration therefore creates an important barrier to consolidation in the sector, but also to accessing credit, which is indispensable to capital and technology improvements, as farmers are required to provide collateral to meet bank lending requirements. Despite further efforts to implement the BAL, existing ambiguity over land rights remains one of the reasons for land conflicts. In 2012, the office of the President recorded 8 305 land disputes, 2 002 of which are likely to turn into violence (Jakarta Globe, 2012). The land tenure system should thus be clarified (Box 2.4), and the registration of land rights to

Box 2.4. **Land rights in Indonesia**

The 1945 Constitution stipulates that all land, water, air space and natural richness are controlled by the State and must be used to assure the people's welfare. The most important piece of legislation regulating land rights is Law 5/1960, known as **the Basic Agrarian Law** (BAL) (Winoto, 2009). Under the BAL, land controlled by the State on behalf of the people is available for distribution to all citizens under various forms of land tenure.

Established in 1988, **the National Land Agency** (*Badan Pertanahan Nasional*, BPN) was responsible for the administration of all non-forest land. Activities of the BPN were grouped under four areas stipulated in the BAL: land reform, use, titling and survey/registration (Heryani and Grant, 2004). Under Law 22/1999, land affairs were devolved to local governments (USAID, 2010), but BPN was maintained as a central agency with a role limited to legislation, performance standards, uniform land registration procedures, training and the provision of some land-related services (Heryani and Grant, 2004; Hendriatiningsih et al., 2009).

The BAL defines the fundamental **types of land rights** that may be held by both private individuals and entities and describes the role of the State in regulating and implementing these rights (USAID, 2010). While foreigners are not eligible for the right of land ownership (*Hak milik*), they can be granted some other types of land use rights as described below. The main objective of the BAL was to remove the legal dualism between colonial law over land and customary rights to land (*Hak ulayat*) based on communal land rights, and land rights exercised by individuals with the consent of the community (Penot et al., 2002). *Hak ulayat* law principles vary widely across regions (USAID, 2010). The BAL explicitly acknowledges that Indonesia's agrarian law is derived from *Hak ulayat*. However, to obtain *ulayat* rights, several conditions must be met: *ulayat* must not conflict with national interests or other regulations set out in the BAL; the land must be under the ownership of a recognised traditional community (*adat*), and its boundaries must be well defined and understood; *ulayat* rights can be registered and certified only after having been rendered into one of the types of formal land rights recognised in the BAL.

The BAL sets seven forms of land rights that can be registered, including the rights, restrictions and responsibilities of the tenure holder. These land rights can be primary titles derived directly from the State or secondary titles granted by other title holders (BAL, 1960).

- ***Hak milik* (*right of ownership*)** is the strongest land right. It is unlimited in time and can be sold, gifted, exchanged, bequeathed and mortgaged. Only Indonesian citizens and special bodies designated by the government, e.g. government banks, co-operatives and religious and social bodies, can hold this right. The right must be registered, and the holder is given a certificate as proof of title. Subsequent government approval is not necessary for sale or mortgage of land if the buyer is an Indonesian citizen. However, this approval is necessary if the buyer is a legal entity. In all cases the State retains the right to regulate the use of land in accordance with any authorised regional or local development plans.
- ***Hak guna-usaha* (right to cultivate)** is the right to exploit the land directly controlled by the State for the purpose of agriculture, fisheries or cattle breeding. It can be granted on land whose area is at least 5 ha. Only Indonesian citizens and corporate bodies incorporated under Indonesian law and domiciled in Indonesia are eligible. It is transferable and can be used as collateral. It can be granted for a maximum period of 35 years and extended for a further 25 years.
- ***Hak guna bangunan* (right to build)** applies to rights to construct and own buildings on land. Only Indonesian citizens and corporate bodies incorporated under Indonesian law

Box 2.4. **Land rights in Indonesia** *(cont.)*

and domiciled in Indonesia are eligible. It is transferable, can be used as collateral and can be granted for a period of up to 30 years and extended for a further 20 years.

- ***Hak pakai* (right to use)** is the right to use and to harvest from land that is directly controlled by the State or belonging to other persons. It is transferable under certain conditions. Its eligibility is wide and includes Indonesian citizens, foreign citizens domiciled in Indonesia, corporate bodies incorporated under Indonesian law and domiciled in Indonesia and foreign corporate bodies having representation in Indonesia. The use right is granted for a definite term or for as long as the land is used for a specific purpose.
- ***Hak sewa untuk bangunan* (right to lease for buildings)** represents the entitlement to use land owned by another party for the purposes of building construction. The user of this right is obliged to make rental payments to the owner of the property. There is no fixed term for this type of land right. The eligibility is the same as for the "right to use" and includes Indonesian citizens, foreign citizens residing in Indonesia, corporate bodies established under Indonesian law and domiciled in Indonesia and foreign corporate bodies having representation in Indonesia.
- ***Hak membuka tanah* and *Hak memungut hasil hutan* (right to clear land and right to collect forest products)** can be held only by Indonesian citizens. There is no private or community land ownership or land rights for forest areas, only forest concessions. BPN becomes involved in forest land areas only when it is converted to non-forest use.

Source: OECD (2012b), *OECD Review of Agricultural Policy*, Indonesia.

facilitate access to credit for smallholders should be accelerated. Creating a unique and dedicated agency to accelerate land rights registration should be a priority.

Another reason for subdued productivity growth is the low level of investment. The share of agriculture in total realised investment, at 10.7% on average in the last 10 years, is lower than its share in GDP, imports, exports and employment. Promoting investment in agriculture is crucial to bridge the productivity gap between staple and export crops. Investment in agriculture should be encouraged via subsidised loans, but also by removing restrictions on foreign ownership in large-scale horticulture businesses, warehousing and cold storage, which are hampering growth in agriculture (cf. below).

Encourage further diversification

Diversification away from traditional crops is another avenue for productivity growth. Upgraded marketing channels, and shared market-based information on which crops are attracting the highest prices, would help farmers make the best crop-choice decisions. But diversification has been limited by institutional factors: public agricultural extension services (advice to farmers), research and agriculture education are indeed deeply rooted in traditional agricultural crops, especially rice. For example, in the area studied by Jeon (2013) the most commonly planted crops were staples, which are highly regulated by government. The dominance of staple crops in some regions means that farmer groups and the supporting agricultural agency receive comparatively little guidance on cash crops or high-value specialised crops. This is detrimental to farmers' income prospects. The focus on staple crops is misplaced and should be abandoned in favour of more diversification. At the same time diversification efforts should be complemented with better market-price information for farmers. Smallholders should also be better linked to local and national markets to make the most of their diversification efforts. This requires better transport infrastructure, improved market-price information for farmers, and phasing out export and import restrictions (see below).

In addition to diversification, insurance schemes can help farmers to deal with income variations caused by price and output fluctuations, thereby encouraging them to take more risks. A well-developed insurance scheme against adverse climatic or price developments would thus discourage farmers from returning to the safe option of government-regulated staple crop production for (own) consumption. Trials of insurance programmes for rice and cattle have been carried out in some areas. These pilots should be assessed and, if successful, made available in other districts and extended to a range of commodities outside the area of government interest in order to encourage diversification. In the long term sound insurance schemes would allow for a more stable policy framework and reduce the need for one-off support payments to farmers. The short-term challenge is to demonstrate to farmers the value of having insurance and overcoming the domestic barriers that have prevented the private provision of such schemes to farmers. In this regard, a temporary subsidy for insurance purchase to "jump start" the market may be justified.

The government has in place programmes to encourage greater fertiliser use to improve productivity. Nitrogenous fertiliser is the most widely used (64% of total consumption in nutrient terms in 2008), followed by potash (27%) (FAOSTAT, 2014). With little livestock, most farmers do not apply manure. Among food crops, the highest application rates per hectare are for rice, maize and soybeans (OECD, 2012b). Indonesia's fertiliser application rates averaged 98 kg/ha in 2007-09, which is higher than in the Philippines (69 kg/ha) but remains much lower than in such countries as China (427 kg/ha) and Vietnam (233 kg/ha). In an attempt to stimulate fertiliser use, the government has set up a subsidy programme which includes: planning of the quantities requested and produced, setting a ceiling price (HET), fixing the amount of subsidies to cover the costs of provision at the HET, and distributing subsidised fertilisers to eligible farmers. Around 75% is distributed at subsidised prices and subject to strict regulations, and 25% is sold at market prices in village kiosks (Pandin, 2008).

Currently, there are five fertiliser producers. All are state-owned, and in 1997 they were combined into a single holding company, PT Agro Kimia Indonesia. The current system, however, is inefficient. The lack of competition, insufficient gas supply and obsolete technologies (most factories are more than 20 years old) are major reasons for low capacity utilisation, around 20-30% below potential, and high production costs. Moreover, field surveys indicate that subsidised fertilisers are not available in required quantities, deliveries are often delayed, and only 40% of fertiliser subsidies reach smallholders (OECD, 2012b). These subsidies, which cost 1.3% of total government expenditure on average over the last three years (Box 2.5), should be phased out. The savings could be used to finance vouchers that could be used by farmers to purchase any inputs leaving them free to decide how to use those funds. Privatising the five producers and reducing import and export restrictions for fertilisers would raise efficiency in the sector. Privatisation could also be useful to launch the voucher reform.

Indonesia has made improvements in agricultural productivity when viewed over the longer term, helping to place downward pressure on food prices. For example, crop yields have risen, including in staples. This, along with economic growth has contributed to falling rates of undernourishment: its prevalence is currently estimated at 9% of the

Box 2.5. Government financial support to agriculture

Government financial support to agriculture is growing. The PSE (Producer Support Estimate as a share of farmers' gross receipts) increased to 19% in 2010-12, on par with the OECD average, due to higher domestic prices compared with those on international markets (OECD, 2014c). PSE was only 3.4% in 1995-97 and 9% over 2006-10 (with some significant fluctuations), which was then far below the OECD average of 22% (OECD, 2012b). As for the Total Support Estimate (TSE), it was at 3.4% of GDP in 2010-12 (up from 1.9% in 2006-10), well above China (2.25%), the OECD (0.8%), Brazil (0.49%) and South Africa (0.22%) (OECD, 2014c). This high TSE figure is also due to agriculture's relatively large share in GDP. Market price support is the dominant form of support. It reflects border protection for certain agricultural commodities, subsidies on inputs, such as fertilisers, and output price support for rice and sugar. In 2010, support for rice alone represented one-third of the total PSE.

population, half of what it was only a decade ago. Food security remains high on the policy agenda. This takes various forms such as rice reserves, priority to domestic production, price support, delivery of rice at subsidised prices to poor households (RASKIN), and export and import restrictions and licenses. These policies have severe drawbacks: the domestic price of rice was 60% higher than the international reference price in 2010-12 compared to 8% in 2000-02, and simulations show that these policies would increase the rate of undernourishment under various risks scenarios (OECD, 2014c). In addition, according to the FAO, at 13.1% the cereal import dependency ratio is already one of the lowest in the region and has not moved much since 1998. It is on par with Thailand (12%) and Vietnam (13.4%) but much lower than wealthier countries such as Malaysia and Japan both at 80.7% (2011 data, three-year average) (FAOSTAT, 2015). By removing trade restrictions (see below) and phasing out price support, Indonesia could lower prices for both domestic and imported food, making costly self-sufficiency policies less necessary and improving well-being, especially for the poor.

As an alternative to RASKIN, which does not always reach its target population and suffers from high administrative costs, food vouchers or cash transfers would improve diversity and be more cost effective (Hidrobo et al., 2014). They would also further encourage crop diversification. In order to reduce food poverty through trade, export and import restrictions should be eliminated over time, in co-ordination with other ASEAN members. Import restrictions, especially in areas where Indonesia has no comparative advantage, are especially burdensome. For instance, import quotas on raw sugar are forcing the country's 11 refineries to operate below capacity, despite fast-rising demand.

Reducing trade restrictions

Since 2005, the value of Indonesia's agro-food exports has been consistently more than twice the value of agro-food imports, and their share in total exports increased from 12.5% in 2000 to 23.3% in 2011. Asian countries are the main export destinations, with their share rising from around one-half in 1990-92 to two-thirds in 2011-13 (China alone accounted for 12.4% of the total in 2013). Major agricultural imports include wheat, cotton, soybeans, dairy products, sugar, tobacco and beef. The United States and Australia are the most important suppliers, with market shares in 2008-10 of 19% and 17%, respectively (OECD, 2012b). This pattern of trade reflects Indonesia's comparative advantages in producing perennial tropical crops such as crude palm oil and rubber, which fit its land and

Box 2.6. **Palm oil in Indonesia**

Indonesia is now the world's largest exporter of palm oil, and more than 70% of its production is destined for export. About 70% of production is in Sumatra, and small producers provide 42% of it. The main export markets in 2012 were India (27.5% of exports), China (14.8%), Malaysia (7.5%), the Netherlands (7.1%) and Singapore (5.1%) according to CEIC data. Partly due to increased labour costs in Malaysia, another major palm oil producer, its companies have shifted plantations to Indonesia, which explains the large palm oil share exported back to Malaysia.

Besides its role as a cooking oil in Asia, palm oil is used in the production of margarine, sauces, soaps, detergents, cosmetics and household care products, and applied in the leather, textile, metal and chemical industries. Palm oil can also be burned directly as fuel and used as a raw material for biodiesel production.

There are major environmental issues related to the increase in palm oil production, especially deforestation (cf. last section below).

climate well, and importing cereals or livestock for which Indonesia does not have a comparative advantage (Box 2.6).

Still, Indonesia is restrictive regarding farm trade compared with other Asian emerging countries. For instance, back in 2010 the government initiated several policies limiting the export of unprocessed agricultural commodities. It imposed export tariffs on raw cocoa beans and crude palm oil in order to encourage the development of higher value added agricultural activities and ensure that local industries do not lack affordable raw materials. In 2012, Indonesia also banned the export of raw and semi-finished rattan in an effort to induce businesses to export furniture instead.

As for imports, they are subject to many licensing requirements. For instance, livestock producers are supported through border protection keeping domestic prices above international levels, in particular for poultry and beef (OECD, 2014c). In August 2013, Indonesia adopted two ministerial regulations on the importation of horticultural products, requiring importers to obtain three permits: a Registered (or Producer) Importer permit from the Ministry of Trade; an Import Recommendation of Horticultural Products from the Ministry of Agriculture; and an Import Approval from the Ministry of Trade. Import approvals and recommendations are valid only for six months and come with many additional administrative requirements attached (USTR, 2014).

The Horticulture Law 13/2010 has now come into force. It restricts foreign ownership to large-scale horticulture businesses by capping it at 30%, down from 95% previously. The deadline for compliance was 2014 for all companies, including those in the business before the law was passed (no grandfathering). Similarly, a plantation bill setting stricter rules on foreign ownership in that sector (especially palm oil) is currently being drafted. By limiting foreign equity, the law is hindering innovation and restricting the inflow of qualified experts. Such ownership restrictions should be removed to accelerate productivity growth in the face of growing demand for food. Similarly, border protection should be removed to let farmers take advantage of international trade and comparative advantages. Onshore value adding should indeed be encouraged, but by attracting domestic and foreign investment, rather than taxing the export of raw commodities.

Recommendations to manage agricultural resources better

Encourage further diversification

- Encourage diversification into specialised cash crops by reducing institutional support to staples.
- Provide better information for farmers on market prices for crops and an insurance system to help them take more risk.
- Better link smallholders to local and national markets by improving transport systems and access to information and communication technologies.

Ease constraints on investment and encourage consolidation

- Clarify and simplify the land tenure system, and develop a long-term strategy for farm restructuring.
- Increase farmers' access to credit by accelerating land titling.
- Expand partnership agreements between smallholders and large estates to provide technical assistance and training.

Gradually remove producer support and allow more market-based mechanisms to operate

- Phase out fertiliser subsidies and privatise fertiliser producers to raise efficiency.
- Lower food prices by decreasing trade restrictions.
- Phase out market price support, including replacing RASKIN with more cost effective cash transfers or food vouchers.

Indonesia's reliance on fossil fuels poses policy dilemmas

Fossil fuels, whether for domestic consumption or export, are central to Indonesia's economy. Coal is both the country's main source of electricity generation and its first export by value (Figure 2.2, Panel A). Even though its output has been declining for years, oil is still an important (and until recently heavily subsidised) component of Indonesia's energy mix. Indonesia's ramping up of its natural gas capacity, both as a way to replace oil domestically and to meet growing demand from its neighbours, will contribute to lower its CO_2 emissions.

The expansion of coal production is reaching its limits

Indonesia has abundant proven reserves of steam coal (Figure 2.9, Panel A) with its share of the world's output and exports rising fast (Panel B). It is thus well placed to take advantage of growing coal demand as the five biggest coal importers in 2013 were all in Asia: China (327.2 Mt), Japan (195.6 Mt), India (179.9 Mt), Korea (126.5 Mt) and Chinese Taipei (68 Mt), all of them buyers of Indonesian coal (Figure 2.10). In 2013, Indonesia produced 485 Mt (million tonnes) of coal, placing it fourth for output but first for exports, as in 2011 and 2012 (Figure 2.11). Indonesia's coal is mostly steam coal used for heat and energy production (Box 2.7).

With 400 million people still without electricity, ASEAN countries will rely increasingly on coal as a cheap way to generate electricity. It is hard to know, however, how long Indonesia will be able to take advantage of that growth, given talk of an Indonesian ban on low calorific value coal exports and the staunch commitment of the new Chinese government to more efficient, sustainable and environmentally friendly growth. In

Figure 2.9. **Indonesia and the world coal market**

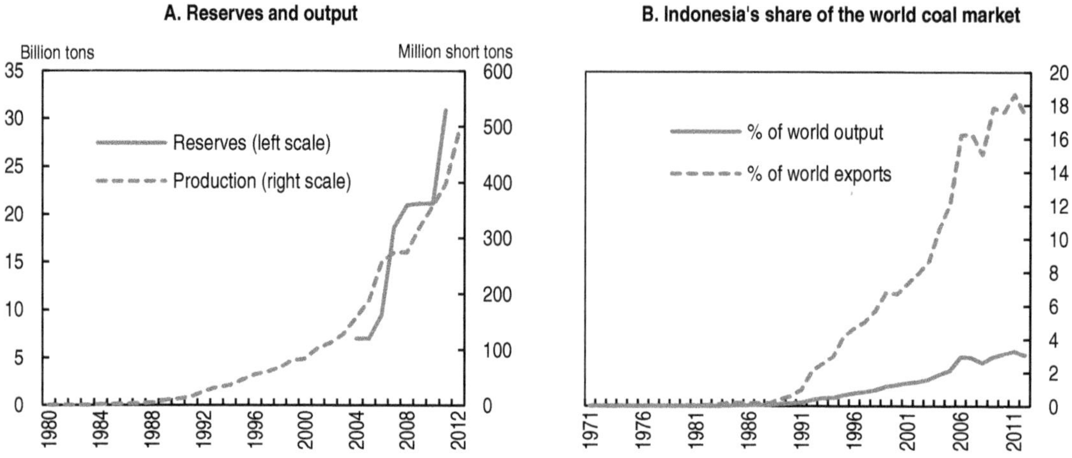

Source: *IEA Database* and Ministry of Energy and Mineral Resources.

StatLink http://dx.doi.org/10.1787/888933200413

Figure 2.10. **Coal import sources, selected countries, 2012**

Million tonnes

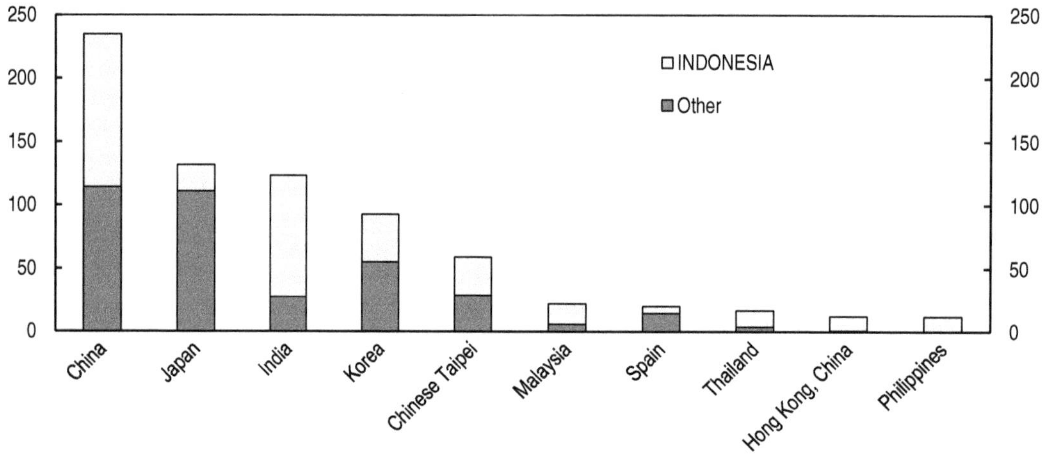

Source: *IEA Database.*

StatLink http://dx.doi.org/10.1787/888933200429

addition, the transition of the US economy towards shale gas and light tight oil is taking place at the expense of coal, whose share in US power generation has collapsed. Given that the United States was until recently the second biggest consumer at 1 000 Mt per year, this change in the US energy market will reduce its demand for coal and increase its exports.

In Indonesia, more electricity generators are shifting to coal. Indeed, coal remains a cheaper option than gas for generating electricity in many provinces. However, Indonesia's coal-fired electricity generation efficiency is still lagging both by world and Asian standards (Figure 2.12). The efficiency of coal-fired plants (measured by the ratio of the energy services delivered, i.e. electricity and useful heat, to the fuel input) depends on a range of factors including the technology employed, the type and quality of coal used, and the operating conditions and practices. Given the share that coal-fired electricity is going to play in its energy mix, improving energy efficiency should be a priority for Indonesia as it offers both significant fuel savings and lower CO_2 emissions, as coal-fired plants are

Figure 2.11. **Main coal producers and exporters, 2013**

Million tonnes

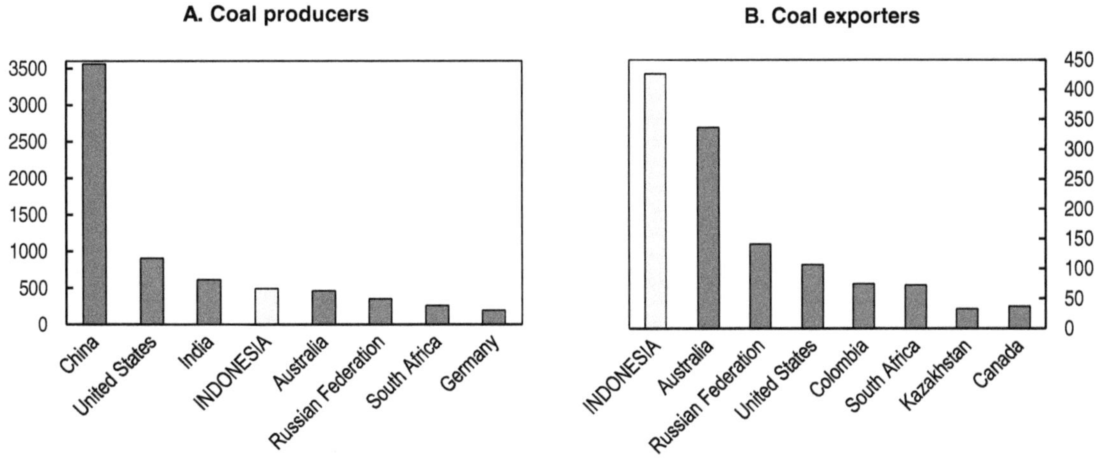

Source: *IEA Database* and IEA (2014), *Coal Information 2014*, OECD/IEA Publishing.

StatLink http://dx.doi.org/10.1787/888933200434

Box 2.7. **Types and uses of coal**

Coal is the world's most abundant fossil fuel resource and its fuel for electricity production. It represents 28.8% of the world's primary energy supply, behind oil at 31.5% but ahead of natural gas at 21.3%.

Coal is commonly classified by its rank (degree of alteration from the original plant source), its calorific value or its carbon content, which are loosely related, with higher ranked coals generally being less polluting. In decreasing order of transformation, from high to low rank, there is anthracite, bituminous and sub-bituminous coal, lignite and peat. A common distinction is between hard and brown coal. Hard coal corresponds to anthracite, bituminous and sub-bituminous coal, which includes coking (or metallurgical) coal for steel-making purposes and steam (or thermal) coal used to produce heat and electricity. Brown coal corresponds to lignite and peat. Hard coal has a higher carbon and energy content.

Unlike oil, coal is primarily a domestic fuel: 85% of it is consumed in the same country where it is mined. Coal is primarily used for electricity production (41.3% of worldwide electricity production in 2011). While a cheap source of energy, coal has many environmental drawbacks. It is the fossil fuel causing the largest amounts of greenhouse gas emissions, and burning coal causes considerable amounts of air and water pollution. Moreover, the lower the rank the more the air pollution. Default carbon emission factors measured in tonnes of carbon per terajoule (tC/TJ) are: 15.3 for gas, 16.8 to 27.5 for oil products, and 25.8 to 29.1 for primary coal products.

where the largest potential gains lie. For instance, coal and other non-gaseous fossil fuels can be converted into electricity in combined gas cycle if the fuel is gasified in advance. Encouraging FDI in the sector will be key to helping Indonesia alleviate such constraints and make the most of its coal endowments while containing its emissions.

The future of coal mining in Indonesia is also looking steadily towards low-rank, lignite-grade coals. This shift in quality means that the amount of tonnage being mined, trucked and barged will increase over time to maintain existing energy-equivalent levels. Given that all these operations are diesel-powered, the amount of diesel consumption in

Figure 2.12. **Coal-fired heat and electricity generation efficiency, 2011**

Per cent

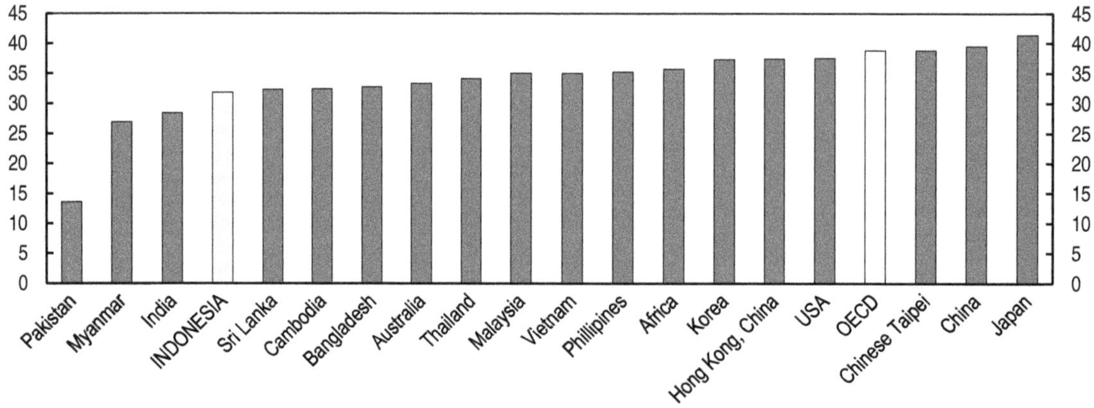

Source: IEA (2013a), *Coal Medium-Term Market Report*, OECD/IEA Publishing.

StatLink http://dx.doi.org/10.1787/888933200446

mining is expected to climb, exposing the industry to volatile fuel prices (Lucarelli, 2010). More and more mining companies are contemplating producing electricity on site via coal-fired power plants. There are then physical, economic and environmental limits to the amount of coal Indonesia can mine, burn at home and supply to the world.

Indonesia's coal bias harms its environment

Coal combustion will be by far the main source of rapidly rising electricity production in Indonesia, followed by oil and gas (Figure 2.13). The role played by fossil fuels is not peculiar to Indonesia but rather applies to a number of developing countries, especially in ASEAN, where non-fossil energies such as hydro and nuclear power are marginal, if not non-existent (Figure 2.14). In Indonesia the trend has long been reinforced by an implicit negative carbon price for all types of fossil fuels due to Indonesia's fuel and electricity subsidy system. While petrol subsidies are about to be removed completely, the heavy use of coal in electricity production is going to challenge Indonesia's commitment to

Figure 2.13. **Indonesia's future energy mix**

Million tonnes of oil equivalent

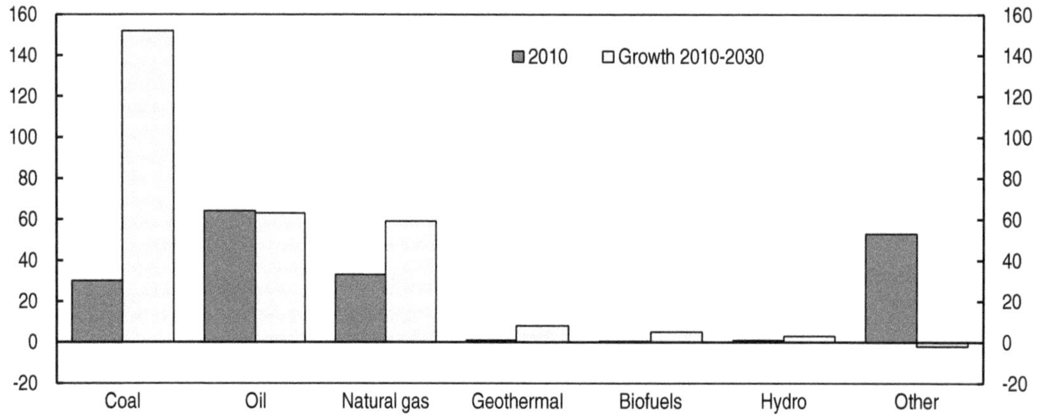

Source: McKinsey Global Institute (2012), *The Archipelago Economy: Unleashing Indonesia's Potential.*

StatLink http://dx.doi.org/10.1787/888933200459

Figure 2.14. **Sources of electricity production, selected countries, 2011**

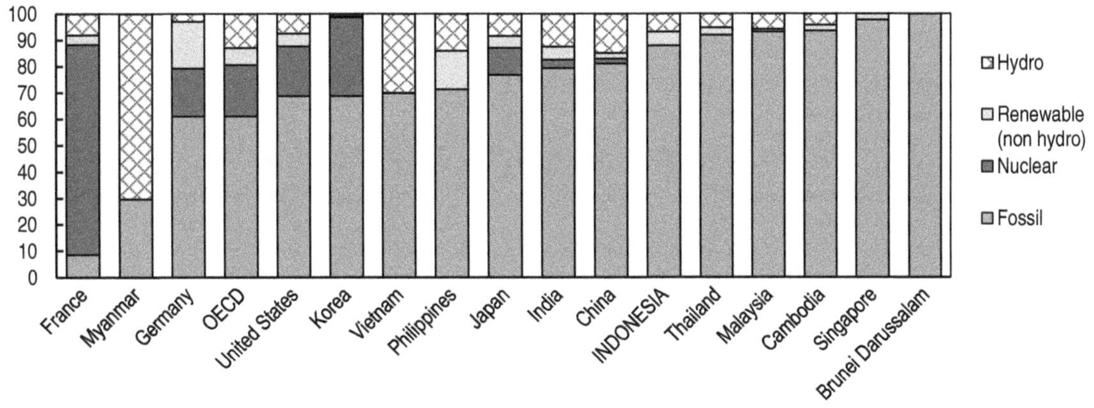

Source: OECD (2014b), *Toward Green Growth in Southeast Asia*, OECD Publishing.

StatLink http://dx.doi.org/10.1787/888933200462

greenhouse gas (GHG) reduction. In order to reduce demand for fossil fuels, the implicit carbon price of electricity in Indonesia should be brought back to positive levels by phasing out electricity subsidies.

Revitalising the oil sector

Crude oil, together with natural gas liquids, refinery feedstocks and additives as well as natural gas, generate about one-fifth of Indonesia's consolidated budget revenue in the form of taxes, royalties, revenue-sharing contracts and the profits of the state-owned oil producer Pertamina. Yet, Indonesia is in dramatic need of an overhaul of its exploration and exploitation policy, as output and FDI have been falling. The critical oil sector is at risk of falling behind.

Indonesia has been active in the oil industry since 1885, when oil was first discovered in North Sumatra. It switched to become a net oil importer in 2006 (Figure 2.15) due to growing domestic demand (4% annual growth over the last 15 years) alongside declining domestic output. Output has indeed been falling since the late 1990s in the face of

Figure 2.15. **Indonesia's oil balance**

Million tonnes

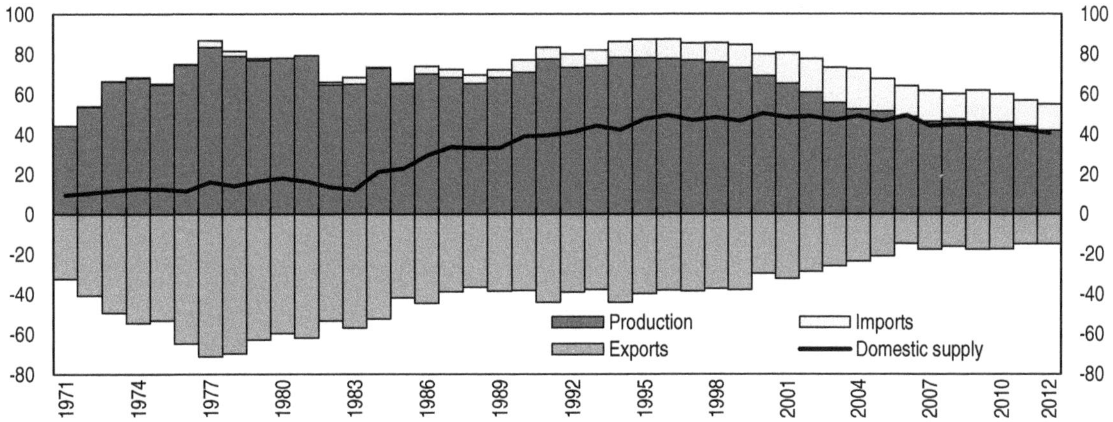

Source: IEA Database.

StatLink http://dx.doi.org/10.1787/888933200474

maturing oil fields and decreasing exploration and investment (Figure 2.16). The required increase in imports, together with skyrocketing prices in the mid-2000s, has been highly detrimental to Indonesia's economy, including contributing to the blowout in the current account deficit between mid-2011 and 2013.

Figure 2.16. **Indonesia and the world oil market**

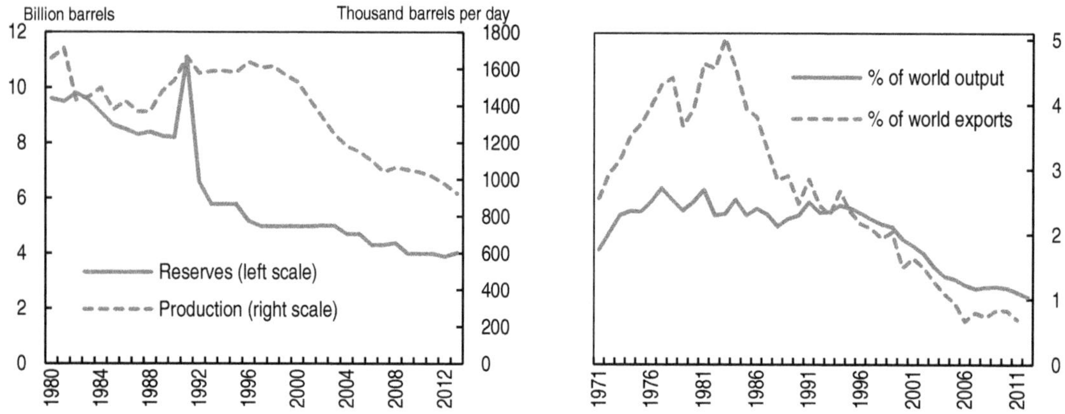

Source: US Energy Information Administration (EIA) and *IEA Database*.

StatLink http://dx.doi.org/10.1787/888933200488

Until now, Indonesia had been subsidising fuel and electricity to keep energy affordable for the poor and to raise household purchasing power. In recent years fuel subsidies had been absorbing over 20% of government spending (Figure 2.17). But the subsidies did not work as intended, as 40% of subsidy benefits went to the top income decile and less than 1% to the poorest (World Bank, 2014a). Subsidies also had unintended consequences in the form of increased demand, traffic congestion and environmental damage, whose deadweight loss has been estimated at USD 4-8 billion annually (Davis, 2014; see also OECD, 2014d). Declining production from maturing oil fields (requiring more

Figure 2.17. **Energy subsidies as a percentage of government expenditure and GDP**

Per cent of total government expenditures

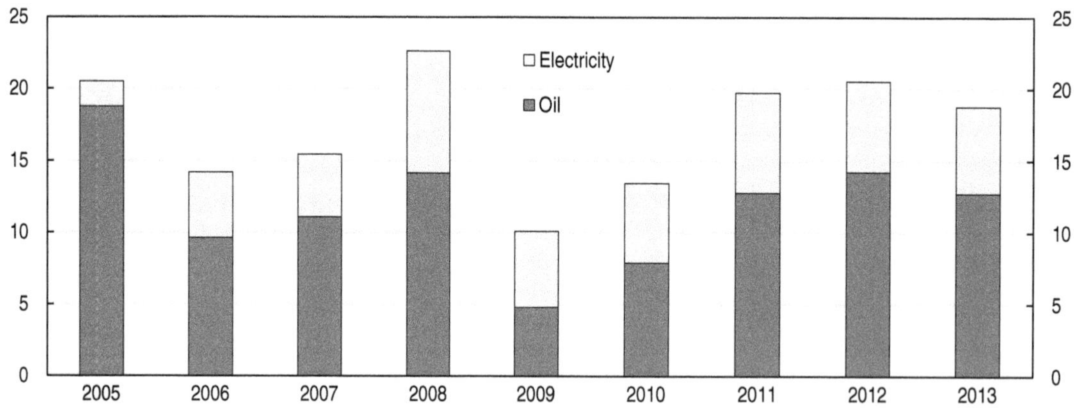

Source: CEIC.

StatLink http://dx.doi.org/10.1787/888933200495

imports) add to the problem. Fuel subsidies were reduced in June 2013 and again in November 2014, bringing subsidised fuel prices closer to market prices (Figure 2.18). Then, at the beginning of 2015, the government grasped the opportunity offered by falling world oil prices and scrapped its existing petrol and diesel price-setting regime. Both domestic petrol and diesel prices are now linked directly to world prices, with only diesel getting a fixed subsidy of IDR 1 000 (USD 0.08) a litre. The 2015 budget originally contained fuel subsidies worth more than 13% of total government expenditure, but this has now been whittled down to only 1%.

Figure 2.18. **Prices for oil and petrol**

IDR/litre

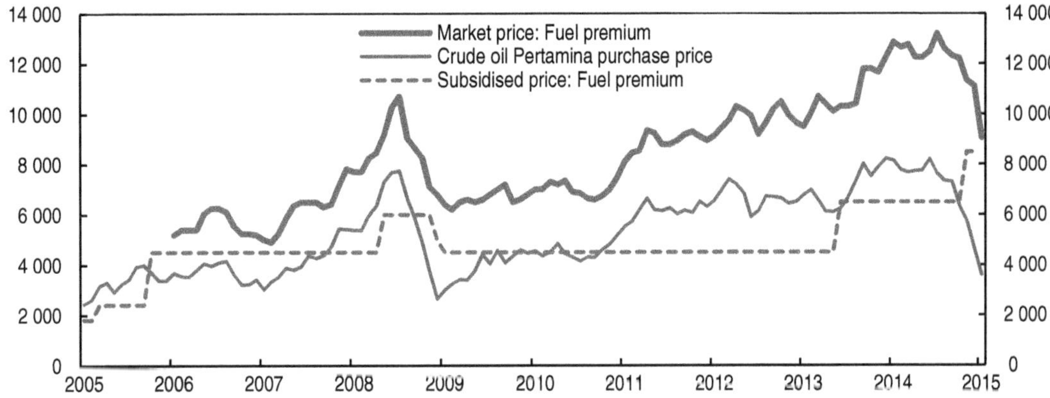

Source: CEIC.

StatLink http://dx.doi.org/10.1787/888933200508

Additional measures have recently been taken. For instance, in 2012 the government banned cars and vehicles used in mining and plantation operations from buying subsidised fuel. In 2007, it introduced a gas conversion programme to reduce the burden imposed by subsidies to diesel and petrol, involving the development of natural gas infrastructures as well as the distribution of free gas converter kits for public transportation (Andadari et al., 2014). This kerosene-to-liquefied natural gas programme should be expanded, as gas is abundant and cleaner.

Electricity subsidies remain an issue, and because most generation capacity takes the form of coal- and oil-fired power plants, this is indirectly a fossil fuel subsidy. Electricity subsidies amount to around 8% of total government expenditure. The ongoing reforms in this area should continue, including gradual price reforms until electricity pricing fully recovers the ongoing costs of maintaining and improving Indonesia's electricity system.

Indonesia should embrace an ambitious oil (and gas – see below) revival programme. It is well placed to take advantage of growing regional and world demand, but it needs to change the way it operates in the oil sector, as it is looking steadily less attractive to exploration companies. In addition to legal uncertainty following the controversial 2009 Mining Law, Indonesia's oil industry also suffers from excessive government control via Pertamina and overlapping regulations. The resulting lack of incentive to explore and develop upstream oil production capacity (increasingly located in the east and offshore) has contributed to falling output and revenues. In a series of interviews conducted with Indonesian policy makers and ministries Boyd et al. (2010) noted that resource nationalism, corruption (Indonesia ranks in 107th place out of 175 countries surveyed on the 2014 Transparency International Corruption Perceptions Index) and decentralisation have all contributed to the decline of Indonesia's oil industry. The recent reform of the Mexican oil energy sector and its corporate governance, including the establishment of autonomous regulators for licensing, safety and environmental protection and the fostering of greater competition, could be used as a model (OECD, 2015).

Greater use should be made of private-sector expertise in exploration, exploitation and refining. Similar to agricultural development, it is imperative for Indonesia to simplify land titling and resource licensing, and to better protect private investors' interests. It should streamline and advertise simple guidelines and, when involved, limit the number of interlocutors for private companies by creating, for instance, a one-stop shop that would handle the entire process. In the meantime greater co-ordination among the government agencies involved in the licensing process should be encouraged. The alternative is for Indonesia to become increasingly dependent on foreign oil at a time of rapid and sustained growth in demand. Indonesia's fuel deficit is forecast to rise 5.3% to 640 000 barrels a day in 2015, to be compared to a domestic output of about 825 000 barrels a day (Bloomberg, 2014).

Using gas to bridge the gap until more renewable energy comes on line

Natural gas is set to become one of the three major sources of world energy, with a market share expected to double from 17.3% in 2000 by 2035, thanks to its widespread availability, competitive supply costs and environmental advantages over other fossil fuels (it releases about half as much carbon as coal). As of 2012, Asia represented 46% of global international gas imports, ahead of Europe (45%) for the first time in history. Currently the world's 10th largest gas producer and holding the largest reserves in Asia (Mujiyanto and Tiess, 2013), Indonesia is advantageously positioned to profit from Asian demand growth. China is now its fifth biggest market, and 8.1% of its imports come from Indonesia. Gas represents only 5% of China's primary energy mix at the moment (still far below coal's share of about two-thirds) but its use is rising sharply.

However, the output of Indonesia's gas industry has steadily fallen from its 2010 peak, accelerating the trend decline in its share of world output and exports (Figure 2.19). This fall reflects domestic hurdles to increasing production, such as delays in field development

Figure 2.19. **Indonesia and the world natural gas market**

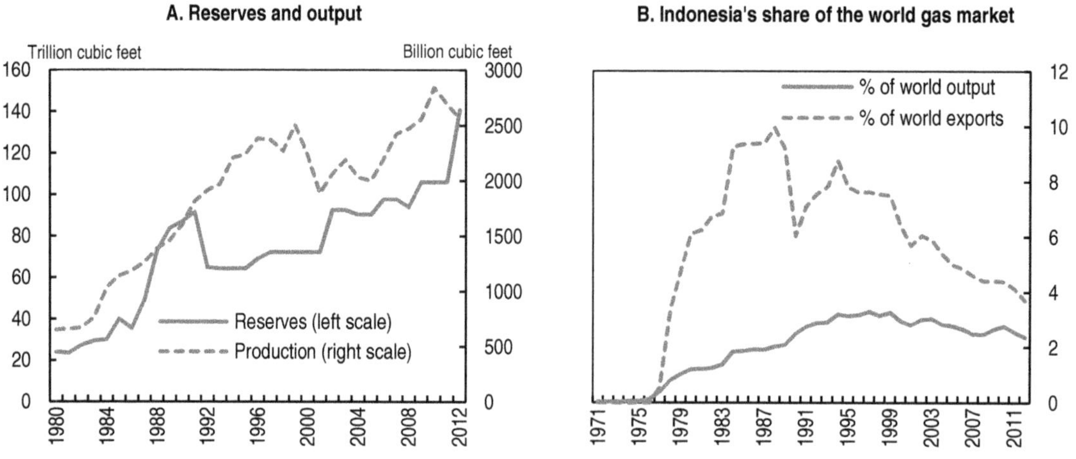

Source: US Energy Information Administration and IEA *Database*.

StatLink http://dx.doi.org/10.1787/888933200513

or regulated domestic prices being too low to attract new investment. In 2012, Indonesia saw a decrease in both production revenues and volumes (-5% for the latter), yet demand increased by 1.5%. So Indonesia's oil and gas sectors face the same issues. The development of new production and export facilities should be accelerated by removing administrative barriers and hurdles. While Indonesia has been among the largest exporters of liquefied natural gas (LNG) for many years, it completed its first LNG importing facility in 2012 (the West Java floating storage terminal and regasification unit) and began to import LNG in 2013.

The future of Indonesian LNG exports is uncertain, however, due to competition from Asian countries with vast unexploited reserves, such as China (Aguilera et al., 2014), or from countries with a well-established gas industry, such as Russia. For instance, Russia and China have sealed a deal that would see Russian Gazprom supply China National Petroleum Corporation with 3.75 billion cubic feet a day for 30 years starting in 2018. China's current demand is about 16 billion cubic feet a day and rising fast. And there is more than 7 billion cubic feet a day of Australian LNG capacity due to come on-stream by 2017 (*Wall Street Journal*, 2014). Due to limited scope for pipeline development in the region, additional liquefaction and export terminals should be developed.

Indonesia will soon find it increasingly difficult to allocate its gas output between growing domestic and international demand. It will probably have to boost its supply, perhaps using unconventional sources such as horizontal drilling with hydraulic fracturing (fracking). However, given Indonesia's mixed record in terms of environmental protection, the development of fracking should be carefully monitored and tightly regulated. Five companies have actually already delivered a joint study regarding shale gas potential in northern Sumatra, and around 70 proposals to drill exploration wells have been submitted (IEA, 2013b). While the risk for the environment is high, developing shale gas could help plug the gap until renewable energies gain in importance.

Recommendations relative to the energy sector

The recommendations from the previous section regarding land rights also apply to the exploration and exploitation of fossil fuel energies. In addition, a series of specific measures should be taken:

Coal

- Increase the energy efficiency of coal-fired power plants in order to limit their harm to the environment.
- Further develop transport infrastructure, especially in the form of port and rail freight capacity, which will also benefit the rest of the economy.

Oil

- Continue phasing out fuel and electricity subsidies (and compensate the poor, as necessary) to allow a reprioritisation of government spending programmes, and communicate on the many benefits to be expected from their removal.
- Expand the kerosene-to-LNG conversion programme to switch demand from oil to gas.

Recommendations relative to the energy sector *(cont.)*

Gas

- Consider developing shale gas as a transitional fuel. Accelerate development of new production from conventional sources.
- Due to limited scope for pipeline development in the region, develop additional liquefaction and export terminals.

Restoring a favourable environment for mineral extraction and processing

Given its ample mineral endowment and assuming no land use restrictions and best practices, Indonesia ranks fourth out of 96 jurisdictions in the "Policy/Mineral Potential index" in the Fraser Survey of mining companies. Despite its potential, no clear uptrend can be observed in mineral output, as most of the value gains have come from rising prices rather than volumes. Moreover, while Indonesia attracted 3-5% of global mineral exploration funding in the 1980s and 1990s, its recent share has been less than 0.5% (Castle, 2013). Mineral exploration investment is quite low by comparison: it was only USD 80 million in 2011 (*Energy and Mining Journal,* 2012), in contrast with USD 2.9 billion in Australia (Australian Bureau of Statistics, 2014). The causes of this disappointing performance are numerous: restrictive legislation on land use, uncertainty concerning the interpretation (or enforcement) of existing regulations, fairness regarding legal processes and corruption.

To understand the current situation, it is important to step back in time. According to the 1945 Constitution, all resources belong to the central government, which enjoys the exclusive right to manage and license their exploitation. While not necessarily a problem, as seen in the case of Botswana, this can reinforce nationalistic views and deter foreign investors. In the 1960s, eager to attract foreign investment, President Soeharto's government introduced Law 1/1967 on Foreign Investment and Law 11/1967 on the Basic Provision of Mining. It established a new legal structure, the Contract of Work (CoW), which was a contract between the government and a foreign mining company that set out the company's rights and obligations including all taxes, royalties and fiscal charges. Under a CoW, the company retained management control and responsibility for all its activities (PricewaterhouseCoopers, 2010). Importantly, CoWs provided competitive and stable royalty rates compared to neighbouring countries. Absent private ownership, the CoW proved successful in attracting investment and developing the sector, which was then dominated by foreign companies. After the 1997-98 crisis, CoWs went through a series of changes (or "generations", eight in all) reinforcing the position of the government, shortening the contract period and raising the percentage of equity to be held by domestic interests beyond simple majority ownership.

CoWs were finally abandoned in the 2009 Mining Law, which came into force in 2014, in favour of mining business licenses, or *Izin Usaha Pertambangan* (IUPs). With this new regime, exploration and exploitation rights are now separated, meaning that the right to develop a deposit is not automatically granted to the exploring entity that found it. In addition, the 2009 law no longer protects companies from changes in royalty rates (Gandataruna and Haymon, 2011). This uncertainty adds to investment risks in the mining sector. Also, the fact that the maximum timeframe for mineral exploitation of 30 years is now a decade shorter than under the 1967 law might also be dissuasive. The government should reconsider the 2009 Law in favour of best practices regarding mining contracting. In particular, it should suppress the dual-licensing system by moving back to a unique exploration and exploitation license in order to create the right incentives for foreign mining companies. Divestment requirements should also be removed and replaced by attractive terms of operations for both Indonesian and foreign companies.

The law also requires that all IUP and CoW holders add value to their mining products via onshore processing and refining. By value, approximately 40% of total mineral exports are currently processed, but the government aims to raise domestic value added. In May 2012, the Ministry of Energy and Mineral Resources (MEMR) issued Regulation 7/2012 asking producers to formulate smelting plans and imposing a ban on the export of raw mineral ores. While mineral ore exports such as nickel and bauxite are now banned, exports of so-called mineral concentrates (copper, iron, manganese, lead and zinc) will be permitted for the next three years under a new regulation taxing semi-processed mineral exports at 20-25% of sales revenues (to rise to 60% by 2016) (World Bank, 2014a).

Such import-substitution strategies have been used elsewhere, although with mixed effects. If successful, they can launch new growth engines. Airbus successfully entered the world aircraft market thanks to strong support from European governments. In Indonesia the tax on crude palm oil (CPO) exports succeeded in keeping it as an affordable input into many domestic industries rather than being exported at high prices. In all instances the global context needs to be taken into account. In Airbus' case, it penetrated an uncompetitive market characterised by high monopoly rents, making the rationale for government support stronger. In the case of the ore export ban, the net benefits may well depend on the details of the extraction and refining processes, however. For instance, about 96% of copper's market value is derived from the first step of concentration, with only 4% of final value generated in copper smelting (World Bank, 2014a). Copper mining in Indonesia is dominated by two major companies, Freeport McMoran and Newmont Mining, and both already process their copper ore into concentrates and supply part of it to the only smelter in the country, P.T. Smelting (USAID, 2013). But for nickel, refining generates more value.

For most minerals, the purification process is highly capital-intensive and subject to significant economies of scale. It also requires reliable and affordable access to water and electricity. For copper, lead and zinc, additional investments in processing appear unlikely to be economically viable under current conditions, given low margins from global overcapacity in smelting and refining (World Bank, 2014a). That said, some companies are going ahead with these investments, such as the Chinese firm Hongqiao, which has recently been building several alumina refining plants in Indonesia. In the end the government should facilitate the provision of infrastructure, skills and other fundamental inputs, as well as ensuring efficiency and well-functioning institutions and factor markets (see Chapter 1). With these in place, domestic value added may well be viable without having to resort to export bans and other distortionary measures.

In the meantime, the ore ban will have costs as the mineral extracting sector, and the tax revenues it provides, will be hurt because of falling exports. The production of bauxite, for instance, was only 2.8 million tonnes during the January-August 2014 period, versus 58.7 million tonnes throughout 2013. In the copper sector Newmont has faced sharply reduced sales since the ban took effect in January, halted mining operations in June, but operations have resumed after it agreed to an increase in royalties to 3.75% (from 1%) for gold, to 4% (from 3.5%) for copper, and to 3.25% (from 1%) for silver. It will also scale down its mining areas in eastern Indonesia by almost a quarter and pay a deposit bond amounting to USD 25 million as a guarantee that the company is serious about building a smelter. Earlier Freeport also came to a similar agreement with the government. Indonesia should also consider moving away from its current tax regime based on royalties, which is distortionary, and implement a tax on profits instead (Box 2.8).

Box 2.8. **Taxing mineral rents**

Indonesia derives rents from its mineral wealth. In recent years, the mining sector has contributed approximately 5% to GDP. This is significant and raises the question of how best to tax the rents. Royalties are based on the amount of resource extracted (either quantities or production revenues) and are therefore easy to collect. But they drive a wedge between the world price and the price that producers receive for each unit of output, decreasing the quantity supplied to below the efficient level. By contrast, a resource-rent tax (or profit tax) extracts a portion of the rent and ideally has no effect on output. But it usually requires the government to pay out cash to the private company in years of financial losses and get a positive profit share in years of profit. Because cash payments by government are unpopular, they are usually replaced by delayed taxation, which is more complex to implement. In Indonesia, IUP holders are required to pay *ad valorem* royalties, with rates varying between 2 and 7% of revenue depending on the mineral. There are also land taxes based on the surface area mined. Royalties and land taxes are deductible from taxable income, which is subject to the standard 25% corporate income tax (Arnold, 2012). Indonesia should eventually do away with royalties and move to taxing profits directly.

The Decentralisation Law 22/1999, which came into force in 2001, resulted in a transfer of authority and responsibility from the central to regional governments. This law contributed to blurring the governance picture by handing additional powers, notably of taxation, to regional authorities eager to increase their revenues but lacking the capacity to handle their new responsibilities. As a result too many licenses were granted to unqualified businesses as a quick way to raise revenues. It also contributed to the development of illegal mining, as control by the central government diminished (Box 2.9). While decentralisation should be consolidated, more focus should be placed on regional capacity building in order to train local governments as to mining rights (IUPs) allocation and ensuing responsibilities. Regional governments should also be made liable for any negative externalities stemming from a lack of proper vetting and regulation of licence holders.

Box 2.9. **Illegal mining in Indonesia**

Illegal mining in Indonesia is known by the name of PETI (*Penambangan Tanpa Izin*, "Mining Without Permits"). Illegal coal mining is widespread in Kalimantan, while Java and Lombok host many illegal gold mining operations.

Prior to the introduction of reforms in 1999, the government exercised tight control over the nation's mining operations. It made it difficult for illegal mining operations to develop, despite the government's longstanding push towards smaller-scale mining ventures as a

Box 2.9. **Illegal mining in Indonesia** *(cont.)*

way to spread the mineral wealth. Since the end of the Soeharto administration, the government has been faced with the spread of illegal mining operations. As the 1997-98 crisis forced many laid-off workers back to their home provinces, looking for work in agriculture or mining, the shift to decentralisation at about the same time introduced several inconsistencies between central- and local-government policies and left holes in the mineral resource management framework, which were exploited. As illegal miners started to spread, they formed alliances with landowners, support contractors, suppliers of mining equipment and transporters (basically every link in the supply chain). They soon became politically influential, challenging the concessions given to larger, authorised companies. Local government officials often benefit from those operations by getting a share of their profits, receiving royalty payments and reclamation fees and absolving miners from environmental responsibility (Lestari, 2007). Importantly, demand for illegal mining products is fuelled by lower informal prices, up to 40% below the official market price in the case of coal, for example.

In the case of open-cast mining operations, when the government and a mining company reach an agreement over a concession, the latter is legally required to follow guidelines regarding the setup of operations, including operating and clean-up protocols. They include carefully clearing the land of any forest cover or vegetation, removing and storing the topsoil for use during the post-mining land-rehabilitation procedure, and, when the soil is replaced, restoring the land's original fertility characteristics. Once the topsoil is removed, the overburden is cleared away exposing the coal seams below, and dumped in the mined out areas at the back of the active pit. Like the topsoil, the overburden is typically reused during land reclamation after mining operations are terminated (Lestari, 2007).

None of these operations is conducted by illegal mines, which create a lot of damage. In addition to not following guidelines imposed on official mines, illegal mining produces degradation of its own: logging or burning the forest to clear the land (resulting in serious smoke haze); abandoned open pit sites filled with acidic run-off leaking into the surroundings and poisoning water bodies; and illegal coal-loading ports built with no regard for environmental safeguards (coal destined for domestic consumption is barged from one island to another).

It was estimated that illegal coal mining amounted to 20 million tonnes in 2010 (Lucarelli, 2010). In the case of gold, while also difficult to estimate, BaliFokus (an Indonesian environmental organisation) estimates that 65 to 100 tonnes of gold were illegally produced in 2012 by small-scale gold miners, to be compared with a legal production of 60 tonnes. This represented as many as 850 gold mining and production areas across the archipelago in 2013, up from about 575 in 2006. In addition to environmental damage, studies done in other regions of Indonesia, including work by the University of Mataram, showed elevated mercury levels in people processing gold, and dysfunctional motor skills among local children (*New York Times*, 2014).

Recommendations to get the most out of mineral extraction

- Adopt best practices regarding mining contracting such as a fully stable mining regime and competitive taxation, while ensuring that a large share of the rents from extraction benefits the Indonesian people.
- Revise the blanket mineral export ban based on a careful evaluation of the costs and benefits of onshore processing for each mineral.
- Eliminate the dual-licensing system by moving back to a unique exploration and exploitation license. Raise the threshold on foreign ownership restrictions.
- Build capacity at the regional level to allow local governments to better handle mining rights (IUP) allocation and revenue collection.

Protecting the environment through regulations and control of illegal extraction

Rapid economic growth combined with rising urbanisation has led to pressures on the environment. The joint ADB-ILO-IDB Environmental Performance Index positioned Indonesia 134th of 163 countries in 2010 and only 12th among the 13 Southeast Asian countries in terms of environmental sustainability and performance (OECD, 2012b). One major issue is the growing role that fossil fuels are playing in Indonesia's energy mix. Other pressing environmental concerns relate to deforestation (which is Indonesia's main source of CO_2 emissions), particle pollution coming from transport and fuel combustion, and water pollution coming from industry and illegal mining. Palm oil sustainability is also considered a major agro-environmental issue. Its rapid expansion since 1990 (Figure 2.3) has often taken place at the expense of natural forests. It also contributes to increased carbon emissions and has endangered biodiversity, not to mention the impact of haze-generating forest cover burn-off on neighbouring countries.

Indonesia's record regarding GHG emissions and pollution is poor

Given the large and increasing role played by fossil fuels in Indonesia, it is not a surprise to see that its GHG emissions doubled to 1.9 billion tonnes (bt) in 2012 up from 1.1 billion tonnes in 1990, making Indonesia the fifth biggest GHG emitter among OECD and key partner countries. China ranks first (10.8 bt) ahead of the United States (6.7), India (2.7) and Russia (2.5). While CO_2 emissions per unit of GDP (at PPP) is about average for Asia (but quite high compared to OECD countries), its record regarding CO_2 emissions per kWh of electricity and heat is poor, reflecting the dominant role played by coal. As for the PM_{10} index (Particulate Matter up to 10 micrometres in size), Indonesia ranks last among ASEAN countries, with ensuing negative impacts on human health and life expectancy (Figure 2.20).

At the 2009 G20 summit, the Indonesian government committed to reducing the country's carbon emissions by up to 26% by 2020 against a business-as-usual trajectory. Indonesia's energy strategy is laid out in the National Development Plan 2010-14, which supports an increased utilisation of renewable energy, including geothermal, generating electricity from phasing in solar power, micro-hydro and nuclear power. Following the Presidential Regulation on the National Energy Mix Target 2025, policies are also geared towards reducing carbon emissions through energy diversification and conservation.

Activities like mining also contribute to environmental degradation, mostly through water pollution and damage to the ecosystem. As a result, Indonesia's record regarding

Figure 2.20. **Pollution indicators**

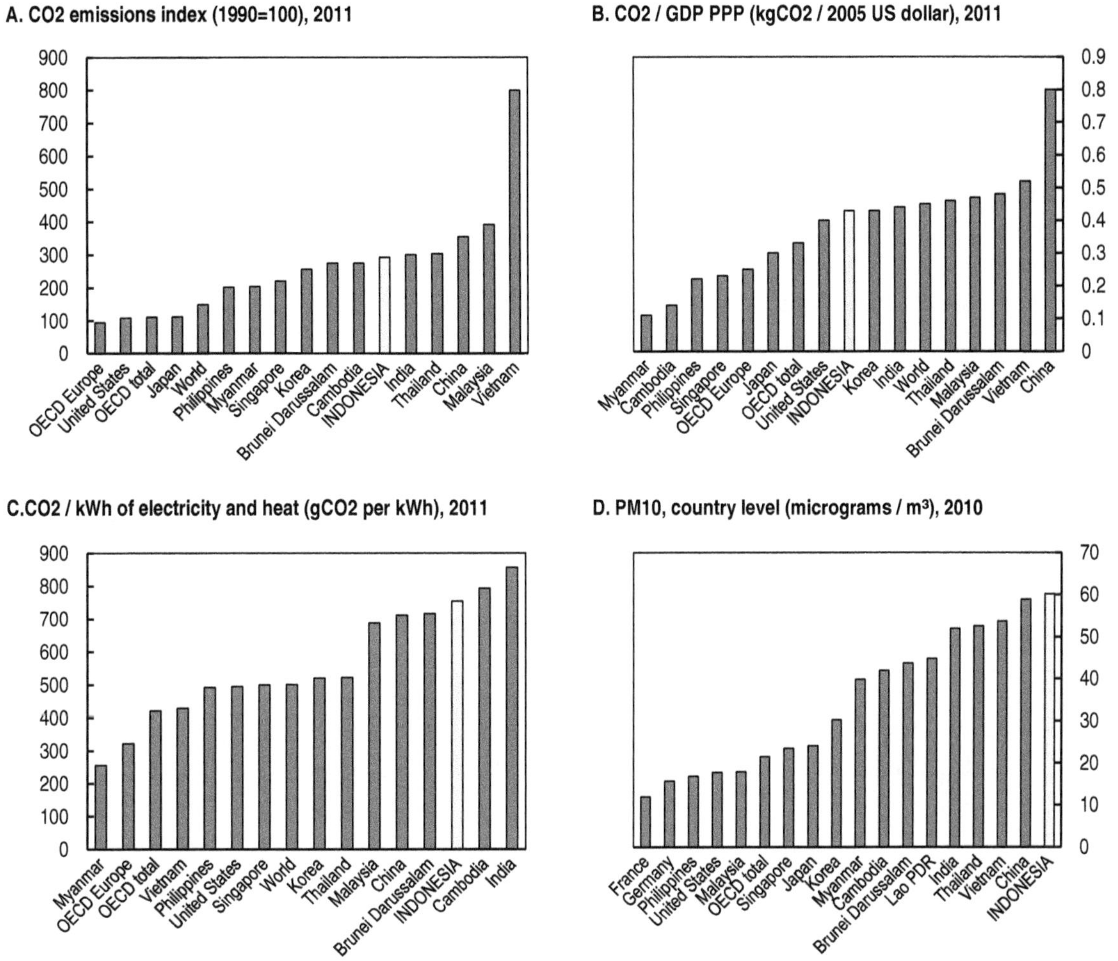

Source: OECD (2014b), *Toward Green Growth in Southeast Asia*, OECD Publishing.

StatLink http://dx.doi.org/10.1787/888933200525

organic water pollutants (measured by the amount of oxygen that bacteria in water will consume in breaking down waste) is also poor (OECD, 2014c). For instance, most coal mining operations are open-cast and carried out in remote, pristine areas, increasing the risk of environment damage. The Indonesian Coal Mining Association, an organisation comprising 130 of the country's most influential miners, has set out a plan to ensure that all coal mining operations are conducted responsibly. Several large coal mining companies, such as Adaro Energy, are pursuing rehabilitation programmes, which aim at restoring the environment to a state as close as possible to that which existed before mining activities started. But a lot of the mining-related pollution actually comes from smaller, often illegal mines that do not have the willingness or the means to repair the harm they do (Box 2.9). Of the 3 922 permits for coal exploration, 1 461 are listed as not clean and clear, according to the Ministry. Better monitoring of illegal mining and stricter enforcement of existing regulations should be pursued. The requirement that mining companies deposit funds to ensure they carry out rehabilitation and reclamation program should be a pre-requisite to starting operations.

Deforestation should be reversed

In Indonesia, forest cover as a share of land area shrank by more than 10 percentage points from 1990 to 2011, on a par with Cambodia and Myanmar (Figure 2.21). Forests function as carbon sinks and help reduce greenhouse gas emissions. Deforestation makes Indonesia the world's fifth largest emitter of greenhouse gases and leads to loss of biodiversity, peat fires, soil erosion and flooding, and also affects local communities whose existence depends on forest resources. Illegal logging, conversion to agricultural land, deliberate forest fires and mining are the primary causes of deforestation. In addition, a number of regulatory and institutional issues have facilitated deforestation during the last 20 years. Specifically: unclear roles and responsibilities of different levels of government following decentralisation; land tenure and access issues putting local communities against private firms; inappropriate land pricing and rents; and weak enforcement of existing laws and protocols at the national and local levels (OECD, 2012b).

Figure 2.21. **Change in forest coverage**

Per cent of area

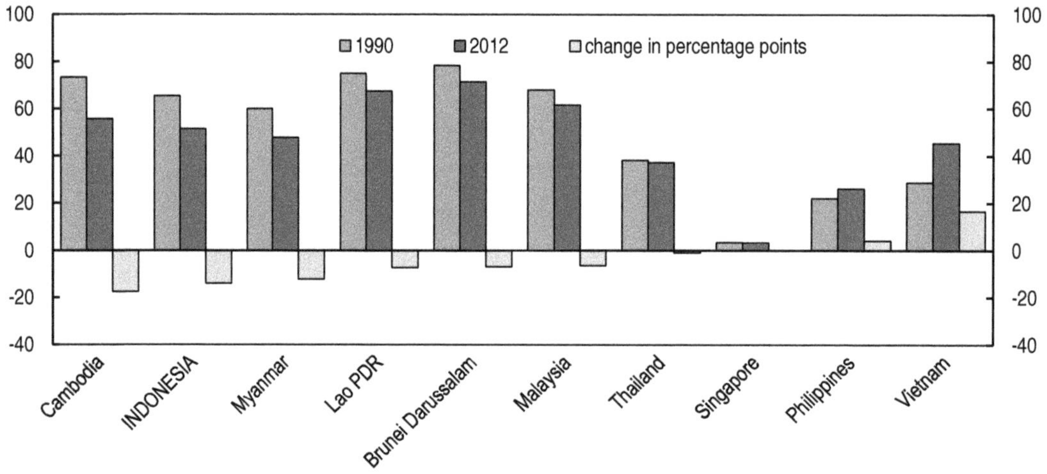

Source: World Bank, *Development Indicators 2015*.

StatLink http://dx.doi.org/10.1787/888933200536

In reaction, in 2009 Indonesia established the Reducing Emissions from Deforestation and Forest Degradation (REDD+) agency as part of the government's 2020 emissions reduction commitment. Its programmes include the one-map initiative (a single, all-encompassing map of Indonesia containing all relevant information regarding forest licensing and land-use claims) and the implementation of the Measurement, Reporting and Verification (MRV) system to monitor carbon flux and estimate the size of carbon reservoirs. In addition, Indonesia is trying to directly increase forest restoration by 500 000 hectares per year. However, many challenges remain, given weak monitoring of the forest sector. For instance, the Corruption Eradication Commission said that 89% of the nation's 128 million hectares of forest were under no regulation or permit, making them difficult to protect. The government should then make sure that every hectare of forest, whether private or government-owned, has well defined property rights and is under clear regulations in order to prevent illegal activities. It should increase the resources devoted to reforestation and combatting illegal logging, and punish illegal deliberately set forest fires more severely. A well-resourced and powerful agency should also be created to actively combat illegal logging and mining. New agricultural activities should be authorised only on scrub land and abandoned cultivated land.

Indonesia should tap its unique renewable energy potential

Indonesia's renewable energy potential is huge and can contribute to energy access in off-grid areas. Given the role of agriculture in Indonesia and the scattered population, developing biomass is a first option. Basically any agricultural by-product that people currently cart away is biomass that can be used to generate power. Potential liquid biomass includes biodiesel from palm oil and bioethanol from sugarcane and cassava. Yet, both carry threats to biodiversity and the forest. Potential solid biomass can come from palm shells from palm oil, coconut shells and fibre, bagasse from sugar refining, rice husks and corncobs. Several initiatives have already taken place, such as the recent signing of a memorandum of understanding between state-owned energy firms and General Electric for the development and deployment of biomass gasification systems.

In addition to biomass, Indonesia boasts an estimated 40% of the world's reserves of geothermal energy, an energy source that is expensive to develop, but clean, abundant and not subject to supply (and therefore price) volatility. Currently, Indonesia utilises less than 5% of its estimated potential (Mujiyanto and Tiess, 2013). In August 2014, the House of Representatives approved a revised geothermal law allowing for the exploitation of geothermal sources in the country's conservation forests. It also returns the power to issue permits or conduct tenders related to geothermal energy exploitation to the central government. As the new regulatory environment becomes operational, the government should accelerate the exploration and tendering of new geothermal projects. In order to attract investors the ceiling price for electricity generated from geothermal power plants should be raised. Other renewable energies include hydropower, the largest resources being located in Papua. Wind energy potential is limited due to the lack of wind along the equator. But its location makes solar resources significant, though it is still underdeveloped and appears mostly in the form of solar roof-panel systems. The rise in CO_2 emissions should be limited by reducing the share of coal in energy production and increasing its efficiency, and by increasing the share of gas, geothermal and other renewables in the energy mix as part of the push for more and better infrastructure. Nuclear power should also be considered.

On the investment side, restrictions on FDI in Indonesia are less severe for green investment than for the average sector (OECD, 2014b). It is also much lower than in other ASEAN countries (Table 2.2). While this favourable regime should be maintained, more support should be provided to international companies willing to enter the market. Rather than ad hoc ministerial decrees, a comprehensive and attractive regulatory framework for renewable energies should also be created (GIZ, 2012). Indonesia also promotes organic farming and the transition away from chemical to organic fertilisers. For more than 30 years the government has sought to encourage greater fertiliser use by farmers as a way to enhance agricultural productivity. The gradual reduction of chemical fertiliser subsidies in favour of their organic counterparts would be appropriate.

Table 2.2. **FDI restrictions in renewable energy**

Per cent of foreign ownership permitted in greenfield FDI and mergers and acquisitions

	Biomass	Hydro	Solar	Wind
Indonesia	**95**	**95**	**95**	**95**
Malaysia	30	30	30	30
Philippines	100	100	40	40
Thailand	49	49	49	49

Source: Golub et al. (2011), adapted from *World Bank Investing Across Borders Database*, 2010.

Recommendations to protect the environment from resource extraction and develop renewable energies

- Create a strong regulatory environment to encourage investment in renewables, especially geothermal, solar and biomass. Construct more energy-efficient coal-fired power plants, and gradually phase out old ones.
- Better monitor illegal logging and mining, and create a well-resourced and powerful agency to strictly enforce regulations.
- Limit the rise in CO_2 emissions by reducing the share of coal and oil in energy production and increasing those of gas, geothermal and biomass but also of nuclear and solar power.
- Start ambitious reforestation programmes in areas that have been damaged, and ensure that every hectare of forest has well defined property rights, whether private or government-owned, and is under clear regulations.
- Bring the implicit carbon price from electricity use back to positive levels by phasing out energy subsidies.

Bibliography

Aguilera, R.F., J. Inchauspe and R.D. Ripple (2014), "The Asia Pacific Natural Gas Market: Large Enough for All?", *Energy Policy*, Vol. 65, pp. 1-6.

Alston, J.M. and P.G. Pardey (2014), "Agriculture in the Global Economy", *Journal of Economic Perspectives*, Vol. 28, No. 1, pp. 121-46.

Amin, L.I. (2011), "Challenges and Future Needs for Irrigation Management in Indonesia", *Paper* presented at International Workshop on "Sustainable Water Management for Food Security: An International Policy Dialogue on Progressing Water Policy Reform for Agriculture, with Focus on Indonesia", Bogor, Indonesia, 13-15 December.

Andadari, R.K., P. Mulder and P. Rietveld (2014), "Energy Poverty Reduction by Fuel Switching. Impact Evaluation of the LPG Conversion Program in Indonesia", *Energy Policy*, Vol. 66, pp. 436-49.

Arnold, J. (2012), "Improving the Tax System in Indonesia", *OECD Economics Department Working Paper*, No. 998, OECD Publishing.

BAL (1960), Basic Agrarian Law, Undang-Undang Pokok Agraria – UUPA, the Directorate General of Agrarian Affairs of the Department of Home Affairs.

BAPPENAS (National Development Planning Agency) (2011), *Master Plan for the Acceleration and Expansion of Indonesia's Economic Development 2011-2025*.

Bloomberg (2014), "Indonesia Looks Overseas in $25 Billion Refinery Overhaul", 11 December.

Boyd, M., A. Devero, J. Frias, J. Meyer and G. Ross (2010), "A Note on Policies for the Oil and Gas Sector", *Bulletin of Indonesian Economic Studies*, Vol. 46, No. 2, pp. 237-48.

Brandt, N., P. Schreyer and V. Zipperer (2013), "Productivity Measurement with Natural Capital", *OECD Economics Department Working Papers*, No. 1092, OECD Publishing.

Castle, J. (2013), "Indonesia's Mining Malaise and Deeper Challenges to Growth", *Global Asia*, Vol. 8, No. 4, pp. 200-25.

Davis, L. (2014), "The Economic Cost of Global Fuel Subsidies", *American Economic Review: Papers & Proceedings*, Vol. 104, Iss. 5, pp. 581-85, May.

Energy and Mining Journal (2012), "Transforming the Nation's Mining Industry. Indonesian Coal Giants Look to Take the Next Step", pp. 52-59.

FAOSTAT (2015), *FAOSTAT Database*, available at *http://faostat3.fao.org/faostat-gateway/go/to/home/E*.

Fraser Institute (2013), *Survey of Mining Companies 2012/2013*, Fraser Institute, Vancouver.

Fuglie, K.O. (2010a), "Sources of Growth in Indonesian Agriculture", *Journal of Productivity Analysis*, Vol. 33, pp. 225-40.

Fuglie, K.O. (2010b), "Indonesia: From Food Security to Market-Led Agricultural Growth", in J. Alston, B.A. Babcock and G. Pardey (eds.), *The Shifting Patterns of Agricultural Production and Productivity Worldwide*, Midwest Agribusiness Trade Research and Information Center, Iowa State University, pp. 343-81.

Fuglie, K.O. (2012), "Productivity Growth and Technology Capital in the Global Agricultural Economy", in K.O. Fuglie, S.L. Wang and V.E. Ball (eds.), *Productivity Growth in Agriculture: An International Perspective*, CAB International, Oxfordshire, United Kingdom.

Gandataruna, K. and K. Haymon (2011), "A Dream Denied? Mining Legislation and the Constitution in Indonesia", *Bulletin of Indonesian Economic Studies*, Vol. 47, No. 2, pp. 221-31.

GIZ (2012), *Legal Frameworks for Renewable Energy*, Federal Ministry for Economic Co-operation and Development, Bonn.

Golub, S.S., C. Kauffmann and P. Yeres (2011), "Defining and Measuring Green FDI: An Exploratory Review of Existing Work and Evidence", *OECD Working Papers on International Investment*, 2011/02, OECD Publishing, *http://dx.doi.org/10.1787/5kg58j1cvcvk-en*.

Hendriatiningsih, S., A. Hernandi, A. Budiartha, K. Sarah and R. Abdulharis (2009), "Comparative Study of Customary and Formal Land Tenure System in Bali, Indonesia", *FIG Working Week 2009*, Eilat, Israel, 3-8 May.

Heryani, E. and C. Grant (2004), "Land Administration in Indonesia", *Paper* presented at the 3rd FIG Regional Conference, Jakarta, 3-7 October.

Hidrobo, M., J. Hoddinott, A. Peterman, A. Margolies and V. Moreira (2014), "Cash, Food, or Vouchers? Evidence from a Randomized Experiment in Northern Ecuador", *Journal of Development Economics* Vol. 107, pp. 144-156.

IEA (2008), *Energy Policy Review of Indonesia*, OECD/IEA Publishing.

IEA (2013a), *Coal Medium-Term Market Report*, OECD/IEA Publishing.

IEA (2013b), *World Energy Outlook 2013*, OECD/IEA Publishing.

IEA (2014), *Coal Information 2014*, OECD/IEA Publishing.

Jakarta Globe (2012), "South Sumatra Shooting Puts Government in Cross Hairs", 30 July.

Jeon, S. (2013), "Agricultural Transformation and the Escape from the Middle-Income Country Trap: Challenges Facing Small Farmers in Indonesia in a Time of Green Restructuring", *Ph.D. thesis*, The Graduate Institute, Geneva.

Lestari, N.I. (2007), "Illegal Coal Mining in South Kalimantan – A Mining Company Confronts PETI Operations Through Engagement", *Artisanal and Small-Scale Mining in Asia-Pacific Case Study*, No. 4.

Lewin, M. (2011), "Botswana's Success: Good Governance, Good Policies, and Good Luck", in *Yes Africa Can, Success Stories from a Dynamic Continent*, World Bank.

Lucarelli, B. (2010), "The History and Future of Indonesia's Coal Industry: Impact of Politics and Regulatory Framework on Industry Structure and Performance", *Freeman Spogli Institute for International Studies*, Stanford University.

McKinsey Global Institute (2012), *The Archipelago Economy: Unleashing Indonesia's Potential.*

Mujiyanto, S. and G. Tiess (2013), "Secure Energy Supply in 2025: Indonesia's Need for an Energy Policy Strategy", *Energy Policy*, Vol. 61, pp. 31-41.

New York Times (2014), "Small-Scale Gold Mining Pollutes Indonesian Lands", 2 January.

OECD (2008), *OECD Economic Surveys: Indonesia Economic Assessment*, OECD Publishing.

OECD (2009), *Natural Resources and Pro-Poor Growth, the Economics and Politics*, OECD Publishing.

OECD (2010), *OECD Economic Surveys: Indonesia 2010*, OECD Publishing.

OECD (2012a), *OECD Economic Surveys: Indonesia 2012*, OECD Publishing.

OECD (2012b), *OECD Review of Agricultural Policy, Indonesia*, OECD Publishing.

OECD (2013), *OECD Review of Fisheries, Policies and Summary Statistics*, OECD Publishing.

OECD (2014a), *OECD Tourism Trends and Policies 2014*, OECD Publishing.

OECD (2014b), *Toward Green Growth in Southeast Asia*, OECD Publishing.

OECD (2014c), *Agricultural Policy Monitoring and Evaluation 2014: OECD Countries*, OECD Publishing.

OECD (2014d), *Modelling of Distributional Impacts of Energy Subsidy Reforms: An Illustration with Indonesia*, OECD Publishing, forthcoming.

OECD (2015), *OECD Economic Surveys: Mexico 2015*, OECD Publishing.

Pandin, M.R.L (2008), "Portrait of Indonesian Fertilizer Industry", *Economic Review*, No. 214, December.

Penot, E., G. Wibawa and C. Geissler (2002), "Perennial Crops Trigger Land-Use and Land-Tenure Changes in Indonesia (Example of the Province of West Kalimantan)", *Paper* presented at the World Bank Workshop on Land Issues, Phnom Penh, Cambodia, June.

USAID (2010), "Property Rights and Resource Governance – Indonesia Country Profile", *Country Reports Series*.

USAID (2013), *Economic Effects of Indonesia's Mineral-Processing Requirements for Export*, April.

USTR (2014), "National Trade Estimate Report on Foreign Trade Barriers, Indonesia", Washington, DC.

Winoto, J. (2009), "Taking Land Policy and Administration in Indonesia to the Next Stage and National Land Agency's Strategic Plan", *Paper* presented at the Workshop in International Federation of Surveyors' Forum, Washington, DC, March.

Wall Street Journal (2014), "China and Russia at the Altar of Gas", 18 February.

World Bank (2012), *Indonesia Economic Quarterly*, World Bank Group, Jakarta, March.

World Bank (2014a), *Indonesia Economic Quarterly*, World Bank Group, Jakarta, March.

World Bank (2015), *World Development Indicators Database, http://data.worldbank.org/data-catalog/worlddevelopment-indicators*.

ORGANISATION FOR ECONOMIC CO-OPERATION AND DEVELOPMENT

The OECD is a unique forum where governments work together to address the economic, social and environmental challenges of globalisation. The OECD is also at the forefront of efforts to understand and to help governments respond to new developments and concerns, such as corporate governance, the information economy and the challenges of an ageing population. The Organisation provides a setting where governments can compare policy experiences, seek answers to common problems, identify good practice and work to co-ordinate domestic and international policies.

The OECD member countries are: Australia, Austria, Belgium, Canada, Chile, the Czech Republic, Denmark, Estonia, Finland, France, Germany, Greece, Hungary, Iceland, Ireland, Israel, Italy, Japan, Korea, Luxembourg, Mexico, the Netherlands, New Zealand, Norway, Poland, Portugal, the Slovak Republic, Slovenia, Spain, Sweden, Switzerland, Turkey, the United Kingdom and the United States. The European Commission takes part in the work of the OECD.

OECD Publishing disseminates widely the results of the Organisation's statistics gathering and research on economic, social and environmental issues, as well as the conventions, guidelines and standards agreed by its members.

OECD PUBLISHING, 2, rue André-Pascal, 75775 PARIS CEDEX 16
(10 2015 08 1 P) ISBN 978-92-64-22968-6 – 2015

www.ingramcontent.com/pod-product-compliance
Ingram Content Group UK Ltd.
Pitfield, Milton Keynes, MK11 3LW, UK
UKHW051505290926
15471UKWH00008B/1437

9 789264 229686